THE
TELEVISION
SERIES

Trevor Griffiths

MANCHESTER
1824

Manchester University Press

THE
TELEVISION
SERIES

series editors

SARAH CARDWELL

JONATHAN BIGNELL

JOHN TULLOCH

Trevor Griffiths

Manchester University Press
MANCHESTER AND NEW YORK

distributed exclusively in the USA by Palgrave

Published by Manchester University Press
Oxford Road, Manchester M13 9NR, UK
and Room 400, 175 Fifth Avenue, New York, NY 10010, USA
www.manchesteruniversitypress.co.uk

Distributed exclusively in the USA by
Palgrave, 175 Fifth Avenue, New York, NY 10010, USA

Distributed exclusively in Canada by
UBC Press, University of British Columbia, 2029 West Mall,
Vancouver, BC, Canada V6T 1Z2

British Library Cataloguing-in-Publication Data
A catalogue record for this book is available from the British Library

Library of Congress Cataloging-in-Publication Data applied for

isbn 0 7190 6858 4 *hardback*
ean 978 0 7190 6858 4

First published 2006

15 14 13 12 11 10 09 08 07 06   10 9 8 7 6 5 4 3 2 1

Typeset in Scala with Meta display
by Koinonia, Manchester
Printed in Great Britain
by CPI, Bath

Contents

List of illustrations

Every effort has been made to obtain permission to reproduce copyright
material in this book. If any proper acknowledgement has not been made,
copyright-holders are invited to contact the publisher.

General editors' preface

Television is part of our everyday experience, and is one of the most significant features of our cultural lives today. Yet its practitioners and its artistic and cultural achievements remain relatively unacknowledged. The books in this series aim to remedy this by addressing the work of major television writers and creators. Each volume provides an authoritative and accessible guide to a particular practitioner's body of work, and assesses his or her contribution to television over the years. Many of the volumes draw on original sources, such as specially conducted interviews and archive material, and all of them list relevant bibliographic sources and provide full details of the programmes discussed. The author of each book makes a case for the importance of the work considered therein, and the series includes books on neglected or overlooked practitioners alongside well-known ones.

In comparison with some related disciplines, Television Studies scholarship is still relatively young, and the series aims to contribute to establishing the subject as a vigorous and evolving field. This series provides resources for critical thinking about television. Whilst maintaining a clear focus on the writers, on the creators and on the programmes themselves, the books in this series also take account of key critical concepts and theories in Television Studies. Each book is written from a particular critical or theoretical perspective, with reference to pertinent issues, and the approaches included in the series are varied and sometimes dissenting. Each author explicitly outlines the reasons for his or her particular focus, methodology or perspective. Readers are invited to think critically about the subject matter and approach covered in each book.

Although the series is addressed primarily to students and scholars of television, the books will also appeal to the many people who are interested in how television programmes have been commissioned, made and enjoyed. Since television has been so much a part of personal and public life in the twentieth and twenty-first centuries, we hope that the series will engage with, and sometimes challenge, a broad and diverse readership.

Sarah Cardwell
Jonathan Bignell

Acknowledgements

Because this book focuses on the 'texts' of Trevor Griffiths, both in his own authorship and in various modes of production, circulation and reception (as in the studio, in the auditorium, in newspaper reviews and in academic presses), my thanks are due first of all to Trevor and Gill Griffiths for complete access to a huge body of work (some of it in a series of manuscripts which never went to air) and to photographs from the productions; and then to the actors, production personnel, marketing professionals, reviewers and academics named in the chapters that follow, who all put their particular signatures on Griffiths' work. I would also like to thank the actors from both the Richard Eyre/Trevor Griffiths productions of *The Cherry Orchard*, at Nottingham Playhouse and on BBC1 Television, nearly all of whom were interviewed, but some of whom are not quoted here for want of space. Tom Burvill from Macquarie University assisted me in *The Cherry Orchard* interviews, as well as being a wonderfully productive colleague in thinking about that part of the research. Particular thanks are also due to the publicity personnel at the Northcote Theatre, Exeter, both for giving me their valuable time in interviews and in facilitating the audience study of *Comedians* in Chapter 7. Finally, my thanks are due to Nobby Clark for the location and studio photographs we have used in this book.

Introduction

Old socialists never say die. They just retreat further into history. Having done battle with the 20th century – from the 100 days that shook the world to the 12 years that turned Britain blue – Trevor Griffiths has turned his fire on the French Revolution. Hope In Year 2, tonight's BBC Screen Two play, is an elusive and passionate exploration of the revolutionary consciousness ... Griffiths notches up setbacks like battle scars. The son of a Manchester chemical worker who died of lung cancer at 54, he carries from his childhood an unshakable sense of 'naturalised inequality', together with a passion for talking to strangers. (Claire Armistead, *Guardian*, May 11, 1994)

Trevor Griffiths has been a critical force in British television writing for over three decades. His television works have offered an acclaimed oeuvre through which Griffiths has negotiated the issues of genre, politics, identity, class, history, memory and television form with a sustained creativity and integrity. This has paralleled an equally eminent career in theatre (there are discussions in this book of early theatre works like *Sam, Sam*, and of his much later *The Gulf Between Us* and *Piano*), as well as his sometimes difficult forays into film-collaboration in *Reds* with Warren Beatty, and *Fatherland*, directed by Ken Loach (Tulloch 1990).

From the early 1970s when his theatre plays began to have major critical impact, Griffiths was controversial. Highly respected newspaper critics like Milton Shulman and Michael Billington spoke of Britain as potentially being on the verge of a revolutionary situation, and praised Griffiths for the powerful pertinence of his work. Discussing Griffiths' *The Party* in the *Guardian* in January 1974, Billington took to task his fellow theatre reviewers for being very negative about 'one of the most mind-stretching and politically sophisticated works I have seen on the modern stage'. He concluded his review, 'Griffiths has ... paid a British audience the unusual compliment of assuming it will be interested in a discussion about the future of our society and the possibility of revolution: a timely enough topic, I should have thought ... At a moment when our whole mode of life is being challenged and when the bland affluence we have so long taken for granted is crumbling, there comes before us an eloquent, witty, well-written play about the need for social change, and seemingly all we can do is wrinkle our noses with distaste and primly rearrange our critical skirts' (January 24, 1974).

Most reviewers certainly did wrinkle their political noses. With titles like 'Reds on the Bed' (Jeremy Kingston), 'Looking-glass revolution' (Harold Hobson), and 'Socialist Sunday School' (Benedict Nightingale), the majority of theatre critics in the British press would have agreed with John Barber, in his *Daily Telegraph* review 'Playing the party game', which said that 'the best political drama is devious ... Griffiths' new play for the National Theatre is not, and therefore fails' (January 7, 1974).

All of Griffiths' work was immediately read as 'political'. His first major play *Occupations* had been reviewed in similar vein to *The Party*. Frank Marcus began his *Sunday Telegraph* review 'Back to the barricades!' (October 7, 1971). Irving Wardle headed his review in *The Times* 'Bitter eloquent look at revolutionaries' (October 14, 1971). Peter Lewis wrote in the *Daily Mail* that 'A clever revolution fails to catch fire' (October 19, 1971). And Michael Billington, challenging the charge by many reviewers of Griffiths' supposedly dogmatic political naturalism, wrote in the *Guardian*, 'if the aim of political drama is to take the scales off one's eyes and activate both brain and conscience, then ... the derided form of naturalism seems to me the best way for conveying the many-sidedness of most questions. And significantly the two best plays about politics I've seen this year (John McGrath's "Trees in the Wind" and Trevor Griffiths' "Occupations") have both used this method' (October 25, 1971).

Even these few early newspaper references to Griffiths' work indicate a key set of conjunctures. His work was immediately noticed. It was thought to be political in a highly contemporary way, even if disliked and dismissed. He was seen to be working in the powerful context of other writers (Billington's reference to John McGrath), the loss of which Griffiths' was to comment on much later in his career. And the form and style of his work became a preoccupation with audiences, critics and academics alike, as this book will explore.

A television maker of texts

Griffiths' first tilt at television drama came as a writer for the 1972/3 Granada TV series *Adam Smith*, about a Scottish minister and a young doctor, in which social exploitation in both Scotland and South Africa, and sexual tensions between the doctor and the minister's radical daughter were, as it was written under a pseudonym, more than once pared back or directly censored. Griffiths left the second series in protest, and Poole and Wyver make the telling point that this was the first time that Griffiths encountered the fact that 'meaning is produced by television as an institution, as a collection of contributing individuals and as a set of practices and relationships. The writer is one element within that, but his or her meanings will be overlain with many others in the creation of a final text' (1984, 26). Similarly, Griffiths' first television piece for London Weekend Television, *The Silver Mask* (1973), was part of a six-part series *Between the Wars*, based on literary texts from the 1920s and 1930s, and commissioned by Verity Lambert. *The Silver Mask* was based on Hugh Walpole's 'psychological' short-story of the same name, and apart from Griffiths making more overt Walpole's (and the series') 'deep-seated and widespread fear of social upheaval' there was 'very little impress of specific "authorship"' (Poole and Wyver 1984).

As originally a stage play, Griffiths had more control of *Occupations* which, when first performed at the RSC in 1971, was in the immediate context of worker occupations in the Upper Clyde and elsewhere. The play focused on the Turin occupations by workers of the Fiat factories in 1920. The collision in the play between the intellectual Gramsci and the pragmatic Kabak who represents party discipline and Stalinist political expediency, was both an early attempt by Griffiths to work through his own position as working-class intellectual, and an engagement with current debate and practice in intellectual Left circles. Like *The Party*, its contemporary relevance was the Paris of May 1968. A Granada TV adaptation of *Occupations* followed in September 1974, with some indicative changes to Griffiths' design instructions, specifically a more naturalistic and lavishly affluent set for Kabak's apartment, and with the dying countess 'banished to an adjoining room' where her 'power as a symbol of a dying order is much reduced' (Poole and Wyver 1984, 41).

The Party (National Theatre 1973, adapted for BBC television in 1988) examined the contradictions faced by a revolutionary socialist writer (like Griffiths himself) and a fellow-travelling television producer working within capitalist cultural industries that they critiqued or wanted to destroy. The background of the piece was the May 1968 student/police confrontation in Paris, and the extended dialogue of the play traced the issue of hard-line political organisation as against the 'soft' debate of different Left intellectual positions taking place in a well-heeled middle-class home.

All Good Men (BBC *Play for Today*, January 1974) featured the passionate debate between a 70 year old Labour politician and former trade union radical Edward Waite who now owns a country house (and is about to accept a peerage) and his son William, a sociologist from Manchester University, all of it recorded by a suave BBC television producer Massingham for a documentary which, as William tells him, can never be neutral or objective. *Absolute Beginners* (BBC *Fall of Eagles* series, April 1974) was Griffiths' attempt to insert a revolutionary content into an otherwise conservative series about the collapse of the Romanov, Hapsburg and Hohenzollern dynasties. It focused on Lenin's centralisation of the Bolsheviks and isolation of the Mensheviks at the 1903 Second Congress, contrasting the party discipline of Leninism with the personal, and social morality of socialist humanism. In all of these class-oriented plays, Griffiths questioned whether socialist humanism had the focus and coherence to defeat capitalism; and this same debate became the basis of his peak-time television series *Bill Brand* (Thames Television, June–August 1976) which featured the hostility between 'humourless' Left radicals in the 1970s Labour Party and its compromising leadership.

Griffiths' *Through the Night* (BBC 1975) was ostensibly more personal, written in 'anger and fear' after his wife Jan went into hospital for a biopsy and woke from the anaesthetic to find her breast had been removed. Griffiths drew on Jan's journal recounting her emotions and events in hospital, and it became one of his most popular television plays, with an audience of 11 million viewers and a huge letters campaign in the *Sunday Mirror*. As with all of his work, the personal was embedded in a systemic social critique, in this case of medical professionalism. And as *The Radio Times* preview said, Griffiths saw the terms of reference as wider still, as relevant to factories as to doctors' waiting rooms.

Comedians (Nottingham Playhouse 1975, BBC *Play for Today*, October 1979) embedded highly personal angst within the broader socioeconomic reality of the capitalist entertainment system, tracing the ambition (to make it out of the working class) of a group of amateur comedians, focusing on the opposition and empathy between their liberal-minded teacher Eddie Waters and his favourite, 'hard' pupil Gethin Price, and exploring the final sell-out by most of them (but not Price) to Waters' commercially-fixated arch-rival who comes to audition them at a working-men's club.

Sons and Lovers (BBC2, January–February 1981) and *The Cherry Orchard* (Nottingham Playhouse 1978, BBC1, October 1981) marked a generic shift as Griffiths turned to the 'classics', D.H. Lawrence's strongly autobiographical novel and Chekhov's last play. In both cases Griffiths reworked the originals, countering the strong middle-class, upwardly mobile mother-son relationship of Lawrence by emphasising other (working-class and female) subjectivities; and in the case of Chekhov reconfiguring the dominant western stage interpretation (Tulloch 1985) that sees the gentry sadly and 'inevitably' lose their beautiful home and orchard to the twin forces of capitalism (represented by the merchant Lopakhin) and revolution (represented by the student Trofimov).

Country (BBC1 *Play for Today*, October 1981) addressed the historical moment just after World War II when many people (including the landed upper-class) feared that a social revolution was imminent as Churchill was swept aside by the Attlee Labour government in the 1947 elections. It focused on the personal/psychological decay of the old-school, hunting/shooting beer-brewing patriarch, Sir Frederic Carlion after the recent death at war of his eldest son and heir, Frederick, and the conversion of his next oldest son, Philip, who is gay/bisexual and has left his social class and stately home to become a left-leaning journalist dabbling in sleazy gossip columns. The play marks his rebirth as the new Tory – tough, pragmatic and locking the family fortunes into the confident march of multinational beer corporations.

Griffiths' *The Last Place on Earth* mini-series (Central TV, February–March 1985) was also historical, comparing the nationalistic contexts of the 'professional' Norwegian Amundsen and the 'amateur' Englishman 'Scott of the Antarctic' in their race to be first at the South Pole. It was a highly controversial series (Tulloch 1990, chapter 5), mainly for adopting biographer Roland Huntford's claim of an affair between Scott's wife and the Norwegian ambassador/explorer Nansen while Scott was at the Pole. In contrast, Griffiths' *Oi for England* (Central TV, April 1982) was determinedly contemporary, written and produced at great speed after the Southall, Toxteth and Brixton 'race riots', and featuring the neo-Fascist tendencies of an Oi-rock band.

What Billington called Griffiths' naturalism, and others (Tulloch 1990, Bignell 1994) described as critical realism, was central to all of these television works. But his last decade of television work has been seen (Garner 1999) as more overtly reflexive and 'filmic'. *Hope in the Year Two* (BBC 1994) explored the final few hours of the French revolutionary leader, Danton (though Griffiths also leaves open the possibility that this may be someone standing in for Danton), before his execution in Year 2 of the new Republic. The two-hander play focused on Danton and his very ordinary, pragmatic gaoler in asking the question: where does revolutionary hope lie (after the failures of the French and Russian Revolutions)?

Griffiths' most recent television work, *Food for Ravens* (BBC Wales, November 1997), was specially commissioned for the centenary of the Welsh radical Labour leader Aneurin Bevan's birth, and, directed by

Griffiths himself, played between the key relationships of Bevan and his Labour Party wife Jennie Lee, and with 'the Boy', a fresh-eyed youth who may be the son Bevan never had, or his angel of death (since Bevan is dying of cancer in 1960, on the verge of his quest to lead the Labour Party away from the reformist compromises of Hugh Gaitskell).

This, too briefly stated, is one history of Trevor Griffiths – of the television *maker* of texts, biographically involved and reflexively aware of his interventions in history across a range of communication forms. But there are many other histories. For the purposes of an academic series that shows 'how critical approaches can be applied to actual programmes', I want to offer some parallel histories too, because they will complicate the simple newspaper reviewers' conjunctures I started with.

Other histories

First, there is the history of media/cultural and theatre studies' various engagements with Griffiths over that same three decades, as academics grappled with the television impact, politics and forms of his works (Chapter 1). Any history of Griffiths, including this one, is bound to be both selective and paradigm-related, and we start with this chapter to outline that academic field which has 'spoken' Griffiths. Closely associated with the shifts in theoretical field described in Chapter 1 have been shifts in academic focus and methodology, and this book as a whole takes note of this history, with different chapters on textual and intertextual analysis, on the production of Griffiths' texts, on the circulation of his texts (via books and articles, printed playscripts, reviews, theatre marketing and programming), and on audience reception of his texts. Second, there is the history of synergy, interaction and conflict between television, theatre and academic industries, as Griffiths *himself* engaged, in both his works and written previews, with social theory (Chapter 2) in offering his printed works to potential producers and audiences. Third, there are – as Poole and Wyver note of *Adam Smith* – the different histories and idiolects at work when Griffiths is in production, and is constructed as 'author' by actors, directors, cameramen, lighting and sound directors, editors and set designers (Chapter 3). Fourth, there is the history of Trevor Griffiths as constructed in other parts of the media itself – as in previews and reviews in daily newspapers, weeklies, and regional and fringe press (Chapter 4). Fifth, there is a new history of authorship, as we return to a concept maligned by media studies for many years, but drawing on its resources in emphasising the power of intertexts. This is to write about a Trevor Griffiths historically active within his own work as his dramas play intertextually off each other, and off history-as-text (Chapters 5, 6). Sixth, there are the various audiences who make meanings from Trevor Griffiths' works. Poole and Wyver note the 'bizarre' comment by actor Ben Kingsley after winning an Oscar for *Gandhi* that he began preparing that role by playing 'the Italian communist *non-violent revolutionary*' in Griffiths' *Occupations*. 'This misreading', Poole and Wyver argue, 'highlights in how maverick a way dramatic meaning often circulates' (1984, 30). In fact, two decades of 'active audience' studies in the 1980s and 1990s suggested that audience readings are not maverick but socially embedded, and in Chapter 7 there is a study of audiences for Griffiths' theatre play *Comedians*, which is both relevant (because of all his works, this was one in which Griffiths wanted to engage with the subjectivities of a live audience) and poignant (because by the time this audience study was done in 2001 Griffiths was having to turn back to the theatre as a place where his works could still be produced). And finally in Chapter 8 there is another history, of works by Griffiths that were not produced at all, that were written and commissioned TV texts but for various economic and political reasons never seen on air. In an important sense, Griffiths is still writing these works, and in a study of his *March Time* we have the advantage of seeing Griffiths' approach as writer to the same text across three decades.

Finally, and inevitably, there is my history of Griffiths, sharing many similar theoretical/political positions with him, yet – through the pages of this book – constructing him dialogically, in relation to these *other* voices, discourses and histories. Since this selection and reconstruction is inevitable, it is best to be upfront about it reflexively – as Griffiths always is himself – and leave readers to continue their own dialogic performances with him, some of which, I am sure, will be found reflected in the pages of this book.

Because the book *Trevor Griffiths* is about the construction and circulation of histories, it needs to take account of its own. Written in 2002/3 about a writer who produced the bulk of his television drama work in the last thirty years of the twentieth century, any 'authorship' history must necessarily be retrospective. This is especially the case, given the stance of Chapters 5 and 6 where I asked Trevor Griffiths himself, in 2002, to nominate the 'case studies of several of the practitioner's most significant works', as this series' brief asks. Griffiths chose *Country*, *Oi For England*, *The Last Place On Earth*, *Hope In The Year Two*, and *Food For Ravens*, and in Chapters 5 and 6 I focus on four of these works (the other, *Oi For England*, is looked at in Chapter 1). Obviously, any choices of 'significant works' will be voiced from one position or other, and within one set of discourses or another: so for example I look at academics' choice of significant works in Chapter 1, and reviewers' in Chapter 3. Chapters 5 and 6, therefore, offer Griffiths the same authority of choice, as author looking back from 2002.

This is not privileging nostalgia, but simply offering authority to the current historical moment as Griffiths reflects on his work and on the histories woven through and around his texts. There are obviously other ways that the author could have been inserted into the 'significant text choices' of Chapters 5 and 6; for example, by referring to Griffiths' own sense of priorities as located in each of the decades he worked through, as evidenced for example in his recorded and written interviews at those times (to some extent, that is the stance of Chapter 2). But I have preferred here – as indeed Griffiths has preferred textually and histori-cally throughout his career – a history of significance *spoken* from the present moment.

Then there is also the future of the present moment. Neither Griffiths nor I believe we are engaging with the 'spectres' of Marx, as Stanton Garner Jnr does in a recent book. We do believe we are – must – engage with the reality of a 'New World Order', a frightening (but not so new) international imperialism which tells its truths and its lies (as about 'democratisation' and 'weapons of mass destruction') with equal clarity and obfuscation. Griffiths continues (against so much resistance both in the media and in my own academic field) to sign his affiliation as 'Other' to all of that; as indicated in his Preface to the re-issue of *Occupations*: which he signed 'Trevor Griffiths, Palestine, Summer 1995'. In a surveil-lance world that ludicrously (except as ideological ploy) signs itself as pre- and post-September 11, 2001, we should remember that continuity in Griffiths' signature between 1973, 1995 and 2004.

A biographical sketch

Each of the differently voiced 'Trevor Griffiths' chapters of this book contains or implies its own biographical sketch: the contrast in Chapter 1 among academics between those who embed their analyses of Griffiths in his working-class biography against others who co-opt him for post-'linguistic turn' theory; the often crass and reductive 'socialist' repre-sentation of Griffiths among newspaper reviewers (Chapter 4), and Griffiths' own sense of a powerfully intimate yet generically distanced relationship with his former wife in *Through the Night* (Chapter 4) and his father in *Sons and Lovers* (Chapter 2), *Bill Brand* (Chapter 4), *Food for Ravens* (Chapter 5), and even *Country* (Chapter 5).

It is important that each of the different 'Griffiths' biographies has its place and space in this book. Griffiths himself, for example, would prefer more of the nuanced intertextual analyses of his works (as in Chapters 5, 6 and 8), much less on the 'Leftist' Griffiths constructed by reviewers (Chapter 4), since he feels they have had more than enough space already to speak about him. But it is *all* those different 'Griffiths' biographies, as appropriated in the various media of production, circulation and consumption which work together to present and receive his texts.

On the other hand, I have already made my own position clear: that I do believe in an experiential continuity working through Griffiths' career. The biographical facts of Trevor Griffiths' early life are easily schematised. He was born in Manchester into a working-class northern British family in 1935. His mother was Irish, and his chemical process worker father was the son of a Welsh miner. His father became unemployed when he was very young, and he lived with his grandmother till he was reunited with his parents at five. As Garner notes, he was an early beneficiary of the 1944 Education Act, passing the 11 plus exam to go to a Catholic Grammar School, and then being awarded a state scholarship in 1952 to Manchester University where he studied English. After a stint in the army, he taught English at a private school in Oldham. Politicised by other staff at the school and by his meeting with his first wife, Janice Stansfield, a militant working-class sociology student, Griffiths got involved in the Campaign for Nuclear Disarmament and the New Left Movement of the 1950s and 1960s, becoming chair of the Manchester Left Club in 1960 where he first interacted with many of Britain's leading Left intellectuals, Raymond Williams, John Coates, John Rex, Peter Worsley, Christopher Hill, Perry Anderson, Stuart Hall. Stanley Garner Jnr tells the story well:

> The early New Left registered its mark on Griffiths' life and work in a number of ways: through its opening of socialism to the unfettered debate of ideas, its historical and sociological emphases, its emphasis on education, its focus on culture as lived experience, and its expanded articulation of the political roles of intellectual and cultural worker … Given its emphasis on socialism as something done by people for people and its reclamation of human agency and moral choice, it is no accident that the New Left would generate some of its richest and most prolific work in the fields of history and drama. It is also no accident that Griffiths, who came of political maturity in the vigorous air of New Left thinking, would choose these fields as his principal artistic territory.
> (Garner 1999, 22–3)

Between 1961 and 1965 Griffiths lectured in the Liberal Studies

Department at Stockport Technical College, and after consideration for Labour Party pre-selection in Stockport, he let his Party membership lapse in 1965 because of his disillusionment with the Wilson government. In 1965 he joined the BBC as a further education officer in Leeds where, as Garner says, 'He was exposed to the structures of power and interest that characterized the television establishment in Britain, even as he investigated the educational contributions of broadcast technology on people's lives' (Garner 1999, 25). He resigned from the BBC in 1972 to become a full-time writer, having already seen his play *Occupations* produced in late 1971 and been approached by Kenneth Tynan to write *The Party* (in which Olivier would star) for the National Theatre.

Each part of the schema of biographical details I have listed here was to resonate within very different forms, temporalities and histories throughout his working career. As late as the 1990s Griffiths was planning a series tracing his Irish family story through his mother. It was never made. His father, whose body had been systematically burned while loading sulphur into hoppers and cleaning out acid vats, is a key biographical link in *Sons and Lovers* (1981), where Griffiths recognises both the male domestic power and the at-work exploitation of Paul Morel's miner father (Chapter 2). Griffiths' father is also represented briefly but with reflexive significance in the death of Bill's father in *Bill Brand* (1976, Chapter 4), and more indirectly perhaps, metamorphosed into the class he voted for but could never join in the working-man made landowner, Sir Frederic in *Country* (1981, Chapter 5). In his television play, *All Good Men* (1974), Griffiths brought together different parts of his biographical schema – working-class fathers and sons, his college lecturer and university background, his disillusionment with the Labour Party, and his sense of 'the structures of power and interest that characterised the television establishment in Britain' – in the personalised debate between Edward Waite and his son William. In his theatre (and then television) play *The Party* (1973/1988), Griffiths extended this reflexive media theme, examining the possibilities both of 'strategic penetration' and of the appropriation of people like himself via working within mainstream theatre and television. *Through the Night* (1975, Chapter 3), as we saw, engaged with his former wife's mastectomy, and *Bill Brand* played through much of Griffiths' 1964/5 thinking when being pushed for Labour nomination, and (as with *All Good Men*) his disillusion with a compromising Labour Party.

What is really crucial, and highly complex though, is not a litany of biographical 'influences' on Griffiths' television and theatre works. More important are the ways in which personal class (and gendered) biography, education, new intellectual ideas (Raymond Williams' cultural approach to Griffiths' subject of English, John Rex and Peter Worsley's radical sociology absorbed both through Jan and at the Manchester Left Club, the New Left's socialist humanism, and Griffiths' developing reading of Bertolt Brecht, Walter Benjamin, Georg Lukacs, E.P. Thompson and others) mixed, melded and innovated in his develop-ment of new television forms in his own rediscovery of working-class agency. And then how those innovative forms were circulated and received by British publics.

The grammar schools that working-class boys like Griffiths entered after the 1944 Butler Act produced a majority that did not complete their studies, and, among those who did, a majority who rejected working-class neighbourhood life, their working-class families' values, and who shifted to Conservative politics in 'a conscious and articulate rejection of a way of life' (Jackson and Marsden 1966, 212). But the grammar schools also produced others like Trevor Griffiths who played out the tension (or border, as Griffiths put it) between class-background and new aspira-tions and agencies via 'his choice of realism as a dominant aesthetic; the interest in television as a cultural medium; an awareness of class more pervasive, nuanced, and personally grounded than that of many of his contemporaries' (Garner 1999, 3). Garner rightly notes Griffiths' profound interest in 'the working-class as subject and audience' which has made itself felt throughout his work – 'from *Sam One* in Griffiths' autobiographical play *Sam, Sam* and the aspiring performers of *Come-dians* through the wall builders of *The Gulf between Us* and Danton's guard Henry in *Hope in the Year Two*' (1999, 3).

Sam, Sam (first performed in 1972) was a play about two brothers in which Griffiths explored his own familial distance between brothers on either side of the Education Act (he did it again in *The Party*). But by writing both Sams for the same actor, Griffiths also exposed the tension between social origin and new identity in himself. Sam 1, the older brother, an unemployed worker, performs, like Gethin Price in Griffiths' later *Comedians,* a hard, stand-up comic routine directly to the audience, brutally parodying (but also living experientially) the dirt and smells of his wife, mother and real poverty, while also playing, as Garner notes, on the kitchen-sink realism of contemporary theatre and film. The younger Sam 2 is, like the young adult Griffiths, a teacher who understands the relationship between education and capitalism and seeks revolution. Sam 2 lives a comfortably 'progressive' open marriage in which he and his wife both take lovers, yet he feels trapped and angered by her lovers and by her affluent parents, all of whom give her a power over him that is displayed on-stage in a sexualised class struggle between the equally humiliated partners. Griffiths said of *Sam, Sam* and the cultural and educational impact of the New Left on him in the 1950s and 1960s 'Then began for me a very long struggle to hold on to where I had come from and also to get a hold on this new thing which, outside of its class aspects, dealt with intellect, with feeling, objectivity to some extent, standing outside one's own being and seeing things from another position. So I was living a massive contradiction which I couldn't, unaided anyway, resolve' (Griffiths, interview by Boireau, 1985, 3).

Later chapters of this book will explore the path of that 'long struggle' through a range of media discourses and identities, because, crucially, it was there that much of Griffiths' struggle focused. Inevitably, there are some implicit disadvantages in this book's emphasis on the different media voices constructing 'Trevor Griffiths'. There is less space here for the intertextual analysis of some of his texts, as I have offered in Chapters 5, 6 and 8. There is little space for the important interweaving of Griffiths' stage plays, films and television works (covered excellently by Stanton B. Garner Jnr in his *Trevor Griffiths: Politics, drama, history*) – though there is a different approach to this issue offered here from inside the theatre and television industries in chapter 3. The rhetorical mode of address of different chapters will differ to some extent, since theoretical analysis of television texts in production, circulation and reception (which this book is about) vary in methodological focus, register and emphasis.

But there are also major advantages in adopting this strategy. First, it covers a much wider field of media theory than textual analysis of Griffiths' plays alone would do. Second, it encourages academics and students to follow Griffiths himself in being reflexive about their own work (which is one reason I begin the book with an account of the academics' 'Trevor Griffiths'). Third, it examines the industries of television, theatre, and academia which Griffiths' work must engage to reach the audiences he aspires to, and it begins to look at what happens when those audiences respond.

It has been these complexities and mediated identities that have constituted the writing life – and the writing around that life – of the following chapters.

John Tulloch

Mapping Griffiths and cultural studies: from New Left to Derrida, *The Party* to *Oi For England* and *Food for Ravens*

1

Utopia has its place in a re-mapped world; the achievement, for Griffiths, lies in 'imagining such a thing'. (Stanton B. Garner Jnr, 1996, 389)

The most recent sustained academic account of Griffiths' work has been within a postmodernist context. In his book *Trevor Griffiths: Politics, drama, history*, Stanton B. Garner Jr, describing Griffiths' stage play, *The Gulf Between Us*, speaks symptomatically about Griffiths' shift from 'grand narratives'.

O'Toole is a fallible narrator, given to narrative ellipses and memory breakdowns ... Such moments of slippage and fragmentation reveal much about the dramatic and epistemological world of Griffiths's recent work, an arena that opens up in the failure of the great nineteenth century narratives. Characterized by shifts and improvisations in the face of both the obsolete and the uncharted, it is an increasingly postmodern territory, operating out of and within the fissures of politics and representation (1999, 235–6).

I begin with Garner's study not only because it is a fine account of Griffiths' work, but also because it indicates so clearly the way in which Griffiths is 'spoken' by the discourses that describe his 'epistemological world'. There is even an implied sense in Garner's account of a parallel historical development between postmodernism and Griffiths' changing dramatic form, though Garner's is too subtle an analysis for that parallel to be used reductively. He argues that 'by the late 1990s it is the stage of *history* that has changed most intricately' (1999, 6, my italics).

But for Garner, 'In the twilight of organised Marxism, history in Griffiths' dramatic and filmic practice becomes the site of retrospect, both interiorized and public, and the boundaries of the past, present, and future are troubled by the spectrality that Derrida identifies as the signature of a post-Marx historical conjuncture' (1999, 16). Garner's book is written self-consciously and rhetorically *within* the 'twilight of organized Marxism' and in the context of new, postmodern master accounts, which speak of the 'traces' of history, of 'spectres', 'slippage' and 'fragmentation' that supposedly now map Griffiths' work.

While admiring Garner's account, I take issue with it, especially when it wants to use the 'lens' of Derrida to look right back to Griffiths' early works. Thus Garner argues that

> even in the heyday of early 1970s radicalism Griffiths's plays and films derive much of their power, and their poignancy, from their awareness of loss and dispossession .... If, as Derrida suggests, a certain spectrality – not yet, no longer, not here, not now – has been constitutive of Marxism's claim on the present since its earliest emergence, then the spectropoetics of Griffiths's most recent work can help rethink the workings of mourning and hope, nostalgia and utopia, in even the most overtly revolutionary phase of post-war British political theatre (1999, 16–17).

In my view there are more useful ways to examine how Trevor Griffiths is 'written' – and how he *writes* – within academic discourse than simply via the lens of Derrida's retrospective. In this and the following chapter, I will focus on a cultural studies much broader than Derrida in looking back at Griffiths' early television plays, and on Griffiths' own account of the 'not yet, no longer, not here, not now' through his works.

Cultural studies and Trevor Griffiths

The quarter century of Trevor Griffiths' television activity coincides almost exactly with the emergence of media and cultural [M/C] studies, as well as with significant developments of cultural analysis within theatre studies. There are two ways of examining the construction of Griffiths within these academic discourses. The first is to map 'Trevor Griffiths' across the changing hegemonies within academic paradigms. Thus M/C studies has successively been dominated by the (often overlapping) contributions of Marxism, feminism, semiotics, psycho-analysis, screen theory, ethnographic production analysis, 'active audience' theory, Derridean (and other post-modernisms), to mention only the major theoretical discourses that have engaged with Griffiths' work that I will survey in this chapter. The second way is to consider Trevor Griffiths and those academic critics who write about him as themselves situated within *contiguous but different industries*, thus contributing different languages and representations in the same time period, and yet imbricated in facing similar national/global histories, identities, ideologies and politics. This second approach must include Trevor Griffiths as a television and theatre writer who *positions* that other industry of

academia. I will look at this dialogic relationship between Griffiths' television work and the academic industry in Chapter 2.

Mapping 'Trevor Griffiths'

Within M/C studies Trevor Griffiths has different moments of citation within a field shifting its preferred discourses across a thirty-year
period, and along the way engaging with the same range of substantive
issues that inform the various signatures of Griffiths himself: authorship, genre, text, production, audience, ideology, identity.

Authorship studies: Griffiths' revolutionary socialism

As with the newspaper reviewers I have cited, it has been difficult for
academic critics, whatever their paradigm, not to focus centrally on
Griffiths' socialism. A significant difference between academic analysts
of his work has depended on how transparently they have collapsed
Griffiths' texts *on* to his class and political biography, and to what extent
M/C theories have been used to distance, interrogate or extend Griffiths'
own sense of 'seeing things from another position'.

For example, at the more 'transparent' end of this spectrum was
Catherine Itzin, in her book *Stages of Revolution: Public Theatre in
Britain since 1968*. For Itzin, '1968' was a significant political marker.
Consequently, it seemed significant for her that Griffiths was older and
politicised earlier than the generation of other political playwrights she
discussed, like Howard Brenton, David Hare and David Edgar. '[He]
was not politicised like them in 1968, but in the late fifties and early
sixties ... involved in the emergence of the British New Left ... He was
strongly influenced by Raymond Williams' *The Long Revolution* in the
early sixties. "It liberated me"' (1980, 171).

Mindful of her book's benchmark date, Itzin argued that, 'In 1969
he regarded himself as a revolutionary Marxist who believed that
through various means of organisation, it would be possible to create
an insurrectionary moment and then to exploit it for revolutionary
purposes' (1980, 171). This consequently explained his substantive focus
on potentially revolutionary moments in history: the 1920 Turin factory
occupations of *Occupations* (1974), the 1903 moralism/pragmatism split
within the Bolshevik party in *Absolute Beginners* (1974), and the collision
between revolutionary socialist son and reformist Labour Party father
in *All Good Men* (1974).

In Itzin's evolving socio-political biography, Griffiths, was 'motivated
by [his] impotence in the face of the great upheavals of 1968 – Paris,
Detroit, Watts' (1980, 166) to produce *The Party*.

Set at the time of the May Events in Paris, the play functioned as a dramatic commentary on the present political situation in Britain. The main character, Joe Shawcross, is a successful television producer who is shown to be sexually and, by analogy, politically impotent ... His friends include an academic Marxist-Leninist revisionist, Andrew Ford; a Trotskyite working-class leader, John Tagg; a former communist writer, Malcolm Sloman, who is drinking himself to death because 'he can't bear the thought of himself succeeding in a society he longs to destroy'; and others representing student, black and women's liberation groups. In short, Griffiths peopled the stage with a cross-section of the Left in Britain, brought them together in a 'party' to discuss the lack of a political party. (Itzin 1980, 165–6)

Also overtly biographical-political for Itzin was *Occupations*, Griffiths' commitment 'to analysing Marxism and to condemning Stalinism without discrediting socialism in the eyes of the world' (Griffiths, cited in Itzin 1980, 172). Again, she interpreted *Bill Brand* (1976) directly in terms of Griffiths' specific political biography. 'The idea came to him on General Election night in 1974, waiting for the votes to be counted, with the anticipation amongst many of a Tory majority, and the final very narrow Labour victory ... Griffiths said he believed in mass parties, though he couldn't see even the germs of those parties in the present Left groupings, and he wanted to convey this.'

So by 1978, Itzin argues, 'influenced by E.P. Thompson's *The Poverty of Theory*, Griffiths had come to regard himself as a revolutionary socialist faced with the problem of "trying to work out ways in which revolutionary change can occur which don't depend on an insurrectionary moment"' (Itzin 1980, 171–2).

As we can see, this kind of 'authorship' analysis of Griffiths' work (see also Tulloch, 1990) relies very heavily on interviews with Trevor Griffiths himself, and compares (like Billington in his review quoted earlier) his style and his views on theatre and television with those of other Left playwrights like David Edgar and John McGrath (or in Tulloch's case with film/TV makers like McGrath and Ken Loach). Thus Itzin cites an article by David Edgar in *Socialist Review* which points to the problems of Griffiths' attempt at 'strategic penetration' via television naturalism 'in the atomised, a-collective arena of the family living room, the place where people are at their least critical, their most ... reactionary' (cited in Itzin 1980, 169; also cited in Tulloch 1990, 169). Similarly, McGrath is quoted as saying 'In Trevor Griffiths' *The Party*, the character of an old Marxist revolutionary from Glasgow was taken over by Lord Olivier, and became a vehicle for a star to communicate with his admirers, a juicy part for a juicy director' (cited in Itzin 1980, 167–8).

Typically, in Itzin's authored account, Griffiths is quoted defending himself against these charges, believing he was creating 'a sort of alternative drama inside television' in *Bill Brand*. 'The rehearsal process was egalitarian, democratic, destructured, de-starred. We talked with each other, we wrestled with the text. We created such an extraordinary community within the organisation. People were politicised in the course of the series and by the end of it they were challenging management decisions about when the plays would go out and how they would be promoted' (Griffiths, cited in Itzin 1980, 170).

Genre critique and production analysis
Merging comfortably with authorship accounts of Griffiths' work were the analyses of Griffiths as a worker within and against popular television genres, and these academic analyses too were generally authorised by Griffiths' quoted intentions. Thus *Bill Brand* was analysed as a critique not only of current Labour politics, but also of the popular TV series at peak viewing time. Itzin quotes Griffiths as saying, 'If for every *Sweeney* that went out a *Bill Brand* went out, there would be a real struggle for the popular imagination ... And people would be free to make liberating choices about where reality lies. Testing both against their own experience' (Griffiths, cited in Itzin 1980, 169). Similarly based on Griffiths' quoted comments were interpretations of *Through The Night* in the context of the hospital soap genre, of *Comedians* in relation to a recent popular TV comics' series, and of *Sons and Lovers* and *The Cherry Orchard* in critiquing the conventional BBC classics genre. Thus, Mike Poole and John Wyver quoted Griffiths extensively in noting that his 'version of *Sons and Lovers* ... differs crucially from most other classic adaptations in its willingness to go beyond mere replication and offer a genuinely *interpretive* reading of the novel ... Walter Morel ... becomes a study in resistance, an assertion of the positive values of the culture Paul rejects ... Considerably aided by a performance of great power by Tom Bell, full of nuanced use of dialect and gesture, Morel becomes the working-class voice suppressed in the text' (Poole and Wyver 1984, 141, 146, 147).

As the comment on the acting of Tom Bell indicates, this kind of genre analysis of Griffiths' work also slid creatively into the new kinds of production ethnographies which were being published in M/C studies around the time that Poole and Wyver's Griffiths monograph was being researched and written (e.g. Alvarado and Buscombe's *Hazell*, Tulloch and Alvarado's *Doctor Who*, and Millington and Nelson's *Boys from the Blackstuff*). The dramatist's *experience* of tensions in production becomes a key source in this kind of study. In particular, Poole and Wyver draw

on Griffiths' experiences with the production of *Sons and Lovers* to note
how conventional 'heritage' values seeped back into the Griffiths text:

> Griffiths has described in detail how the design process works to produce
> this kind of distortion. 'Designers determine the 'look' of a production
> on the basis of highly selective photographic evidence, which is really a
> poisoned witness to the past. Photography, as it developed in the nine-
> teenth century, was a middle-class practice conducted by outsiders who
> didn't necessarily understand their working-class subjects. They produced
> posed images which convey very little about how lives were actually lived
> ...' The cumulative effect of these small distortions – a child's doll that
> is just too expensive to belong in a miner's home, a parlour that looks a
> shade too lower-middle-class – leads to a loss of overall material texture
> (Poole and Wyver 1984, 143–5).

Tulloch similarly quotes Griffiths extensively in examining the collaboration between Griffiths and Loach on *Fatherland* as an exercise in challenging 'Cold War' and various European film genres (1990, chapter 6).

Semiotics, linguistics and discourse analysis
Other trends within M/C and theatre studies were less keen to accept
the authorial voice of Trevor Griffiths as the basis of their interpretative
act, sometimes erecting a superstructure of theory to redirect Griffiths'
socialism. This was the case with Willam S. Free's analysis of Griffiths'
1972 theatre play, *Sam, Sam*, where he drew on Keir Elam's *Semiotics of
Theatre and Drama* (with its extensive consideration of Edward T. Hall's
anthropology of 'proxemics' and Patrice Pavis' spectator/performance
'perspectives'). As with socio-biographical and generic analyses, Free
still overtly foregrounded Griffiths' 'class politics', but drew on the array
of semiotic theory to extend our sense of the *success* of Griffiths' personal
political project. 'Performance space has become a way of experiencing
the nuances of class structure. Having moved us from the relaxed intimacy of act one to the tense hostility of act two, Griffiths can load our
responses heavily in favour of working-class life by allowing the contrast
of special codes to work its own way upon us. This playing with space as
a key to social and class attitudes makes *Sam, Sam* a strikingly original
play for its time' (1984, 52).

An emphasis on using academic theory to extend the success of
Griffiths' project was also the feature of Romy Clark's analysis of *Fatherland*, which used semiotic, social linguistic and discourse analysis. Clark
drew on Tulloch's 1990 production-based interpretation of the Loach/
Griffiths TV film, *Fatherland* in her own sections on 'the semiotics of
appearance and identity', 'names and their intertextuality', 'naturalism
versus critical realism', 'metaphor, symbolism and the discourse of

German politics', 'passivization and agency', and 'discourse and identity'. In particular, she focused on a scene early in the film when the
dissident East German *Liedermacher*, Klaus Drittermann faces his first
press conference in West Berlin.

> Griffiths chose the name of the CDU politician, Hundhammer, very care-
> fully because it was intended to underscore the political point about the
> continuity between Fascism and the present German leadership which
> Drittermann makes ... The name Hundhammer ... would resonate for
> those members of the audience who are familiar with German politics,
> and particularly in the German version for ZDF ... All of this is lost in the
> film text: as Griffiths said, the name Hennig [which Loach used instead]
> 'comes from nowhere' (1993): it has no history. In addition, the sound
> of Hundhammer is much harsher than that of Hennig. The former is
> made up of three syllables, two of then preceded by the same sound /h/
> and separated by the aspirated dental /t/. The latter, on the other hand,
> is bi-syllabic, ending in a palatial fricative /c/. Drittermann, in the print
> text, speaks in very formal complex syntax and his lexical choices are
> also those of formal political discourse ... I thank is formal discourse:
> thanks or thank you are more everyday informal choices; would remind
> is a conditional form more used in formal interactions than the [film's]
> simple present tense remind. It is a phrase typical of English political
> adversarial discourse ... especially Prime Minister's Question Time ... By
> the phrase citizens of the DDR ... Drittermann indicates that he speaks
> on behalf of, and sees himself as one of, them; he does not distance
> himself from them.

As Clark argues, 'this is another important thread in the film and in
Griffiths' politics: Drittermann is a dissident *socialist*, he is not anti-
GDR. The relative clause "those who stand in the direct line of German
Fascism" ... includes Hundhammer, constructs Hundhammer as a
fascist; the modality is categorical, absolute certainty: the interpretation
of modern Germany and its politicians is not open for discussion'.

Clark suggests that it is because of this syntactic complexity in
Griffiths' text that Drittermann emerges as a politically sophisticated
person who responds carefully and dispassionately to Hundhammer's
speech. This is very different from the film version. Here 'Drittermann
does not present himself as a citizen of the DDR: the representativeness
of the character is lost. Second, "What you say about freedom makes
me laugh" (Text 2, line 55) seems an emotional outburst compared
with the measured response of the print text. The actual delivery of the
lines by the non-professional actor also reinforces this sense of a man
responding emotionally rather than politically' (Clark 1999, 114–16).

Clark's sustained linguistic analysis extends Griffiths' anti-naturalism/
anti-non-actor point (made to Tulloch in interview) that his critical-

realist writing is precise, complex and not readily available for change. While she does refer to Griffiths' views, Clark's discourse seeks to extend what Griffiths 'knew he knew' about his writing via her own academic linguistic competence.

Feminism and psychoanalysis

First-wave feminists like Michelene Wandor were less celebratory of Griffiths' work than Clark, incorporating his early pieces within a theatre of 'cultural debate', wherein the 'sexual violence and the representations of ordinary people ... heralded the arrival of a new generation of angry young men for whom the freedom to use sexual violence as a metaphor for political disintegration was one essential consequence of the abolition of censorship' (Wandor 1973, 10). However, within this context Wandor did see Griffiths' *Occupations* as 'an altogether more serious, and more problematic, confluence of political subject matter relying on sexual metaphor' (Wandor 1973, 10). Drawing on assumptions about women in 'the real world' which later-stage feminists were to critique, Wandor noted that *Occupation*'s set was 'dominated by a bed in which lies Angelica, Kabak's wife, dying of cancer of the womb. She is an aristocrat in whom are symbolized both Kabak's personal emotional crises, and the decay of the ruling-classes. Political disease is represented directly by the image of decay on the site of motherhood. The image is highly emotive, and extraordinarily powerful – but at the paradoxical expense of the representation of the realistic woman' (Wandor 1973, 10).

A more theoretical feminist-psychoanalytical analysis that extended Wandor's concern that women in Griffiths are reduced to 'passive representation' (Wandor 1987, 106) enabling the birth of socialism, was Wendy J. Wheeler and Trevor R. Griffiths' account of *Occupations*, where the play was read in terms of Freud's ideas about the organising of primal fantasy through sexuality and sexual difference. In particular, the 'fantasy structure of *Occupations* exposes the unconsciously *compelling* nature of what Marx described as the terrific dynamism of capitalism' (1992, 193).

Again, here, Griffiths' socialism was taken as a founding 'idea', but in this case embedded within complex structurations of desire that are sexual as much as political. In *Occupations*, erotic, romantic desire was 'confirmed by the structure of the set, with its dominant bed. This scene offers itself to the audience in a way that initially allows it to be read as the aftermath of a scene of seduction ... The audience is, however, quickly required to amend this initial reading (and the fantasies which it puts into play) and to recognise the signs of the scene as something else.

The displacement here is from the supposed scene of sexual seduction to the political seduction initiated by the reference to Gramsci' (Wheeler and Griffiths 1992, 195).

On the one hand, in this analysis, there is Griffiths' (socialist) signature, which situated a performative play of audience displacement and difference. In this respect, *Occupations* 'offers, at the point at which fantasy is constrained by the demands of the law and hence of the symbolic, a form of closure which is an invitation to take up a certain identity which attempts, as human identity *does*, to subordinate the sexual instincts to the ego instincts' (1992, 195), where human identity is defined as 'socialism'. On the other hand, there is 'the textual implication ... of the betrayal of a socialist imaginary: the communist seductions fail, the capitalist seduction succeeds'.

> The sexual instincts are (biologically) directed towards the preservation of the species, the self-preservative (ego) instincts towards the preservation of the individual. The articulation of the dialectic of these two instincts is expressible within a political register as the dialectic between the collective urges of communism and the individualist urges of capitalism. Occupations itself ends with the dominance within the dialectic of bourgeois capital. In fact, neither of these instincts is possible without the other. The political question remains that of the form of the synthesis, and the politico-aesthetic question that of its representation. (Wheeler and Griffiths 1992, 197)

At this point, Griffiths' authorship is about as distanced by theory as is possible, without altogether rejecting it, and is now simply one part of a binary expression of 'ideas' underpinned by (and repressing) the 'structure' of primal fantasies in the text which take the work well beyond the naturalism seen by critic Michael Billington.

Much closer to Griffiths' own voice, while still in part siding with the feminist critique of *Occupations*, is Garner, who argues that on the one hand, Wandor's 'description may not be entirely fair as a portrait of Griffiths' attitude towards gender and sexuality .... He often demonstrates an awareness of female experience and its independent claims and authority: *Absolute Beginners* includes several scenes in which Zasulich and Krupskaya occupy a female space independent of male-directed political manoeuvrings, and *Through the Night* stands as one of the decade's most powerful defences of female bodily experience against the objectifications of a predominantly male medical establishment' (1999, 97).

On the other hand, though, 'Wandor's reading of *Occupations* isolates a set of gender problems that Griffiths' plays and films will never entirely escape: a privileging of the male as a site of political vision and agency, a

fear of the female that (in the early work at least) borders on the antagon-
istic, and a difficulty in imagining the terms by which a cross-gendered
mutuality might be achieved and sustained ... [M]isogynistic attacks
on the female body ... run from Sam I's tirade on his wife's bathing
habits ('dirty bugger') to Gethin Price's physical attack on his female
dummy [in *Comedians*]. Most persuasive of all is the relative invisibility
of women on Griffiths' political landscape and the frequent sense one
gets (as in *Bill Brand*) that they serve as backdrops for the more realised
struggles of men' (Garner 1999, 97–8).

Active audiences against screen theory
A number of the academic analyses of Griffiths' works speak of the
audience. Wheeler and Griffiths' discussion of 'shifts in the audience's
reading' which militate 'against the adoption of a settled subject position', and of the 'structure of the play [that] *allows* [my italics] the audience to take up various positions in relation to the fantasy' (1992, 195) is
symptomatic of both post-linguistic turn structuralist (including 'screen
theory') and post-structuralist emphases on the textual positioning
of 'implied' or 'inscribed' audiences. By the 1980s and early 1990s,
following Stuart Hall, David Morley and others, there was significant
criticism within M/C studies of this construction of audiences-in-the-
text, and wide-ranging empirical audience research was conducted
within a loosely defined 'active audience' approach. Sometimes the
'ethnographic' stance of these approaches also embraced production
studies, loosely applying Stuart Hall's distinction between 'encoding'
and 'decoding' the text.

Trevor Griffiths' work attracted virtually no empirical audience
academic analysis of this kind until Jonathan Bignell's article, 'Trevor
Griffiths's Political Theatre: from *Oi for England* to *The Gulf Between
Us* in 1994 (though see Tulloch, 1990, 149–51). Bignell noted here the
'sense of urgency' that Griffiths felt with both of these plays, with *Oi For
England* playing within a year following Griffiths' exposure to increased
racism at a youth culture conference around the 1981 British 'race' riots,
and *The Gulf Between Us* produced one year after the Gulf War. In both
cases, Griffiths spoke of writing less nuanced scripts than he had with
Country and *The Cherry Orchard*. 'The way you write depends on what
is urgent' (Griffiths, cited in Bignell 1994, 49); and given the overt and
immediately political intent of these two pieces, Bignell made it his task
to examine the *success* (or otherwise) of Griffiths' construction of audiences as political subjects.

Because *Oi For England* was written for television, Bignell (implicitly
taking up the Griffiths/McGrath/Edgar debate) argues that Griffiths

'chose naturalistic forms ... since this was the form with which the TV audience was most familiar', though his embedding of character in 'ideas ... exploring the contradictions of contemporary social issues' was 'in a way which might now be termed realist rather than through the comfortable naturalism of contemporary TV fiction' (1994, 50).

As Bignell notes, after its TV transmission, the play was 'toured around youth clubs and community centres, gradually being changed in the process, each performance being followed by a discussion on the issues it was intended to serve' (1994, 50). However,

> The audiences of young people who watched Oi For England were not only confused about what the play was engaging with in their experience, but also lacked the specific skills to understand theatrical representation ... Therefore, the play was unsuccessful as a political intervention, since it did not provoke debate about issues in the lives of the audience ... Oi was also unsuccessful as theatre, since its naturalistic theatrical form could not easily be decoded, and the cabaret style which gradually replaced naturalism during the tour moved the play towards musical performance interspersed with dialogue. (1994, 50–1)

In his analysis of Oi and The Gulf, Bignell used structuralist notions of spectatorship and 'positioning' of the audience, as in his comment: 'The ending of The Gulf counterposed the pathos and emotion of the dead child with the long polemical address to the audience by Dr Aziz, shifting the audience from one regime of spectatorship to another, from emotional involvement to political argument, and refusing a pathos which might anneal and resolve the play's contrasts' (1994, 52–3). Like Wheeler and Griffiths, Bignell found in the plays a consistent displacing of audiences between personal emotions (or desires) and political ideas. The *difference* in Bignell's analysis was his interest in empirical audience readings, and in actual audience resistances to textual 'audience positioning'. In the case of The Gulf, Bignell's empirical focus was newspaper reviewers of the play as performed at the West Yorkshire Playhouse, where 'Critics were ... confused by the mixed theatrical modes, since naturalistic action co-existed with the "magic realism" of the trans-historical Gurkha figure, and the piece could also be seen as a "work play", with the builders constructing a wall on stage in the real time of the performance. The shifting emotional and polemical registers seemed disjointed' (Bignell 1994, 53, 54). Thus, for reviewers who had the competences to 'understand Griffiths' political signature, the fact that the play was "signed" with his name as author and director, allowed the critics to close down the meanings of the production. Its anarchic form and mixed registers were not perceived as political theatre ... but as the failure of Griffiths to live up to his own signature' (1994, 55–6).

Bignell was drawing strongly in this article on Bourdieu-style notions of cultural competence, which were very influential in M/C studies generally. In particular his binary here is on the one hand 'young audiences' lack of competence' in decoding the conventions of performed naturalism, and on the other hand, the 'highly-developed competences' of a 'specialist audience' of theatre critics. This theory-led construction of his audience analysis allowed Bignell to eschew any empirical 'actual audience' study of theatre or TV audiences of his own (The *Oi* audience data was taken from Mike Poole's *Guardian* article, and the critics' responses, of course, from newspapers also). On the other hand, Bignell's achievement is in bringing together discussion of how Griffiths' works formally signify with at least some empirical 'reader-response' data.

A clear example of how the choice of starting from different theoretical premises leads to different conclusions about the radical potential of the same play can be found in Stuart Cosgrove's analysis of *Oi For England* in *Screen* in 1983. Over the previous decade, the British journal *Screen* had established close to a hegemonic position in M/C studies, particularly in the area of film analysis; and a significant theme of *Screen*'s political challenge had been anti-naturalist. Closely associated with this theoretical position was *Screen*'s emphasis on post-Brechtian devices of film or television reflexivity.

Cosgrove, writing a few years beyond the epicentre of this 'classic realist text' debate in *Screen*, was still influenced by it. Thus, he argued, *Oi For England*'s 'progressive project' was damaged by 'the onerous task of working within the formal constraints of a single-set location, and a naturalist style modified only by the inclusion of short video sequences of the riots' (1983, 93). But he also noted criticism of the TV play 'from inside socialism'. In particular, this focused on 'the graphically racist speech delivered by The Man, in defence of his own attitudes to music and politics' as he 'occupies a pivotal and plausible place within the narrative' (1983, 93).

However, for Cosgrove neither naturalism nor the erotic meta-narrative fascination of fascism was the most significant limitation of *Oi For England*. Rather, this resided in 'the manner in which the narrative moves inexorably towards an unsatisfactory resolution that remains trapped in inarticulacy and idealism' (Cosgrove 1983, 93). At the end, Finn remains behind as the other members of the group leave the basement to loot and riot in the streets outside. Finn is joined briefly by the landlord's black daughter, 'a nervous but sympathetic relationship is struck up between the skinhead and the black girl and after several time ellipses the two of them dress up in martial arts equipment in readiness for ritualised combat in the streets' (Cosgrove 1983, 94). Cosgrove's 'inarticulacy and idealism' charge against Griffiths' ending – seen as an 'inexorable' narrative closure marked by none of Brecht's reflexive articulacy – resides in his view that 'the implication is that Finn will join the black girl and his own sister (who has been ridiculed by members of the group for admitting her Irish origins and being a fan of UB40) in inhabiting a multi-racial society without resorting to racism' (1983, 94).

Yet, in Cosgrove's analysis it is the relation between *production* (rather than audience) conditions and politics that is the critical focus of attention, and which, for him, 'saves' *Oi For England* as a radical text despite its naturalism and idealist narrative closure. It is this production relationship that marks *Oi* as 'a particularly important example of the possibilities of urgent cultural practice' (1983, 94). Griffiths, says Cosgrove, was responding urgently to the 'race' riots in Britain of the summer of 1981. He was quickly both confronting the British viewers with an alternative take on the riots, and refusing his consent to the transparent assimilation of skin culture into fascism.

> To ensure that the play had an impact on the social tensions within youth culture when the riots were still in common memory, Griffiths aimed for an unusually fast production schedule. The entire project from the submission of the script during the winter of 1981 to the play's transmissions in the spring of 1982, was geared towards speed and immediacy. The crew were recruited from Central TV's Crossroads serial and the studio time available to the production necessitated an uncomplicated single-set location. In any sustained critical analysis of Oi For England, its deficiencies have to be measured alongside the rigours of a production context brought about by the political advantages of immediate and urgent cultural representation. Oi For England exemplifies the determining pressures that industrial and production constraints put on formal structures. It bears the traces of a drama restricted by its own urgency. (Cosgrove 1983, 94)

It was this continued and *formally flexible* determination of Griffiths for 'strategic penetration' or 'cultural entryism' which made him, for Cosgrove, 'the most theoretically and politically acute' of the generation of dramatists emerging out of British subsidised theatre post-1968. In addition (but not central for Cosgrove, unlike Bignell's analysis) there was the fact that *Oi* was then toured in working-class, racially sensitive areas (and Cosgrove documents some of the problems surrounding conditions of production in places like Barnsley, Doncaster and Wakefield). Importantly, 'there was always a desire to avoid the new institutionalisation of the fringe, and to aim for non-theatrical venues within working-class territory' (Cosgrove 1983, 95).

Cosgrove thus drew on Griffiths' own caution about writing about the working class from the 'covered stand', arguing that 'In transgressing the normal cultural categories by becoming a live performance after its life as a television drama, *Oi For England* seems to point forward to a relatively uncharted area of political culture. Its recognition of the need to continually regenerate representation within an urgent political moment, and its insistence on addressing an unsafe constituency of politically divided, and perhaps culturally hostile, young people is one of the ways in which independent projects can take part in the decisive action on the terraces' (Cosgrove 1983, 96).

Then, in a final return to *Screen*'s long-term rejection of the 'classic realist text' and 'heritage' histories, Cosgrove noted that *Oi* marked a decisive break with Griffiths' 'multi-track, concept-album nuances' in his previous works, *Sons and Lovers*, *The Cherry Orchard* and *Country*.

Postmodernism
As the twentieth century drew to a close, Griffiths' work began to be reconsidered within post-structuralist and postmodernist theoretical frames. Writing about *Comedians* in 1993, for example, Marybeth Inverso drew on Foucault's notion in *Discipline and Punish* of the Elizabethan period – preceding the modernity of the surveillant prison-panopticon – disciplining via spectacle and theatricality, in particular via the public execution. Adding a touch of new historicism also, Inverso wrote that the 'coalescence' of theatrical and punitive modes made 'sense in an age which treated execution as a public spectacle ... the conflation of stage and scaffold during this period has been attested to by literary critics and historians alike ... Michel Foucault explores the carnivalesque atmosphere which often broke out, especially when the carefully rehearsed, deathly pageant went awry' (1993, 420).

Writing prior to Griffiths' *Hope in the Year Two* which, with the impending public execution of Danton, would have been grist to her mill, Inverso focused on Act II of *Comedians*. Here, Gethin Price 'Slips into the role of executioner. Having made them laugh, he'll make them die laughing. He pins a flower on the woman dummy's dress. Within moments, "*a dark red stain, gradually widening, begins to form behind the flower*" ... Oddly enough, but with perfect symmetry, Griffiths' play sends us back to the concentration camp as Waters explains to Price where his own hate had gone' (1993, 427, 428).

There are, Inverso argues, different relations constructing the various 'scaffold plays' of early- and post-modernity. 'Postmodernist dramatic renderings of the execution spectacle ... can be variously described as a defensive strategy, the "crime" itself, the execution itself, and even as a deliberate counter-attack launched by the performer upon the audience' (1993, 421). Thus, in Price's working-class 'football fan' action against the middle-class audience for *Comedians*, even this postmodernist analysis, which is otherwise distanced from Griffiths' own biography and authorship, recognises his use of the play as a site of counter-struggle.

Finally, in this brief account of the discursive mapping of Trevor Griffiths within M/C studies, we move from Foucault to Derrida. Thus, in relation to Griffiths' *Food For Ravens*, Stanton Garner argues,

> It is hard not to evoke Derrida one last time or to see in *Food For Ravens* ... a realization of the French theorist's deconstructive meditation on time and history: 'Without this non-contemporaneity with itself of the living present, without that which secretly unhinges it, without this responsibility and this respect for justice concerning those who are not there, of those who are no longer or who are not yet present and living, what sense would there be to ask the question "where?", "where tomorrow?", "whither?"' (Derrida, Spectres of Marx, cited in Garner 1999, 270).

It is that shifting between historical moments discursively, between early and post-modernity in Inverso's case, late- and post-modernity in Garner's study – refusing both the overwhelming 'now' of a situated account and the narrative causality of 'then' – which marks both their analyses of Griffiths' work as postmodernist. But their particular academic play, via Foucault and Derrida, between (discursive and spectatorial) histories 'then' and 'now' are, I would argue, themselves 'spectres' of Trevor Griffiths' own engagements with history 'then' and 'now'.

Between television and theory industries: from *Occupations* and *Through the Night* to *Sons and Lovers* and *The Gulf Between Us*

2

Though the story of the play is bedded in a lost moment of European socialist history – the occupation of the factories in Northern Italy in 1920 – there are clear resonances with strategically similar struggles in Europe and Britain at the time of its writing ... Audiences, whether in Reagan's rebrutalised America or later in Thatcher's pantomime Britain, tended to find the play a journey worth the taking. (Trevor Griffiths, Introduction to *Occupations*, 1995)

In 1982 Trevor Griffiths, as writer of a new BBC Television version of *Sons and Lovers*, was watching the production on location in Nottingham, where, 'down the blackbrick nineteenth century street of working-class houses, the unit chippies continue their patient attempts to disguise or dismantle the present tense (aerials, antennae, plastic piping' (Griffiths 1982, 7), when he was left speechless by an 'American journalist down for the day' who 'asked if I realised how lucky we were in Britain to have these perfect and loving reconstructions of period housing "maintained and set aside" for historical filmwork of this kind' (Griffiths 1982, 8).

The anecdote recalls Robin Nelson's comment that a significant attraction of TV costume dramas is 'in the crafting of the serials themselves, in how the illusion of historical reality, the conviction of authenticity, was achieved ... To non-Brits, particularly perhaps Americans and Australians who form the substantial part of the Anglophone overseas television market, period costume dramas may appear to tap into deep history' (Nelson, 2001, 39).

But according to Griffiths' television aesthetic the production naturalism he was witnessing on location was not 'deep history' at all, rather a history that 'squirms and twists, glints and is gone. It's now, we're here, that's that' (1982, 8). The encounter with the American did help generate new aesthetic thoughts in the frustrated Griffiths. He now could see the

wood within the trees. Seventy years ago when these streets were already old, cramped and confining, Lawrence had railed against them and against the economic system that made them possible. 'The great crime which the moneyed classes and providers of industry committed in the palmy Victorian days was the condemning of the workers to ugliness, ugliness, ugliness ... the human soul needs actual beauty more than bread'. Much of his best writing, including Sons and Lovers, had been informed by this sense that the real face of capitalism was ugly and inhuman and that the world it reproduced in its image denied the potentiality for human growth in most of its inhabitants. And yet, beyond the antennae, the plastic piping, the modest dormers, the Ford Escorts parked out of sight round the corner, these same houses and the working people persisted in their millions around the country, the angering perpetuation of a divisive and exploitative system's dehumanising entailments. Lawrence's mother had lived and died in such a house, in such a street; as had my own, and distant relatives still dwell in them. For them, 'historical reconstruction' lies one insulting whisker's width from 'present reality'. It was enough. We would finish. It would be as good as we could make it. It would, with whatever imperfections, speak of these things. (Griffiths 1982, 8–9)

It is there, in the determined agency of 'We *would* finish' that Griffiths speaks *his* (not Derrida's nor Foucault's) sense of the 'insulting whisker's width' between 'historical reconstruction' and 'present reality' via an aesthetic realism (Tulloch 1990, chapter 6) which is constantly evolving according to his sense of the historical relationship between an earlier (in this case Lawrence's, in *Occupations* Gramsci's) reality and his own.

This chapter does not 'map' Trevor Griffiths as an effect of the history of cultural studies and its speakers (Chapter 1). Rather, by way of his own professional and theoretical writings, it will examine Griffiths' own engagement with the 'not yet, no longer, not here, not now' of history, theory and form to suggest that academic critiques which too simply discuss his spectator-positionings miss much of Griffiths' creative play between aesthetic forms 'then' and 'now'.

Trevor Griffiths, Raymond Williams and Georg Lukacs

The biographical authorship position which, directly and indirectly, featured strongly in Chapter 1 is neither 'wrong' nor simplistic. There are indeed intriguing linkages and parallels between Griffiths and various mentors in the New Left movement. Politically, theoretically and formally, this is especially true of Trevor Griffiths' closeness to Raymond Williams, one of the foundation figures of cultural studies. The fact that Griffiths himself is highly articulate theoretically, and, like most M/C scholars of this period, on the Left politically, led to him engaging in debates across the industries of television, theatre *and* academia, as Williams did also. For example, in writing *The Party*, Griffiths engaged with Deutscher's book on Trotsky and Marcuse on repressive tolerance; while *All Good Men* worked with Hobsbawm and Walter Benjamin.

The *dialogical* relationship between Griffiths as radical television critic and the radical critique conveyed by cultural studies (each with their intentions of 'strategic penetration' – of television naturalism, and of the conventional disciplinarity of the university) – is, then, of considerable importance. In Chapter 1, that relationship seemed relatively one-sided, the emphasis being on changing academic paradigms' *appropriation* of Griffiths, though frequently with selected quotations from Griffiths himself. But Griffiths' own critical *re-workings of academic political debate* are both indirect (via his dramas) and direct as he writes his previews and reviews in theatre programmes and his edited collections. Whereas in Chapter 1 I started from academic texts which positioned Griffiths theoretically, in this chapter I begin with Griffiths 'Author's Prefaces', which themselves frequently position academic debate.

For example, Griffiths included with his Introduction to the Faber reprint of *Occupations* in 1995 his 1971 riposte to a critical review of the play by Tom Nairn. In doing this, he reprised the importance to his work throughout his television career of the Marxist aesthetics of Georg Lukacs. 'It's important to respond to historical plays as art-works …. Lukacs says: "Shakespeare states every conflict … in terms of typical human-opposites; and these are historical only in so far as Shakespeare fully and directly assimilates into each individual type the most characteristic and central features of a social crisis." Nairn's it's-either-historically-"accurate" -or-it's-purely-and-only-"symbolic" is just too crude and unfruitful a measure of the value of a play' (Grifffiths, 1995, 5).

In this Preface to the 1995 reprinting of *Occupations*, Griffiths draws centrally on Lukacs' aesthetic of theatre. In particular Lukacs focused on *both* collision *and* synergy between selected past (content) and present moment (of production), which together generate the meaning of drama. Thus, Lukacs argues, author and history commune over the 'tragic events of antiquity which were based on historical-moral experiences inwardly similar to those of his own time; so that the generalized form of the drama reveals the features which the two ages hold objectively in common' (Lukacs 1969, 183). The analogy is insistent not only with *Occupations*, which played between the occupations of factories in 1920s Turin and 1968 Europe, but with so many of Griffiths' other dramas: for example, *The Cherry Orchard, Piano, Hope in the Year Two,* each of these moving reflexively between 'fin de siècles' in constructing changing relevancies for the hope and despair of social change.

Thus, twenty years after writing his response to Nairn, Griffiths introduced the published version of his 1990 play, *Piano*, by offering 'a context for a possible reading of the piece with a passage from the late and deeply missed Raymond Williams' (1990, Author's Preface). Despite the major socio-political changes across those twenty years from *Occupations* to *Piano*, there are significant continuities both between the cultural theorists (Lukacs and Williams) that he positions here, and between their theoretical take on realism and Griffiths' own television production. There is a major formal shift from the series of overt political dialogues in *Occupations* to the 'postmodernist' play within *Piano* between Chekhov's works, Adabashyan and Mikhalkov's pastiche of Chekhov in the film *Unfinished Piece for Mechanical Piano* (1980), and Griffiths' own 'post-socialist' engagements. But there is, nevertheless, via Griffiths' continuing references to Lukacs and Williams, an ongoing theme of relating individual experience (between histories) to societal 'collision' and breakdown.

It is important, as a counter to both the charge against Griffiths of 'individualism' and romantic 'revolutionary nostalgia' that we will see voiced by some academics (this chapter) and some newspaper reviewers (Chapter 4), as well as to the postmodernist 'spectres of Marx' academic reading of Chapter 1, to note two things in Griffiths' Introduction to *Occupations* in the 1995 version. First, there is his opening comment that 'Though the story of the play is bedded in a lost moment of European socialist history – the occupation of the factories in Northern Italy in 1920 – there are clear resonances with strategically similar struggles in Europe and Britain at the time of its writing'. Second, there is his signing off this Introduction with: 'Trevor Griffiths, Palestine, Summer 1995'.

For Griffiths, like both Lukacs and Williams, a key dynamic of history is the relationship between the individual and the societal, between agency and structure, and between 'breakdown and deadlock'. The very moment of 'socialist failure' (whether in Turin in 1920, or in Europe's 'Eastern Bloc' in 1990) is also the moment of new agencies, new dialogues (*'Palestine*, Summer 1995'), and of new formal engagements in Griffiths' work between the reality of human oppression and creative challenges to global power.

Positioning theory and *Occupations*: sociology of literature and European Marxism

The 'academic discourse' discussion of Chapters 1 and 2 is specifically positioned here, at the beginning of the book, because both Griffiths and M/C studies were part of the overtly modernist-*educative* intention of radical reform emerging out of the 1960s. It is not just that these were two (or more) 'parallel' paths. They were imbricated discourses centrally involved in the project that Raymond Williams was so committed to, of popular education, itself embedded in the development of the New Left in the late 1950s and early 1960s. Thus it is no coincidence that *Oi For England* emerged out of a 'Race in the Classroom' conference, attended by both academics and by Griffiths himself. As Garner says, 'socialist humanism ... forms the cornerstone of Griffiths' Marxism, a commitment to such political categories as agency and subjectivity that defines itself against Stalinism as well as capitalism. It is evident in a concern with education that extends from Griffiths' own work in the classroom to his understanding of the media as a whole' (1999, 5).

Those concerns were central to Griffiths' thinking about his productions from the beginning, in the early 1970s when he discussed *The Party* and *Occupations*. As Griffiths says of *Occupations* in his response to Nairn, the play is more about the problems we go on *asking* now over the relationship between agency and control than it is about the 'lessons we learn' about the accommodation between Stalinism and capitalism in autumn 1920 Italy.

> Occupations was written as a sort of Jacobinical response to the failure of the '68 revolution in France. What it asserts is that courage and optimism do not, of themselves, ensure the success of revolution, unless they are harnessed, disciplined, tightly organised; in a word, led. And what it asks – because it's a play that, characteristically, asks rather than asserts – is whether the courage and optimism aren't in some way necessarily damaged, distorted, in that disciplining process. (And that's a 'meaning' for Kabak that Nairn barely smells, he's so often away from the play's muscle, skin and sinew).

This *dialogue* with Nairn (still contained in the 1995 reprint, with its Author's Preface from Palestine) is symptomatic of Griffiths. It *is* a dialogue, not a dismissal of Nairn's piece, given that it responds carefully to each of his critiques about Gramsci, and concludes by thanking the magazine *7 Days* 'for printing such a long, detailed and responsible piece. Of all the notices I've read, it's the one most likely to help me make the next play a better one' (Griffiths 1970, 1995).

Griffiths' more regular dialogue at the time of writing *Occupations* was with Raymond Williams and with theoretical debates emerging from the Marxist-oriented 'sociology of literature' departments at the new interdisciplinary '1960s' universities in Britain, such as Sussex and Essex. It is no coincidence that the first substantial M/C study of Griffiths' television work came out of a conference on 'Literature, Society and the Sociology of Literature' at the University of Essex in 1976. Nestled among papers at the Essex conference on 'Hegemony and Thomas Hardy', 'Jane Austen and Gentry Society', and the 'Problems of Trotsky's Literary Criticism', was a piece by Janet Wolff, Steve Ryan, Jim McGuigan and Derek McKiernan, 'Problems of Radical Drama: The Plays and Productions of Trevor Griffiths'.

Symptomatically, in his introduction to this Essex University collection, Stuart Hall established the new context of cultural studies overtly in terms of the different academic personae of Raymond Williams, 'the theorist who, chronologically, has contributed most to its development as a semi-independent area of inquiry' (1976, 1). In a similar way as I am discussing the different 'Trevor Griffiths' of this book, Hall says he is not speaking about the 'full-bodied person Raymond Williams, but the various theoretical personae under whose different disguises he has appeared in the course of his development' (1976, 1).

'Williams I', in Hall's description, was the left-Leavisite who restored to analysis 'the importance of the experiential' and the concept of 'structure of feeling'. This aspect of Williams' work, best represented by his *The Long Revolution*, carried on a 'covert, continuous dialogue with Marxism', which on the one hand insisted on the integral analytical relationship between literature and society, but on the other hand did not engage at all with the Marxist concept of ideology. Trevor Griffiths spoke of being 'liberated' by his reading of *The Long Revolution* while he was a political journalist prior to 1968 (cited by Itzin 1980, 171)

'Williams II' represented the 'decisive intervention of the continental Marxist tradition into the parochial English field of literary studies' (Hall 1976, 2). Like Trevor Griffiths, like myself doing postgraduate work in sociology of literature at Sussex University, Raymond Williams was profoundly influenced by the recent English translations of Georg Lukacs' humanist Marxist literary criticism, and the work in genetic structuralism of Lukacs' follower, Lucien Goldmann. Importantly for Williams, whereas 'Lukacs had ... been more concerned with a homology of contents, the way in which the historical conditions of a class found direct expression in the literary work in terms of its aspirations, ideas and forms of consciousness, Goldmann made a radical break from this socio-historical emphasis to consider the aesthetic, literary and philosophical structures of a given work' (Hall 1976, 2). In an interview in 1982, Trevor Griffiths indicated how much he had come to understand his work via this period of Marxist humanism. 'I think my practice is probably Lukacian ... the whole idea of a character working as a confluence of important social and political and moral forces within society, in real historical time' (Griffiths, personal interview with Tulloch 1982, 39). As we will see, Griffiths' *Sons and Lovers* and *The Last Place On Earth* drew creatively on Lukacian concepts, while it is arguable that his later work for television, such as *Hope In The Year Two* and *Food For Ravens* were closer to Goldmann's sense of generating specific 'homologous' aesthetic, literary and philosophical structures for specific historical moments such as 'post-modernism'.

'Williams III', Hall argues, engaged with Althusser, Barthes and Linguistics, particularly via Williams' attempt to synthesise European Marxism, language theories and the rediscovered influence of Walter Benjamin and Bertolt Brecht. In particular, there was Benjamin's intro-duction of the 'notion of production into cultural studies' (Hall 1976, 3) and Brecht's contribution to 'the previously untouched area of the reader' (Hall 1976, 3). As Hall argues,

> Brecht attacked the whole notion of realism and posited the 'alienation' effect in disjuncturing the passive role of the audience, the reader .... Alongside the notion of rupture, contradiction and broken progress ... [t]he expansion of the mass media, new modes of production and communication and interest in their material basis are evident in the work of Benjamin and Brecht ... [who] drew attention to the constructed nature of the aspiring naturalism of the sign in realism which presented itself as the real world. (Hall 1976, 3)

Griffiths' developing television form was deeply influenced by this alienation and 'disjuncturing' of 'the passive role of the audience' from at least the time of *Comedians* (where, in Act II he makes his audiences encounter their own prejudiced subjectivities as they enter the diegesis as the club audience, see Chapter 7), *Sons and Lovers* and *The Cherry Orchard* (where he spoke of his version of the vagrant in Act II as a 'massive disjuncture' in terms of audience involvement).

But equally importantly, this debate with continental Marxism, with Lukacs, Brecht and Benjamin around new communication forms, fundamentally influenced Griffiths' whole attitude to television in this period, as it did Williams also. In an interview in *The Leveller* in 1979, Raymond Williams said,

> We have to establish the fringe culture – there's no alternative to that – but if we don't also contest the central institutions then we are giving away too much. You run radical theatre groups wherever you can, but at the same time you really do think seriously about establishment theatre and about establishment broadcasting. You really must get in there with proposals for more democratic structures, which ... are the necessary dimension of any serious challenge to the orthodox position. (Williams, cited in Itzin 1980, 165)

And also in *The Leveller*, Trevor Griffiths said,

> 'Strategic penetration' is a phrase I use a lot about the work of social-
> ists and Marxists in bourgeois cultures ... I simply cannot understand
> socialist playwrights who do not devote most of their time to television.
> That they can write for the Royal Court and the National Theatre, and
> only that, seems to me a wilful self-delusion about the nature of theatre
> in a bourgeois culture now ... It's just thunderingly exciting to be able
> to talk to large numbers of people in the working class, and I can't
> understand why everybody doesn't want to do it. (Griffiths, cited in Itzin
> 1980, 165)

The point to be made here is not that Griffiths was simply 'influenced'
by these kinds of theoretical debate on the Left (his *Leveller* interview
is in fact earlier than Williams'). Rather, he was centrally and produc-
tively *part of them* within the television and theatre industries. This
ongoing dialogue has – outside and inside his plays – helped shape his
content, his aesthetic, his survival politics. He made them the content
of his plays (like *The Party* and *All Good Men*, both of which engaged
with television producers). He developed his television forms in their
context, and he extended theoretical debate in so doing. Griffiths' work
also *formally* extended the debates about Lukacs' distinction between
'naturalism' and 'realism' (and the Brechtian critique of naturalism
within realism) via Benjamin's notions of democratic production, and
via Brecht's concepts of alienation and audience disjuncture. And this
was at the same time (or even before) these debates were circulating in
the more elite discourses of university M/C studies.

Thus, for example, the Wolff, Ryan, McGuigan, McKiernan piece
on Trevor Griffiths emphasises that it wants to engage with the ideas
of Lukacs and Brecht (and other Marxists like Williams, Adorno and
Benjamin) by way of the *conditions of production and consumption of
Griffiths plays*. In his section of the Essex paper, McGuigan examines the
closer affiliation of Griffiths with Lukacs than Brecht as between theatrical illusionism/estrangement, but he argues also that 'in *Occupations*
the audience becomes simultaneously, in certain scenes, both the theatre
(or television) audience and the workers in the factory occupation' (Wolff
et al 1976, 140). He notes that the audience is similarly fragmented in
the play-within-a-play Act II of *Comedians* – and following Benjamin's
emphasis on production, the 'whole of *Comedians* is concerned with
performance, communication and politics. Griffiths' own intervention
in the production of his work ... demonstrates his continuing concern
with the development of the play. He stays with his plays right through
the production process and tries to build a team, whether in television
or theatre, sympathetic and responsive to his projects. In the spirit of

Brecht and Benjamin, Griffiths is interested in techniques of production and modes of perception' (McGuigan in Wolff *et al* 1976, 141).

McGuigan further notes that Griffiths' pessimism about the impact
of socialist theatre in the 1970s compared with Brecht's optimism in the
1930s has 'much to do with their very different respective political situ-
ations' (Wolff *et al* 1976, 142). He emphasises Brecht's insistence (like
both Griffiths and Williams) on fighting for the heartland of *popular*
entertainment so that works are 'intelligible to the broad masses'
(Brecht, cited in Wolff *et al* 1976, 142).

Discussing *Bill Brand*, however, McGuigan goes on to say that
'because of the overwhelming emphasis on ... Brand's personal life in
order to represent the connections and homologies between sexual relations and global political structures', a 'possible audience response is
to sympathise with Brand's personal problems and regard him as just
another individual in a difficult situation ... Brecht long ago pointed
to the dangerous mesh of empathy' (Wolff *et al* 1976, 148). Clearly, for
McGuigan, the Brechtian aspects of Griffiths were in the interstices
of his work, though it is symptomatic of this stage of M/C studies
that McGuigan spoke of 'possible' audience responses, rather than
researching Griffiths' actual *Comedians* audiences. Griffiths had been
fully aware of the 'dangerous mesh of empathy' from the beginning,
which is why his early television and theatre plays like *The Party* and
Occupations carried such sustained position pieces in order not to reduce
and caricature diametrically opposed ideas, and why also he refused
to construct as 'bad guy' Venturi, the Fiat capitalist in *Occupations*.
Janelle Reinelt points out in her book *After Brecht* (1994) that Griffiths
was not aware of Brecht until well after leaving university. However, it
was precisely through his engagement with the critiques of his 'naturalism' and potential 'individualism' *though fellow playwrights* whom
he respected like David Edgar and John McGrath (and indeed through
being aware of the sociology of literature debates being opened up by
Janet Wolff and others), that 'in the early 1970s Griffiths began to read
Brecht's plays and also the theory ... [H]e also read other Marxist theorists (Adorno, Benjamin, Lukacs, Sartre) and played them off against
one another' (Reinelt 1994, 144).

Positioning theory and *Through the Night*: Enzensberger's 'leaky system'

It was this 'written' (by the New Left) Trevor Griffiths who was also actively
dialogic as subject and agent – but also as observer and recipient – of
history and theory, that addressed professional producers and publics

through his published play texts. Symptomatic is Griffiths' reflexive use of what he describes as 'without question, my best-known piece' *Through the Night* to review his educative policy of 'strategic penetration' in his 1977 'Author's Preface'. Here Griffiths quickly dismisses mainstream cinema, where the 'global audience' tends to be 'surrendered by the writer to the expert ministrations of other "ideas men": studio chiefs', and he again worries about theatre because 'To write only for the theatre is to watch only from the covered stand; you stay dry but there's a pitch dividing you from another possible, and possibly decisive, action on the terraces'. Television, too, has its problems for the writer who wants to reach masses of people, because

> A medium as potentially dangerous as this one will need to be controlled with some rigour and attention to detail. 'To inform' and 'to educate' may well be in the charter alongside 'to entertain', but information that inflames and education that subverts will find its producers facing unrenewed contracts and its contributors mysteriously dropped .... What Enzensberger calls 'the consciousness industry' (c.f. H.M. Enzensberger: 'The Industrialization of the Mind' in Raids and Reconstructions, Pluto Press, 1976) has become, more than steel, coal or oil or motorcars, the critical industry in the efficient management of modern societies, capitalist and Stalinist alike; as television has increasingly come to be located in that industry's key sector. (Griffiths, 1977)

Those references, within the few lines of his Preface, to 'education that subverts', to the current history of both the television industry *and* academia (including Griffiths' careful bibliographical reference to Hans Magnus Enzensberger's recent work, to encourage his reader to follow this argument further), and to 'capitalist and Stalinist alike' (to indicate that his words apply as much to the current Soviet Union) are typical of Griffiths. But so, too, is the challenge that follows to those intellectuals on the Left who write 'a puny apology for a theory of the media'.

There are at least two reasons, Griffiths argued, why the pessimism of these Left media intellectuals is misplaced. Firstly, blanket control of the media system would 'demand a monitor that was bigger than the system itself'. Secondly – and here Griffiths was retrospectively responding to the many newspaper journalists who castigated his 1976 series *Bill Brand* for its 'Left' lack of humour (see Chapter 4) and establishing his own 'deep history' – he argued that

> The 'meanings' and 'messages' of plays are often encoded in such a way that the controllers of television output are incapable of decoding them with any precision. (In particular I'm thinking of plays where working-class idioms, speech patterns, behaviours suggest one thing but imply, by defensively developed irony, something quite other, which only a

person of that class or with a deep knowledge of it could be expected to recognise readily. I suspect much of Bill Brand worked that way, with a working-class audience). (Griffiths 1977, 10)

The use in Griffiths' Prefaces to producers and audiences of his plays of current M/C studies discourse – as in Hall's 'encoding' and 'decoding' of the text – is symptomatic. So, too, is his challenge to hegemonic academic discourse, still some years away from 'active audience' publications, and its own postmodernist theories of 'disintegration' and 'fragmentation'.

To argue, then, as many still do, that television is part of a monolithic consciousness industry where work of truly radical or revolutionary value will never be produced is at once to surrender to undialectical thought and to fail to see the empirical evidence there is to refute such an argument ... To work on television as a playwright will be to seek to exploit the system's basic 'leakiness' ... 'The "telly-glued" masses do not exist; they are the bad fiction of our second-rate social analysts .... But the actual men and women, under permanent kinds of difficulty, will observe and learn, and I do not think that in the long run they will be anybody's windfall.' The words are Raymond Williams' and, as with so much he has written in the last twenty-five years, I wish they were mine. (Griffiths 1977, 11)

Positioning theory and *Sons and Lovers*: Lukacs and Brechtian realism

In Griffiths' Preface to *Sons and Lovers* we find Lukacs' 'Balzac-style' D.H. Lawrence at work. Reinelt observes that '[F]ollowing Lukacs, Griffiths sees particular writers as able to capture the historical and social contradictions and transformations of their times, whether consciously or not. He cites D.H. Lawrence's first 150 pages of *Sons and Lovers*: "It's about so many things Lawrence doesn't know it's about, because of the extraordinary breadth of the terrain that runs through it, human experience, concrete, determined, historical. The best writers will apprehend the fault lines, the confluences of change and transformation without knowing it; it will be part of their project, but they won't be scientists in the way in which Brecht wanted' (Reinelt 1994, 144).

Griffiths' direct model here is Lukacs' description of Balzac in comparison with the 'scientific' naturalist, Zola. 'Balzac boldly exposed the contradiction of nascent capitalist society and hence his observation of reality constantly clashed with his [right-wing, monarchist] political prejudices ... [In contrast] Zola's "scientific" method always seeks the average, and this grey statistical mean, the point at which all internal contradictions are blunted, where the great and the petty, the noble and the base, the beautiful and the ugly are all mediocre "products" together, spells the doom of great literature' (Lukacs, 1964, 91).

Whereas Zola, in Lukacs' view, was completely absorbed within the fatalistic objectivism of science, great writers emphasised *hope* in humankind by seeking not the individual but the type. What makes 'a type a type is not its average quality, not its mere individual being, however profoundly conceived; what makes it a type is in it all the humanly and socially essential determinants are present at their highest level of development, in the ultimate unfolding of the possibilities latent in them ... rendering concrete the peaks and limits of ... epochs' (Lukacs 1964, 6).

It was in this sense of contradiction, transformation and the 'peaks and limits' of Paul Morel and his father that Griffiths considered *Sons and Lovers*.

> The tensions for Lawrence, as for Paul Morel, were not merely the familiar ones of town and country, of industrialism and agriculture, but of urban and rural against education, itself a major pull in the long struggle for self-definition. Within the family, the key elements of class-difference and class-perspective caused further fractures and torsions. Lawrence's father, like Walter Morel, was a miner, apprenticed at 11 and destined to spend the greater part of his life underground, on his knees, in two- and three-foot seams, hacking coal out for a pittance. Lawrence's mother, like Gertrude Morel, was of middle-class burgher stock whose family had come down in the world since the 1839 slump in the lace-trade. Along these and other borders, Lawrence's life is shaped and buckled; and it's through these borders, at the novel's close, that Paul uncertainly bursts, as Lawrence had done before him, in the stumbling search for social harmony and human love. (Griffiths 1982, 9–10)

This 'Lawrence' was quite well known within and beyond academia, and Griffiths was not saying in his Preface anything that was particularly new. *Except* that he was preparing, via Lukacian 'typicality', for his own reflexive statement *as text* on 'Griffiths' Lawrence'. Here he went well beyond Lukacs towards the objectifying, disjuncturing and de-centring position of Brecht. Not only, Griffiths argues, is much that is 'rich and textured' lost in reducing a 500–page novel to a six-and-a-half-hour time slot. There is also, crucially, the issue that this is *not* Lawrence's 'Lawrence'. '*Sons and Lovers*, though ostensibly a third-person novel, frequently presents events, relationships and people through the consciousness of its central figure Paul Morel (who, as we have seen, is a version of the author himself). Since no comparable relationship to Paul existed for me in the dramatic re-working, it proved pointless to seek a dramatic device that would support one.'

Griffiths' *difference* from Lawrence 'lies in the way Paul – and all his social relationships – becomes *objectified* within the form of realistic drama ... Hence, as Paul's subjective view of the social reality is de-centred, so the other characters' perceptions acquire a newly-charged subjective dimension ... [T]he shift in the formal focus affects, in some cases crucially, all the other characters in the piece. The Walter Morel that emerges, for example, is now as much victim as anyone else and, incidentally, much closer to the 'father' that Lawrence revalued towards the end of his own life. Gertrude, Clara, Miriam, too, all undergo a significant re-making in our minds, as the plays centre them for the first time as subjects within the structures of their own lives' (Griffiths 1982, 11–12).

Griffiths is as keen for his readers to visit the 'original' D.H. Lawrence as he is for them to read the 'original' Hans Magnus Enzensberger – and in both cases his written Prefaces and Introductions usher readers to these other academic and literary texts. Meanwhile, he is not the least repentant in offering his 'version' of Lawrence as 'a powerful and radical celebration of dignity in resistance within working-class culture in industrial class-societies; as well as a dark, tortured cry against the waste of human resources such societies require as part of their logic. It is no bad thing to be saying when unemployment has reached three million' (Griffiths 1982, 12).

This Lawrence – and it is equally clear from Griffiths' critique of the 2002 TV serialisation of *Sons and Lovers* where Gertrude, Clara and Miriam are again seen 'as subjects within the structures of their own lives', but where the 'subjective' working-class history is in Griffiths' view missing – is re-worked in terms of 'distancing' Paul, and offering audiences the textual 'disjuncture' of a father who both exploits and is exploited. It is via the father of Paul Morel (and indeed, via his own father, whom Griffiths also 'revalued', see Chapter 4) that Griffiths then positions the present (potential) audience of three million unemployed as well as the more likely middle-class BBC audience who, via visuals of Walter that linger a beat for empathy and via pauses and silences in the dialogue, are asked to re-think their conventional middle-class empathies with the novel.

Griffiths is here taking 'Balzac's' realism a significant step further than Lukacs, moving on from the notion of a creative artist (like Lawrence) who captures social contradictions non-consciously via 'typicality'. Beyond this, Griffiths considered the aesthetic and spectator-positioning changes needed when another author *consciously* and *reflexively* re-worked the earlier (*Sons and Lovers*) text. McGuigan's comments on *Bill Brand* and the 'dangerous mesh of empathy' have to be completely rethought in this process. Griffiths worked reflexively *with* the concepts of empathy and subjectivity to create new 'de-centred' aesthetic forms and disrupted spectator positions.

Positioning theory, *Piano* and *Gulf*: theatre studies, feminism and the post-colonial

At the time of writing his Preface to *Piano* in 1990, the world was changing dramatically. With the Soviet Union and the Eastern Bloc disintegrating, Griffiths revisited, by first quoting Raymond Williams, Lukacs' 'great realists' of the nineteenth century.

> The condition of realism in the nineteenth century was in fact an assumption of a total world. In the great realists, there was no separation in kind between public and private facts, as between public and private experience ... [I]t was a way of seeing the world in which it was possible to experience the quality of a whole way of life through the qualities of individual men and women. Thus, a personal breakdown was a genuinely social fact, and a social breakdown was lived and known in direct personal experience ... Chekhov is the realist of breakdown, on a significantly total scale. (Williams, Modern Tragedy, 1966)

> Should Piano prove to be about anything at all, I suspect it may prove, like its illustrious forebears [in Chekhov], to be about just this felt sense of breakdown and deadlock; and thus perhaps, in a nicely perverse irony, about what it's like to be living in our own post-capitalist, post-socialist, post-realist, post-modern times. (Trevor Griffiths, Boston Spa, 24 May 1990)

Work by Janelle Reinelt on Trevor Griffiths, emerging also in the 1990s, represents the strong strands of cultural and feminist studies in theatre research at that time. As Reinelt argues (and this is also a reply to McGuigan on *Bill Brand*), even in describing himself as a 'Lukacian in one sense or another', Griffiths always accepted Brecht's rejection of 'psychologism and individualism ... Somewhere in this century, the world became impossible to account for in terms of people's [individual] lives' (Griffiths, cited in Reinelt 1994, 144).

As Reinelt argues, Griffiths has presented three defences of his version of realism against Brecht. First, 'Griffiths refuses the Brechtian notion that the involvement of empathy and feeling for the fictional lives of characters is destructive of intellectual and analytical response' (Reinelt 1994, 144). This relates centrally to Williams' view that 'a personal breakdown was a genuinely social fact, and a social breakdown was lived and known in direct personal experience', which Griffiths developed further in his engagement with Lukacs. Second, Griffiths also adopts the Lukacian view of great writers capturing – either through the socio-historical 'collision' of drama or via the epic build-up of novelistic details

– the social breakdowns and transformations of their times, whether consciously or not. Third, the 'issues of realism are not clear-cut because realism is itself not a pure form. Brecht polarized against the conventions of realism as if there were two clear-cut and distinct styles, mutually exclusive. Griffiths sees both the nature of the convention and the intervention of history as changing the terms of the debate' (Reinelt 1994, 145).

As Reinelt says, Griffiths writes in a post-Brechtian, post-classical-realist moment. 'Although sharply disagreeing with Brecht's aesthetics and remaining committed to the realist tradition, Griffiths wishes to retain for his own project the critical, socio-political analytic of Brecht's. He describes his own plays as operating within realism but also enabling distance to occur – "in fact insisting upon distance or alienation at particular moments for particular purposes". Nor does his work allow people to perceive theatrical representation as unmediated life' (Reinelt 1994, 145).

Preparing for her analysis of *Piano*, Reinelt argued that *Comedians* surpassed '*Occupations* in bearing [Griffiths'] fullest relationship to Brecht' (Reinelt 1994, 151). Reinelt is self-reflexive in seeing *Comedians* 'through the 1993 lenses of a feminist critic who is disposed to look for representations of difference in all forms and who finds in the play, now, a topical discussion of difference that joins the struggle to articulate difference and a politics of resistance' (1994, p. 157). Thus, she begins, 'The play is about men (there are no female characters) in the homosocial world of working-class urban experience, in which becoming a comedian on the club circuit represents a way of escaping demeaning repetitive work for a "creative" alternative' (Reinelt 1994, 157–8). Nevertheless, Griffiths 'offers spectators several positions for viewing the play' (1994, 138). 'Price does not try [like Waters] to dissolve tensions of class, gender and race by creating a humanist tolerance that merely camouflages the deep divisions of society. His piece articulates and attacks class privilege, creating the upper-middle-class as a pair of unresponsive dummies to whom he is both solicitous and vicious'. Thus Griffiths 'represents the subject-as-Other and succeeds in placing the audience in the object position, identified with the dummies. For a brief time a politics of resistance through cultural production is palpable, one that is thoroughly rooted in and specific to the delineated context (white, male, urban proletariat) while providing a viewpoint for other diverse groups as well (although the violence perpetrated against the female dummy tends to reinscribe the female as object)' (Reinelt 1994, 160).

As Reinelt argues, Griffiths disturbs comfortable (middle-class) spectator positions here via 'a Brechtian attention to meaning produced in the comedy industry, its power relations and ideology', as the racist and sexist jokes are addressed directly to them as the 'club' audience and yet they are also the affluent 'dummies' on-screen. 'Even though, strictly speaking, the play is continuous, illusionistic, detailed – in short realistic – it produces enough epic effects to reflect the Brechtian legacy. In *Cloud 9* [Caryl] Churchill uses cross-cutting to present her characters to the audience as social constructions; Griffiths accomplishes the same goal through the device of the comedy school and club' (Reinelt 1994, 161).

Reinelt then notes an historical shift between *Comedians* and *Piano*. As she describes it, *Piano* is an accommodation by Griffiths to

> the pernicious damage of Thatcherism and the collapse of the Labour Party's productive opposition as factors in the decline of socio-cultural life ... 'I don't think I would be able to "think" Comedians in 1990. It's a struggle play ... Whereas writers are singular now – at least I don't any longer feel part of a broad grouping who share some goals and some modes and means of achieving them' [Griffiths]. Ironically, this new postmodern condition seems to have brought Griffiths back to writing for the theatre; in part, perhaps, because Thatcher's privatization has also wrecked the notion of television as disruptive cultural production that Griffiths once held. (Reinelt 1994, 163)

Thus in *Piano* (a play based on a creative conjuncture of Chekhovian gentry and peasant types) and *The Gulf Between Us* (originally called *Building Baghdad* and focusing on two Brits isolated by an unnamed war and building in real time the wall of a bombed shrine, watched by an Arab guard), Griffiths' 'combination of [Lukacian] nineteenth-century realism and [Brechtian] epic techniques kills the sympathy of the former and diminishes the "distance" of the latter. This is his true post-Brechtian/post-Lukacian style – a hybridized version of them both, containing complexity and particularity' (Reinelt 1994, 164). Reinelt notes overt Brechtian intertextual devices in these plays. As well as reading many Chekhov short stories in addition to the plays for *Piano*, Griffiths read a number of Arab texts, including the Koran and *Tales of a Thousand and one Nights* for *Gulf*.

> The epigram [by the Chekhov 'short story' peasant, Radish] of Piano, and [in Gulf] the storytelling/parable device of The Tales of Arabian Nights set up a controlling framework from which to historicise and interrogate the incidents of his narratives. Griffiths provides the frame for his viewers to enable The Gulf Between Us to make a contribution to what we now call 'postcolonial discourse'. As is always the case, he must still write as a white European male – mostly about other white European males, but in an attempt to interrogate their position, their whiteness. In The Gulf Between Us he accomplishes this primarily by placing the

Arabs, not the Europeans, 'at the ethical centre' and by representing and critiquing British colonial ideology. (Reinelt 1994, 173)

It was *this* Griffiths who signed his 1996 reprint of *Occupations* 'Trevor Griffiths, Palestine, Summer 1995'.

After the writing of Reinelt's book, Griffiths returned to television with *Hope in the Year Two* and *Food for Ravens*, where further hybridisation – of Lukacs and Brecht, and of theatre and film/television – occurred, as we will see in later chapters. *Hope in the Year Two* contained, for example, all of the Brechtian features that McGuigan missed in his 1970s article: anti-illusionist, estranging devices (Danton's direct address to 1990s audiences), reflexivity (the overt reference to theatricality as the piece opens with safety curtains), and a positive (Socialist) conception of theatre.

Nevertheless, *throughout* Griffiths' career the debate between critical-realist Williams/Lukacian 'typicality' and Brechtian (*not* Derridean) 'fragmentation' has been alive in his television drama work, as he has tried to find ways of more democratically participative production and more subjectively 'disjunctured' spectators. The *dialogic* has always been central to both his content (the long, ideological discussion of *The Party* and *Occupations*) and his aesthetic form (e.g. the 'collision' of world-historical individuals such as Lopakhin and Trofimov in *The Cherry Orchard* focused by his 'Brechtian' Act II, Chapter 3).

It is this (Lukacian *and* Brechtian) relationship between lost *opportunities* and always-in-potential *agencies*, between past and present rather than the Derridean 'ghost of Marx' which explains so much of Griffiths' text-and-spectator strategy in his television work, however unfashionable to some cultural studies academics that may now seem. M/C scholars who regard this position as passé (or theorists encumbered with half-understood farewells to the Soviet Union) should remember the deep and determined engagement with *active human hope* in both Lukacs and Griffiths, and ask themselves *where* in the New World Order driven by U.S. neo-conservatism, *they* seek that hope now. Griffiths continues to seek it, in the new cultural/political formulations of the Arab world, and the point is that this position is both contemporaneously relevant *and* consistent with his production theory from the 1970s onwards. But crucially, too, that hope is embedded in the belief that individual writers can *matter* (just as individual U.S. Presidents can matter) in so far as they act at the confluence points of 'social breakdown and deadlock'.

1 Left to right: Jack Shepherd, Trevor Griffiths, Alan Badel and Arthur Lowe in the Thames Television canteen, working on *Bill Brand*, 1976

2 Jack Shepherd and director of photography Ivan Strasburg rehearsing *Hope in the Year Two*, BBC2, 1994

3 Jack Shepherd as the Prisoner and Tom Bowles as Henry, his gaoler, *Hope in the Year Two*, BBC2, 1994

4 *The Last Place on Earth*, Central TV, 1985

5 *The Last Place on Earth*, Central TV, 1985

48

6 Trevor Griffiths and actor Dean Carey-Davies on location in South Wales, shooting *Food for Ravens*, BBC Wales, 1997

7 Trevor Griffiths by the Aneurin Bevan memorial lith at Bryn Serth, South Wales, a location used in *Food for Ravens*, BBC Wales, 1997

In the studio: making and receiving Griffiths' *The Cherry Orchard*

3

Nine o'clock on a Friday night last January. Writer Trevor Griffiths, a thick-set figure in jeans and a sweat-shirt, creeps restlessly round the control box of studio TC8. Just below him, but visibly only on monitors, a complex scene from his version of the Cherry Orchard. It is the last night of five in that studio. Three acts are complete but the twelve remaining pages of Act 2 must be recorded by 10.30. A mistake could mean two more days in the studio, perhaps in two months time, and a vast increase in the budget. Conceivably, it could mean that the production is never completed. (John Wyver, City Limits, October 9–15, 1981)

Whenever he can, and always in pursuit of more participative production involvement, Griffiths spends time at rehearsals and in the studio. There he brings with him his critical engagement with cultural theory – in the case of *The Cherry Orchard*, it was Raymond Williams' analysis of Chekhov. But he also is there to impact on performance and, as in the case of *Sons and Lovers*, to 'de-centre' the accepted social reality of the performed high-cultural text, and centre other characters 'for the first time as subjects within the structures of their own lives' (Griffiths 1982, 12). In his version of *The Cherry Orchard*, this process of 'disjuncturing' performances and spectators focused around de-centring Ranevskaya (who in conventional productions of the play represents quintessentially the frivolous land-owner about to be swept away 'inevitably' by the Russian Revolution) and repositioning the subjectivity of Lopakhin (too often presented in western interpretations as the crass capitalist, (Tulloch 1980, 1985)).

But John Wyver's account of his production experience of *The Cherry Orchard* speaks of something else too. I also experienced as a researcher the time pressure of putting a programme to bed in that BBC studio (Tulloch and Alvarado 1983), the tension in the control room as the clock ticks round to 10.30, the recognition that the technicians will generally 'pull the plug' on time, the disciplined panic that can set in as long-planned complicated shots are abandoned for something simpler, something that will 'work' – just to get the programme in on time.

Directors are there in the control room, producers are often there, some actors and technical operators are there – and occasionally a researcher is there too, examining, via what I call an ethnography of production, the relationship on the one hand between planned television moves and innovations and, on the other, the well-attested compromises that have to go in place under the time constraints of a unionised industry.

The date of production of *The Cherry Orchard,* 1981, was also the time of a new thrust in M/C studies to television production studies, and this chapter marks that conjunction – of Griffiths' theory, our theory and the constraints of the practices of production. On this occasion I was not able to see the production through, but John Wyver was, and with my colleague Tom Burvill I conducted long interviews with the actors, producer, director, writer and technicians of the *The Cherry Orchard* (as well as of the 1987 Nottingham Playhouse production). Hence this chapter is able to examine what happens when a highly articulate and theoretically focused television writer encounters the values of practice of the TV industry.

Repositioning subjectivity: Ranevskaya and Lopakhin

In Act II of the Eyre/Griffiths' BBC 1 television production of *The Cherry Orchard* there is a pivotal acting moment of identity, class and gender construction by Judi Dench, playing Madame Ranevskaya. Lopakhin (Bill Paterson) has just suggested his summer cottage scheme, which will enable Ranevskaya's land (as he said in Act I) to be 'alive again with growing things'. She responds, 'Summer cottages, weekenders – it's all so "bourgeois"', and her brother Gayev (Frederick Treves), chalking his billiard cue absent-mindedly, adds 'Absolutely'. Lopakhin, on his feet in frustrated anger, and divided on-screen from Gayev by the holy shrine which marks the old gentry culture, says 'you people would be enough to make a saint lose his temper'. He storms off, following the line of modern telegraph poles that mark *his* future.

Dench's Ranevskaya springs to her feet, follows him, and in head-and-shoulders shot against a perspective of tall grasses, begs him not to go. Lopakhin, transfixed in front of the waving ferns, stares back at her. Dench begins to turn her face away, with an 'I've got him' half smile, and then, in long-shot draws him back to the bench, swirling her skirt with her body turn, like a bullfighter with cloak, the bull following slowly behind.

Once back at the bench, Ranevskaya begins to fill out the 'wanton' character that Gayev ascribed to her in Griffiths' version of Act I. She tells Lopakhin of her affairs, her marriage to a drunkard who died of a surfeit of champagne, her throwing her money around, her falling in love with her husband's double, and the death of her son while she was with her lover. The camera cuts to extreme close up as she mentions her lost child, drowned in the river. The visual style is soft and impressionistic, as she herself speaks softly, with a tear forming, about this savagely gendered life among the social elite. 'I went abroad, away for good. I swore I'd never look at this river again, I shut my eyes to all responsibilities, grief makes one cruel you know, and went away. He followed me, this second brutal man, fell ill in Menton, and forced me to buy a house there and nurse him. For three years I slaved over him, night and day, until he wore me out and my soul withered.'

Ranevskaya pauses, glances at Lopakhin to whom the camera cuts, also in close-up. He is in thrall, staring at her. Dench, her soft, wide-mouthed face filling the screen, continues, hand holding her head. 'A year ago I sold the house to pay off our debts and fled to Paris. Where he robbed me, threw me over and took up with someone else. I tried poisoning myself ... I couldn't bear the shame ... My life seemed so futile'. This moment of intimate confession to Lopakhin passes, as she turns to Gayev, asks about the music they hear. Gayev speaks about the old Jewish orchestra, Lopakhin sings the music from a performance he had heard the day before and is berated by Ranevskaya, since people like him should examine their own lives rather than 'going to the theatre to observe others'. Lopakhin acknowledges this, still as much in her power as he was as a child to the father he now speaks about, who (like Ranevskaya's lover) beat him and brought him up ignorant and almost illiterate.

The mood changes again, Dench's soft voice matching the impressionistic camera, as she says gently, 'You need a wife, old friend'. The interaction is shot in close, over-the shoulder two-shots, Lopakhin, face impassive, half-believing for a second she is about to offer herself.

Lopakhin: 'Yes.'

Ranevskaya: 'You should marry my Varya. She's a good girl.'

Lopakhin: 'Yes.'

Ranevskaya: (Slow, distinct, simple) 'She comes from sturdy, common stock, works the clock around, and loves you. You've been fond of her for some time, am I right?'

Lopakhin: 'I wouldn't say no, I suppose. She's a good girl.'

There is a pause. Griffiths' instructions say 'They're on the delicate brink of something', and then the moment is lost again as Gayev says he has been offered a job at the bank, and she turns on him in anger and contempt. So much has been conveyed in these eight minutes of Act II – not simply the class aspects which prevent the gentry folk responding to Lopakhin's scheme that will save them, and which also stop Ranevskaya from conceiving her own marriage to Lopakhin who loves her (which would save their fortunes) – but also the gender exploitation that runs deeply across all classes, and which we have already seen performed earlier in Act II between the servants Yasha and Dunyasha. Lopakhin's subjectivity is centred (as both a man who loves the land and his 'betters', and remains in their power), even while Ranevskaya's is fragmented, as *both* bearer of power *and* victim of gender. Griffiths' repositioning of subjectivities was here vividly challenging both the conventional lachry-mose farewell-to-the-gentry past *Cherry Orchard* so familiar in western productions, and the simplistic class reading of Lopakhin in Soviet (and many western) interpretations.

Prior to this Ranevskaya/Lopakhin moment, there had been two scenes in Act II. The opening scene with the alienated Charlotta and Yepikhodov observing the crassly sexual seduction of Dunyasha by Yasha, and the following bench scene of Ranevskaya, Gayev and Lopakhin. The moment is now set for the third sequence, the arrival of Firs who, like the vagrant who will follow him later in the Act, enters slowly from deep in the set, bearing Gayev's coat, and about to speak his lines about the 'Freedom', which, as Griffiths wrote his version of *The Cherry Orchard*, develop the main sub-text of the play.

Writing 'The Cherry Orchard': transforming Williams, rediscovering Chekhov

The Cherry Orchard was a major example of Griffiths drawing on and transforming not only a classic author, but also a major cultural studies academic, Raymond Williams. 'Williams 2' (Chapter 2) had developed his earlier notion of 'structure of feeling' (as a 'tension', a 'stress', a 'latency', 'often an unease' with things as they are), situating Chekhov's *The Cherry Orchard* as a key work in indicating an emerging Russian structure of feeling in the late nineteenth century. For 'Williams 2', a new societal structure of feeling was frequently first evident aestheti-cally, in 'forms and conventions – semantic figures – which, in art and literature, are often among the very first indications that such a new structure is forming' (1977, 130). Above all, the major example of this

new structure of feeling was Act II of *The Cherry Orchard*, 'which as a
theme for voices, a condition and an atmosphere created by hesitation,
implication, unconnected confession, is more complete and powerful
than anything else Chekhov wrote' (Williams 1968, 109). Williams saw
Chekhov's polyphonic form as central to this new structure of feeling.
It was not in his view an Ibsen-style isolated and compromised individual in deadlock with society that was played out in Chekhov's final
play. But rather, 'the crucial emotion is that of the group'. Chekhov 'is
attempting to dramatize a stagnant group, in which consciousness has
turned inward and become, if not wholly inarticulate, at least unconnecting' (1968, 108).

Trevor Griffiths drew consciously on Williams' critical discourse in
his new version of *The Cherry Orchard*, similarly arguing that Act II was
the high point Chekhov achieved in his plays. But Griffiths also criticised
Williams for his 'statuesque symbolism' (as in his understanding of
the breaking string in Act II of *The Cherry Orchard*). For Griffiths, the
breaking string is part of a sub-text of disjuncture which underpins and
alienates the naturalism of the other Acts, and (as with Paul Morel in
Sons and Lovers) 'objectifies' the gentry characters in the play. This sub-
textual narrative of disjuncture stretches, for Griffiths, from the servant
figures who open Act II, via Firs' speech about declining his 'freedom',
to the 'underclass vagrant' who helps close the 'philosophising' of the
Act, both servants and vagrant thus preparing for Trofimov's lines (as
rewritten by Griffiths) 'From every tree in your orchard there are people
hanging'.

> The heart of the scene for me is the arrival of the stranger ... Nobody
> from that underclass has ever appeared ... in Chekhov's kind of drama
> .... Released by the French Revolution a hundred years previously and
> still wandering, still looking for social justice, equality, fraternity – and,
> clearly, failing to find it here. But, in an odd way, by putting this person
> into the set and presenting that person with such extraordinary menace
> ... [Chekhov] destabilises any notion the audience might have had of a
> settled world, their settled world. (1993, personal interview)

As with his version of *Sons and Lovers*, Griffiths' sub-text was offering
the audience a new subjectivity in this play, attempting a transfer of
identity from gentry to servants and underclass.

Griffiths argues that he turned Williams' symbolic Chekhovian
silences into historical utterances in two further ways. First, Griffiths'
work on Helen Rappaport's translation 'restored' lines to Trofimov
which he believed that Chekhov self-censored. The actors who played
Lopakhin in both the Nottingham Playhouse and the BBC television

versions emphasised the importance to them of Griffiths' presence at rehearsal in clarifying this aspect of Trofimov's embodiment. He was not to be played as the feeble and effete 'eternal student'. Mick Ford (the Nottingham Playhouse Lopakhin) said:

> The most important thing to me of the production ... was that, in this case, the eternal student was...not allowed to go on. That is, he was being failed because of activities or interests that he had; which to me made a big difference, just in terms of how you come on and...do it ... You were given the confidence in the production [by Trevor] to give time for the characters to work...And that's what I remember of the production ... People knew what they were doing. (1993, interview with Tom Burvill)

Similarly for Bill Paterson, who played Lopakhin in the BBC television production,

> Trevor bit the bullet here by translating it, 'I'm still a student. If the authorities have their way I suspect I'll always be one' ... That was the first time probably that it had been translated at all in that way ... The later scene between Lopakhin and Trofimov then becomes a great scene because they both know that ... They both feel they have the clue to the new society. Lopakhin's [clue] is the one of the entrepreneur, leading people forward by looking after themselves by earning money and making profit and moving on, and that would therefore be to the good of all in the end. And Trofimov's is having that Socialist view that you have to attend to the needs of the weakest. (1993, interview with Tom Burvill)

Second, Griffiths transformed Williams via a series of what he sees as alienating devices, such as the taped Russian voice of Charlotta at the beginning of Act II – which Griffiths describes as his 'modest Brechtian input to the piece'. He then constructed his sub-textual Act II narrative, where, as he puts it, 'freedom gets threaded through the play like a piece of tapestry' (1992, University of Birmingham).

This subtext begins with Griffiths' emphasis at the beginning of Act II on what he calls 'a field of meaning ... a mesh, a mosaic...rather than a line of meanings, a univalence', where the polyphonic text works to emphasise modernist cultural aspirations (as in Charlotta, Yepihodov, Yasha and Dunyasha), and where for instance, Charlotta is 'a character edging towards Kafka, edging towards statelessness, edging towards ... "Who am I? How can I define ... a self identity, without a state, without values, without history?"' At this point of Act II, among the servants there are just 'these unachievable, almost inarticulate desires for things to be better ... to be other, to go beyond, to be not what they are'. This is the 'unconnecting' Act II of Williams – but this is only the *beginning* of Act II.

There follows Chekhov's sub-narrative of disjuncture, through which Griffiths makes a clear theoretical distinction between his two classical pieces for television, *Sons and Lovers* and *The Cherry Orchard*. He describes his version of *Sons and Lovers* as 'reworking' Lawrence, finding in him (as Lukacs did in Balzac) alternative voices of which he was not himself consciously aware. But Griffiths described his work on *The Cherry Orchard* as 're-discovering' Chekhov, i.e. in putting back aspects of Chekhov's intentions which were partially self-censored and partially confined to the sub-text for both external (censorship) and formal (polyphonic) reasons. Hence Trofimov's re-written lines about peasants *hanging* from the cherry trees both alienate the historically aestheticised references to the orchard (especially within British theatre) and situate him, together with Lopakhin, as the only character with a vision of a future which can work on 'these terrible ... these unachievable, almost inarticulate desires [among the other characters] for things that are better, and yearning to know why they aren't' (Williams 1968, 108).

These two narrative agents, Lopakhin and Trofimov, thus contextualise for Griffiths the breaking cable which, far from being Williams' 'inert symbol', is rather a signifier of discontinuity with the past, of rupture, fragmentation, a 'cable groaning under stress'. Griffiths sees 'a direct relationship between the rupture notion [of the groaning cable] and the shift to the stranger. The stranger is what is ushered in by the rupturing of present and past over which ... the characters on the stage ... have no control' (1993, personal interview). For the audience, Griffiths argues, the vagrant is 'a massive disjuncture'.

Richard Eyre and John Berger: narrative and intertext

Director Richard Eyre spoke a lot in interview about Griffiths' involvement. 'It's an extraordinarily unsentimental play, and an extraordinarily passionate play. And I think that Trevor's translation did it a great service because it's very, very clear, it's idiomatic, and it's uncontrived.' Eyre, agreeing with Griffiths that the writer was rediscovering Chekhov, believed that this version of *The Cherry Orchard* 'doesn't ... at all make special pleading for Chekhov as this crypto-Socialist' (1993, personal interview).

It was shortly after producing Trevor Griffiths' *Comedians* that Eyre commissioned him to translate (with Helen Rappaport) *The Cherry Orchard* for Nottingham Playhouse, because:

I wanted Trevor to translate a play which I felt had always been obscured by translations ... Theatre traditions are really verbal traditions. They're passed from person to person and they're replicated ... The tone was probably established in the twenties ... and it's just resonated ever since, and accumulated a lot of spurious baggage ... So I think that if you do just simply look at the play free of the baggage ... you see there a Chekhov who, far from being elegiac ... is a man passionately interested in social change. (1993, personal interview)

With this view of Chekhov as himself a change agent, Eyre stridently denied the charge that Griffiths inserted an 'extraneous' politics into the play, but rather 'cleans the varnish off the play, renders up the play fairly and truthfully'. Eyre also thought that there were socio-biographical connections between Griffiths and Chekhov's characters. 'There's a lot of Trofimov in Trevor ... There's an element of him that finds Lopakhin very, very attractive ... You know, working class background guy who's worked very, very hard to emerge from his class background' (1993, personal interview). For Eyre, then, Griffiths' connection between *The Cherry Orchard* and earlier plays like *The Party* were both biographical and intertextual.

It is clear from Eyre's reasons for his choice of writer that Trofimov and Lopakhin were central to *his* notion of the play's meaning from the start. For Eyre, Lopakhin is far from being the crass real estate agent of traditional western interpretations.

> He's a builder, and it was very important for me the casting in the televi-sion version of Bill Paterson, who I think is a hugely sympathetic char-acter. I wanted this guy...It's so often you see the audience being invited to take the side of Gayev and Ranevskaya, and kind of think 'the vulgarity of it – he's ruining this beautiful cherry orchard'. What's so wonderful about the play is all its complexities – because the cherry orchard is beau-tiful. It is a magnificent work of nature – but of course a work of nature that has been appropriated and is owned by people who regard nature as their property. And there is this man who is taking over this piece of property, but at least he is using it to give happiness to a lot more people .... It's spreading it around a bit. (1993, personal interview)

It is clear that before selecting Griffiths as his writer, Eyre already had a 'cherry orchard = private property', rather than a 'cherry orchard = wasted beauty' slant on the play. In fact, Eyre indicated an important intertextual citation for this in John Berger's analysis of Gainsborough's painting 'Mr and Mrs Andrews' in his TV series *Ways of Seeing*, which Eyre had been watching shortly before planning the production. 'So... the whole idea of landscape as property was very much in my mind', and the Gainsborough reference was visible both at Nottingham Playhouse and on BBC Television as *mise-en-scène*.

This intertextual production detail indicates the close meshing of the director's concept of the play with that of his writer, Trevor Griffiths, for whom the cherry orchard represented 'an old way of owning and experiencing possession, land'. And Eyre's casting of Scottish accents for Lopakhin (Paterson), Firs (Paul Curran), and the servants was, indirectly, designed to emphasise this 'ownership of people by people' interpretation as well, adding a colonialist dimension to the class one. 'For every English person when they hear a Scottish accent, whether they know it or not, there's a sense of feeling we're superior; that the Scots have been colonised by the English ... That seemed to me to work for a British audience' (Eyre 1993, personal interview).

However, despite this compatibility of writer and director, there were a number of aspects of Eyre's *The Cherry Orchard* that Griffiths was not totally happy with.

Scottish accents and northern voice

First, in Griffiths' view 'there was an attempt to regionalise people via Scotland, which didn't make a lot of sense ... It would have been much clearer and much more potent if they'd been Irish'. (As Bill Paterson pointed out, the Kilroy Irish version of *The Seagull* had fairly recently been a huge success at the Royal Court, and this would have been in Richard Eyre's mind.) Apart from the greater clarity of class and colonialism in Ireland, Griffiths also regretted the Scottish accents because they were *replacing* the north-country English voices of the earlier Nottingham production, for which the translation was prepared, and which were, he felt, funnier.

The poppy field worth forty thousand

Secondly, Griffiths felt that the 'northern voice' also conveyed a tougher, less romantic spirit at Nottingham Playhouse, where Trofimov and Lopakhin were played by Mick Ford and Dave Hill.

> Mick Ford's Trofimov is hugely original, in the sense that he goes all the way towards recovering Trofimov for a radical and serious reinterpretation. In other words, I think he follows the line of the text. Anton Lesser played him on television ... and...I don't think it had the crudeness in some ways, the force anyway, of the text. I think it's slightly romantic. You're invited to feel sorry for him rather than to reckon with him, to deal with him ... I think that's a weakness on one wing, and on the other wing I think Billy Paterson's Lopakhin...misses ... a key passage in the fourth Act when Lopakhin and Trofimov are talking about the future ... Lopakhin begins to talk about the poppy fields in bloom ... and he

talks about how much it's worth. And in my version of that play both things have got to be very strong; both the natural, organic dimension of a poppy field, and the accountancy. Dave Hill got that on the stage, though he leaned towards the natural dimension of the poppy field. Bill never got anywhere near that. He always had a calculator in his pocket. He was clicking up what it was worth. (1993, personal interview)

The difference between Hill's and Paterson's interpretation of the poppy field scene was fundamentally related to the specific decade of each production. For Paterson, Lopakhin represented current intra-conservative mobility in Thatcherite Britain of the 1980s. 'We did it very much of the time: early 1980s ... when the whole question of the upwardly mobile was the burning political question of the day ... The new nouveau riche were beginning to take over ... The Thatcher period, where you had the entrepreneurial class rising above the landed aristocracy, the old Tory class; which had very strong relevance in this country ... We talked a lot about that in rehearsal' (1993, interview with Tom Burvill).

In contrast, Hill's Lopakhin was performed in 1977 in the dying years of what he described as a 'selling out' Labour government, 'when there was no suspicion in anybody's head that around the corner Thatcherism was about to descend upon us from a great height' (1993, personal interview with Tom Burvill). Instead of having an overt, contemporary political reference (as in 'Thatcherism'), Hill had historical memories of his own for Lopakhin. 'Somebody like Alexander Salt, a person who builds a model village for his workers, but would still want to live in the big house ... He had that similarity with a lot of Victorian mill owners. My father was brought up in the cotton trade and there was that ... dream that there would be a decent life for everybody.'

These differences between the Thatcherite neo-Conservative and the Victorian patriarch who builds a model village for his workers then flowed through to the two actors' interpretations of the poppy field reference. For Paterson, though he saw (and played) the complexity of Lopakhin, the 1980s entrepreneur with a philosophy of enlightened individualism was definitely uppermost.

I played it with a sense of ... him getting embarrassed ... 'that's something to behold I can tell you, the poppy field in bloom'. And it was as though it was a sign of weakness because maybe the cherry orchard would have been nice as well but – 'well anyway ... I made the forty thousand and you're welcome to some of it' .... So it would be a cash crop to him ... rather than necessarily a thing of beauty. He may be thinking of it in the same way as a farmer looks at rape seed oil that we get in Britain today, these ... yellow fields ... which are all part of the EEC money that's come in. (1993, interview with Tom Burvill)

In contrast, Hill had been to Eastern Europe in the 1970s and seen their 'very serious dream' of 'getting away and being at one with your-self' by growing things in small country dachas (which were scarcely bigger than allotments). So he felt that he understood better Lopakhin's plan of subdividing the cherry orchard estate.

> He's arguing ... that there's different perceptions of art and beauty, and that to have a small group of people living in this large house and every-body else living in poverty is not a very beautiful sight, however beautiful the house may be. Those lines were a wonderful combination of beauty, almost like it was a painting but also that feeling of getting your hands dirty at the same time, which I think is some sort of key to unlocking the man. That he has the ability to actually get down and dig...and plant the field himself. .... That the beauty of what you gain from life is enhanced by the fact that that's what you've done .... It's all right to take money because you are somebody who is going to use it well and move on, and money as a form of energy has got to be kept moving round. (1993, interview with Tom Burvill)

The gravitas of star performance

Thirdly, Griffiths was less than happy with the 'star' slant of the BBC television production (as were Nottingham actors who had hoped to get parts in it).

> [T]he principal problem with the TV production is that Richard doesn't get to the radical heart of the play in my view .... And this is in part because he's imported a whole set of actors into the production who are sub-stars or stars. And some of the old English sense of Chekhov I think is re-imported when you get a Judi Dench, for example, playing Ranevs-kaya. Because she has such 'weight' as an actress ... against the relative weight of Trofimov and Lopakhin ... she necessarily pulls my play ... out of kilter. (1993, personal interview)

It is arguable that while Trevor Griffiths established a clear sub-textual narrative in Act II, some of the ensemble acting that establishes polyphony was sacrificed to star performance in the television produc-tion. Cameraman Geoff Feld mentioned, for example, one speech in Act III 'where Judi Dench goes to a window which was so intense that we actually had ... to widen the shot ... Just the sheer intensity of her perfor-mance, it was almost embarrassing. You were somehow intruding' (1993, personal interview).

Mick Ford agreed fundamentally with Griffiths' concerns. For him, at Nottingham it was the ensemble that helped the actors, critics and audiences to 'slightly rediscover the play, because it wasn't hampered by star performances. You weren't going to watch Janet Suzman's Ranevskaya, or Alan Bates' Lopakhin ... You know how that can completely capsize a play. Because people start talking about their performance ... A character isn't important just because they've made a lot of films. They're as important as the play makes them' (1993, interview with Tom Burvill).

Designing Act II: an impression of arid landscape

The Cherry Orchard's set designer, Sue Spence said that Richard Eyre had done much more work, generating clearer design concepts, 'than a lot of directors do when they approach a play'.

> One of them was that the nursery ... was to be ... clean and spare and very unfussy ... He didn't want me to use bright colours, or dominating pictures, or anything like that. It was all kept visually quiet ... The floor boards were all very pale. We stained them and dragged them to look a sort of pale beechwood. The walls were white or off-white ... Richard was very keen that the table in there – that the children had done their homework on – had been there for ages and ages ... We found a lovely large four feet diameter pine table, and I had it painted with a Russian design, and then it was ... aged down, and we spilled on it and scribbled kids' names and things on it. I can't remember if we ever saw it close up ... probably not. But we often used to do those sorts of things because it made things feel right for the artists. (1993, personal interview)

This carefully 'authentic' and detailed naturalism of Act I was (as Griffiths in fact wanted) to be sharply contrasted with Act II where, Spence said:

> Richard ... didn't want anything naturalistic at all...just...an impression of...a dry, rather arid sort of landscape ... We really only had a bench ... where quite a lot of the acting went on [i.e. the 'Gainsborough set']. And then we had some perspective telegraph poles going away into the distance ... .It was ... the most difficult of the three sets to achieve ... There were just these very narrow channels for the cameras, which were very carefully worked out. The studio was full of scenery so that we got a lot of depth. (1993, personal interview)

It was these narrow channels for the cameras which were exploited for Firs' and the vagrant's slow entries from back-stage in Act II. But 'a lot of depth' was exactly what Trevor Griffiths did *not* want. His preference in terms of an 'alienation' effect was to have the kind of staging achieved in the Nottingham Playhouse production, where 'it had been done very flat ... It didn't pretend that it had more space than it had, except in a very cardboard way. It wasn't pretending to be three-dimensional ... [It had] a very strange, almost painted tree for example, rather than what we have here [in the television production], which was dried plants brought into the studio and ... shale and elephant grass' (1993, personal interview).

The problem and 'difficulty' for television personnel when they stray from naturalism is clear here, as Sue Spence indicated. 'It was a difficult one to discuss with Richard. With the nursery set it was easy, because we were dealing with four walls and we'd all seen things like that before. But he couldn't help me a lot with the exterior really, other than saying ... roughly what he wanted.'

Spence chose to establish a deep, three-dimensional impression. And the 'dry, rather arid' effect – which in fact some of our student audience groups were to read as 'mid-West America, not Russia' – was achieved by importing spiky grasses. 'It ... helped a lot with the three-dimensional set ... having those tall, spiky things'.

So the 'sort of flattened' look of Act II that Griffiths wanted was lost, along with some of its comedy. Griffiths' crucial Act II concept was being stripped away in the BBC *The Cherry Orchard*, as it had been with his *Sons and Lovers*.

Lighting *The Cherry Orchard*: Josef Israels' 'cube of light'

Eyre's *The Cherry Orchard* was a potentially prestigious production that technical staff felt privileged to be working on. Less conventional professional practices were encouraged, like the use of new lightweight cameras to provide a 'filmic' look. To avoid the 'tennis court lighting' of standard multi-camera TV drama, Richard Eyre turned to a lighting director, Howard King, who was known at the BBC for his innovative work with reflected rather than direct light. This, indirect lighting – which 'bounced' off the ceiling and walls of a platform-based, full four-wall set – would, in Eyre's view, provide texture and also lucidity to what he saw as Griffiths' idiomatic and 'unsentimental' text.

King described his bounced lighting in the nursery scenes as 'deeply satisfactory'. This would not go beyond naturalism, because as King said, 'The work of my life actually was to try and make things look more real. I'm not an artist. I'm a person who observes things very carefully, and thinks, what is the reality of that? How can I get that in the studio?' But, *within* the conventions of television naturalism, there was scope for innovation. 'I had an idea in my mind which nobody else had ever had about how things ... could look on television, and it worked ... It's now a commonplace. People accept it as a way of looking at things' (1993, personal interview).

King felt that Richard Eyre was 'the most professional man I've ever come across ... He went through it literally shot by shot'. But the technical execution of any one shot was King's domain; and his favourite signature on the visual look of *The Cherry Orchard* was an intertextual reading of how 'to make things look more real'.

> I knew the transition I wanted. I wanted the magic of when he puts the blinds up [in Act I] – that magic from one lighting state to another. And in order to get from one state to another, you actually had to have something rather subtle to go before it, so that when the sunlight came through there was this vast difference ... Before this you had early dawn – dawn's a very tricky thing to do on television ... It's a very subtle thing. There's light, but there's no light ... There's no great direction to it at all. (King 1993, personal interview)

Looking for the appropriate indirect lighting concept, King drew on a nineteenth-century Dutch painting by Josef Israels, to establish what he called the unfocused effect of Acts I and IV. This painting which King had seen in Amsterdam, gave him the 'sense of being in a cube of light – in other words, light all around you'. What particularly impressed King about Israels' style 'was the fact that the floor ... was right. So often ... television lighting ... people...are all obsessed with vertical surfaces – in other words, faces and things like that; but not with the horizontal surfaces, like tops of tables, tops of settees ... and floor ... We have light coming down ... and it all accumulates on the floor eventually, with a multiplicity of shadows' (1993, personal interview).

As designed by Spence and Eyre, the 'clean, spare and unfussy' sets of Acts I and IV were both light *and* showed a lot of empty horizontal surfaces. Therefore Eyre's concept of set design, King's bounced lighting innovation and a painting in Amsterdam came together to provide the 'cube of light' in which, in the last scene of the play, Firs dies. This servant's death is the last link in Griffiths' sub-textual narrative which, from its focal point in Act II, 'unleashes freedom throughout the play'. Here, at the very end of the play, Griffiths has Firs speak in a semi-consciously reflexive way about the wrong choices he has made. Yet an important question is the extent to which King's 'cube of light' concept and Eyre's empty white set sentimentalised and individualised Firs, rather than positioning him sub-textually with the vagrant and with Trofimov's peasants 'hanging from the trees'.

The conventional professional practices of television naturalism were always likely to impinge on the production – and there is plenty of evidence that they did in camera style, sound and set design. One example is what lighting director Howard King called the 'disaster' of Act II. The extreme time pressure of shooting Act II last, as Wyver describes, put the designer under severe pressure as she worried about the naturalistic quality of her set. This led to a last-minute use of nets over the cameras, and so to a soft, unfocused 'impressionist' look. 'The designer thought the camera was too sharp, was showing up all these faults in the exterior set – which is always a pretty difficult thing to do in the studios. She got into a panic and said ... it will look terrible, it will look artificial ... [S]omebody said well, we can put nets over the cameras ... The pictures were awful with the nets over them ... I never have believed in this business of degrading the picture to give some flawed effect' (1993, personal interview).

It is arguable that Richard Eyre's challenge to what he calls 'the inert quality of video ... the head-and-shoulders visual style of TV' – via 'film-style' single-camera work, using true reverse shots rather than the 'cheated' ones of TV multicamera set-ups, and with the director working on the studio floor not in the gallery – in fact interacted with set design, lighting and sound to establish an impressionistic visual style that sentimentalised Act II (especially Judi Dench's speech about her 'brutal' men) at the very times that it should have been, in Eyre's and Griffiths' views, most tough and alienating. But Richard Eyre, who was one of the first directors to bring film techniques to BBC television, disagreed with this interpretation. 'Television is ... very difficult to light well ... because it has no texture and it always shows you too much, unlike film ... To get texture we mostly lit indirectly .... It was all ... indirect light, which is why it's got that soft and you could say impressionistic quality. I don't actually think it's at odds with the lucidity [of the translation], because it gives it a texture and it gives it a beauty which makes it more accessible ... It doesn't romanticise it' (1993, personal interview).

Trevor Griffiths wasn't so sure. 'There's a number of ways you can ... actually image the second act. And one is to do it sort of tight, almost two dimensional; not create an impressionistically natural set. And Richard went the other way. On the [Nottingham] stage ... you always knew you were in a theatre. There was never any attempt to recreate a great sort of parkland ... You understood the space ... but they were just signifiers. There was no attempt at naturalism ... [But on TV] they imported tons and tons of shale ... And suddenly you could see people looking for angles that were natural, rather than alienating, looking for shots that went on forever' (1993, personal interview).

Camera and sound: the new technology

In this chapter, one of the running themes has been the attempts – and failures – to achieve Griffiths' 'alienation' effect in Act II of BBC1's *The Cherry Orchard*. But possibly the most significant reason for this television naturalism was the new camera technology, at a time when the BBC was still prepared to innovate in drama production. At the time of the production Chris Griffin-Beale wrote of the enormous innovation and organizational breakthrough of bringing lightweight cameras into the studios for an entire production. The gulf between the prevalent rehearse/record technique which broke TV drama down into small sections and film practice 'still seemed unbridgeable. *The Cherry Orchard*...prove[s] the gulf can be bridged within – just within – the productivity demands of studios: five days for the 130 minutes of *Cherry Orchard*' (1981). As *The Cherry Orchard*'s cameraman Geoff Feld described it:

> In the late seventies we got the first generation of relatively high quality lightweight cameras. Just about that time I worked with Richard Eyre for the first time on Comedians, and got on with him very well ... And shortly after that I managed to get an attachment with a film cameraman who was shooting Richard's Imitation Game ... really learning about the use of single camera techniques and lightweight cameras ... Richard wanted to do The Cherry Orchard and I said why don't we try something different? (1993, personal interview)

Griffin-Beale explained that 'it was only possible to record shot by shot within that time, because Eyre planned each shot in meticulous detail beforehand. (That is intriguing, since multi-camera techniques are often associated with the disciplines of preparatory planning, and single-camera shooting seen as comparatively undisciplined)' (1981, 25). Eyre's detailed planning for the production depended on close co-operation of cameraman and director.

> The whole set was designed around lightweight cameras, particularly the nursery set, which is Acts I and IV. The set was actually built up on rostrums, on real wooden floors ... which affected the sound of the thing ... You couldn't have done that with multi-cameras ... because big cameras need a studio floor ... And we shot it mostly single camera, by being very organised. Unusually, I went to outside rehearsal for two days before the studio, and we worked the whole play through in camera terms, so that by the time we got to the studio we were very well prepared. And I had an almost shot-by-shot knowledge of how we were going to shoot it, and so did Howard King with his lighting ... Particularly Act I and Act IV were ... something quite different for studio drama. (Feld 1993, personal interview)

Virtually every television professional that we spoke to who worked on *The Cherry Orchard* regarded it as one of the pinnacles of their professional career. Partly this was a matter of Richard Eyre's meticulous preparation and control, which at the same time left space open for individual innovation. This was also facilitated by the greater openness of the BBC at that time, Feld believed.

> One of the great strengths of television in the sixties and seventies was that lots of writers ... learned their craft because it wasn't a million, two million pounds every time you made something ... People could afford to fail because we had a cheap way of making programmes. But no-one takes chances anymore ... .Now the international market is so important to the BBC. Everything has to have a potential sales value ... When something comes in from a writer the first question is, will it attract co-production money? So that immediately changes the potential of your production ... Studio drama is almost a thing of the past. (1993, personal interview)

Feld emphasised that the technological and visual innovation of the new cameras allowed an ever more complete naturalism.

> Inevitably in multi-camera your close-up shots are done on ... telephoto lenses, so ... you tend to crush perspective quite a lot ... You remember the most marvellous moment in the first Act when they open up the curtains? ... Now if that was done as part of a multi-camera technique the lighting could never have been organised in such a way to give you that wonderful moment ... The whole of Acts I and IV were shot single camera. So we did it shot by shot .... There is a visual unity in terms of the lens angles we used. This was unlike a normal multi-camera thing where you're all over the place, where getting the shot requires using different focal length lenses, which actually alters the visual texture. (1993, personal interview)

Sound director, Richard Partridge – who had to use microphones on hand-held 'fishpoles' since booms were impracticable – also emphasised these two Acts as innovative and special. 'It sounded like a real room with all the proper floorboards, and all the walls around you; so it sounded much more like being on location in a real set' (1993, personal interview). Greater naturalism, organic unity, consistent depth of field, historical accuracy in set design, the 'real' sound of real floorboards: Acts I and IV (which were shot first) were the pinnacle of *The Cherry Orchard*'s achievement in the eyes of its technical producers. In contrast, Act II, shot last in some 'panic' because 'under tremendous time pressure' (Howard King), with camera decisions like the use of nylon stockings decided 'in a real hurry', was, in King's view, 'criminal' in parts. Feld agreed with him. 'I always felt Richard was least happy doing that one. I had the most problems shooting it. And it is somehow very different to the other three Acts' (1993, personal interview).

'Different to the other three Acts' was what Trevor Griffiths intended it to be. But, unlike Acts I and IV, the technical professionals had no clear concept for Act II, other than 'It was very stylised ... almost unreal ... It didn't look like an outside at all ... dreamlike' (Feld), or it was 'performance against the naturalism' (Partridge), or 'terribly difficult to do ... dry, rather arid' (Spence).

If any concept did guide the studio production of Act II stylistically, it was Eyre's dislike of standard television. As Feld describes it, this was a major reason for the 'soft look' of the Act. 'One of the things about the electronic image is this sharpness and edge ... And Richard had an abhorrence of that. And so it started off ... as a way to lose that very gritty image ... When we got to the studio there was some experiment with how soft we wanted to make the image ... filters, net, all sorts of things – to soften this edge' (1993, personal interview).

But other technical problems then compounded the problem, as Richard Partridge describes:

> Howard had lit the set almost entirely with bounced light ... And so, with every new set-up, he'd be moving his lights around, bouncing off a wall that we were looking at a moment ago. The result was that the wall tended to be brighter than the faces – because the camera was nice and sharp on all the bright bits, and less sharp on all the darker bits, due to a design feature ... This meant that it always looked as if the cameraman had focussed on the background instead of the faces ... It looked as if the cameraman has got his focus wrong some of the time. (1993, personal interview)

Add to these problems what Howard King called the 'criminal' softening and diffusion of the image with stockings in Act II, and it is unsurprising that there was 'a strong reaction against it ... from the engineering side of the BBC' (Feld). 'They said that the image wasn't good enough. They said it's all right when you're in a good reception area. But you had to remember that so many millions of people don't have good reception of the BBC, so it's not the right sort of image.'

A whole range of technical, professional and ideological values of practice were at work here – making Act II indeed the most 'alienated' of the play, though not in quite the way that Trevor Griffiths intended. On the one hand, as Griffin-Beale argued, the prestigious drama one-off series had been shown a pathway to the future by *The Cherry Orchard*'s use of film cameras. 'At a time when prestigious productions can be expected to attract a considerable return from subsidiary sales, it seems a false economy to insist on the compromises of traditional studio

methods, particularly when the end result must bear repeated viewings by a consumer who has paid hard cash for a videogram or for his
cable and satellite subscription' (1981, 25). On the other hand, camera
'impressionism' and set naturalism were likely to convey a very different
symbolic meaning from the performance than Eyre and Griffiths had
achieved at Nottingham. But how would 'actual audiences' decode this
production?

Audiences: Griffiths' voice at Loughborough University, England

This chapter represents 1980s developments in M/C studies, just as it
reflects 1980s developments in television. In particular it brings together
qualitative studies of the many different professional signatures (and
potential fragmentation of authorship (Tulloch 2000)) in production
with the emphasis on 'actual audience' analysis that emerged strongly in
the early 1980s. In particular, because of the strong cultural studies (i.e.
Raymond Williams) interrogation going on in the writing of Griffiths'
Cherry Orchard text, we were particularly interested on this occasion
in the response of student audiences. Interviews and questionnaire
surveys were conducted with over 200 university students at 17 universities in Britain, the U.S.A. and Australia who watched the Eyre/Griffiths
Cherry Orchard. Fuller quantitative and qualitative analyses of these
audience groups are reported elsewhere (Tulloch, forthcoming). But to
give some sense of a student audience response to the production, I
will discuss briefly a Loughborough University drama group which had
studied Trevor Griffiths.

Responding initially to Griffiths' BBC *The Cherry Orchard*, they felt
'You couldn't have told it was him really'. In this focus group their *immediate* reading, at the beginning of the interview, was about 'stars' and the
authorship of Trevor Griffiths.

> 'It wasn't that different from past interpretations [of Chekhov] ... Consid-
> ering the names involved, I would have thought it would have been a
> bit ...'

> 'More radical.'

> '... political.'

> 'That's one of the things I didn't like about it, the number of stars in it.'

> 'It pampered to a BBC Saturday night audience.'

> 'It did, didn't it? ... It's that kind of ... Elizabeth R costume drama – you
> felt that a lot.'

'This ... was kind of different, but it was basically what you expect seeing when you go to see a Chekhov play. The same kind of thing as ... people expect when the RSC start doing things – what you expect from a Shakespeare play. There was a certain ... look of the sets, a certain way characters spoke. And ... the ... way in which Chekhov is considered ... seems to be like that ...'

'They spent too much money. That's always the problem, isn't it? ... You know, the sets and costumes ... It disables us as viewers and makes us much more passive. Theatre is quite active anyway, live theatre. But especially when you transfer all the chintz of life on to TV as well, you just become redundant. Emotionally it's engaging, but it's nice to get to use your brain ...'

Int: *'What does Trevor Griffiths mean to you?'*

'Comedians.'

'Yeah.'

'Left-wing playwright; used to write a lot for television; till television stopped liking Left-wing playwrights.'

The student emphasis on 'too much money spent on sets and costumes' may well have been prompted by 'all that stuff [on Griffiths] I've seen and read', including the problems with sets and costumes Griffiths had recently encountered with *Sons and Lovers*. Like the Loughborough students, Griffiths wants television that makes viewers more active. In both his sequential 'country house' dramas, *The Cherry Orchard* and *Country*, Griffiths challenged the conventional melodramatic naturalism of the genre, and offered audiences alternative subjective positions to the genre's upper class world view and conventions. In contrast, in the play that the Loughborough students particularly remembered Griffiths for, *Comedians*, he drew on dark and biting satire to challenge the deeply sexist, racist and classist conventions of working-class British humour – subverting on this occasion popular rather than (as in *The Cherry Orchard*) high cultural forms. At least some of the Loughborough students knew this work of Griffiths, recognised the problems of 'Left wing' playwrights working on television, criticised the conventionality of standard 'BBC heritage' genres, and rejected television's high naturalism. Within this group in particular, then, the space seemed available for a 'Left/Realist' reading formation debate about Chekhov.

There were some early pointers to this happening. Most of the students seemed comfortable with the use of Scottish accents in the production, and related this immediately to class issues.

'In ways, they might as well have been given Northern accents which although it is wrong many people use as a stereotype ... I did like the use of the different accent, it kind of stood out as working class.'

'If you get to set the play in Britain, I think Scotland's where you put it. It's certainly not a southern play.'

There were indications here of an acceptance of the social contemporaneity of Chekhov, as well as a recognition, as British students, of the deep class/political divide between north and south of the country. The focus group discussion thus moved on to a characterisation which was narratively central to Griffiths' own sub-textual 'class' reading: Trofimov in relation to the servants and the vagrant.

'[Trofimov] was taken a bit seriously I thought in that production ... There was that scene where he's sitting on the bench with Anya and waxing some political stuff. And ... it just seems to me that the one thing ... they're not doing is falling in love, and not kissing each other, and that's why he's talking. But it seemed like the play was actually ... listening to him in this production ... [Anya was] actually listening, "what are you saying about it? What do you mean?" ... I thought it was strange to actually give him credit, or credibility, for his politics ...'

Int: 'Does everybody feel that? That it seemed strange to give Trofimov's politics credibility? Did that surprise you given what you know?'

'The usual presentation of that ... character in Chekhov is the kind of the rambling student you don't really take much notice of ...'

'And so in that sense it was odd that they gave a space for him to be taken notice in ...'

'When he says that line that all the values that they have are just shimmering on the skyline or whatever, that ... acts as his counterbalance to what you've seen going on beforehand and the whole auction thing. Perhaps this was the strength of the production, the thing which was different ...'

'There's also the discussion of the people that had worked for them, hanging from the branches of the trees of the orchard. So from his point of view...it was inevitable that the orchard had to go, really, for something new to happen'.

'I guess it missed the point of the fact that he's saying – it's like Monty Python – we shouldn't just sit around just talking about this, we should go out and do something. And he's ...'

'He's sitting talking about it all the time, isn't he? ... There was that moment when he'd just said all this, and then there was that dirty old tramp came up and asked for some money. And I thought the production felt distinctly uncomfortable at that point. It didn't know what to do with itself for about five minutes ... That awful shot where they all say, "oh someone's coming", and there's that long pan and you see him stumble up the path. And nothing is said, and they just wait for him. It's almost like someone said the line too early or something. And it's three minutes while he walks up the path and says this. And it seems dreadfully heavy handed.'

Int: 'What did you think he was, this tramp?

'... An escaped convict. I thought something like that'.

'An extra from Hellraiser' (laughter).

'It's quite frightening.'

'I think there was for me that revolutionary kind of feel.'

'That was in the sense that he wasn't afraid to exploit them because he knew that very soon they were going to be on similar sort of levels. But I thought it was done very badly ...'

'He could have almost just come on and...said, "Oh sorry, wrong play!" and gone off again.'

Int: 'What play should he have been in?'

'Oh, Samuel Beckett, Waiting for Godot.'

'And Lear ....'

This Loughborough focus group conversation about Trofimov opens as a negotiation between (i) the canonical Chekhov (Trofimov, the student 'above love'), (ii) the performed Eyre/Griffiths television text (where there is, as the student says, a foregrounded loss of personal credibility as Anya leans forward to kiss Trofimov, and he fails to respond), and (iii) the interviewer's prompting to students to respond to the production 'surprise' about Trofimov *via* their knowledge of Trevor Griffiths ('Did that surprise you given what you know?').

But this 'Trevor Griffiths' conversational cue is ignored by the students, as they reach for a canonical interpretation via 'that usual type of character in Chekhov'. Griffiths' textual markers are, however, harder to ignore; and some of the students do begin to string together the Act II sub-text: Trofimov's rhetoric, the peasants hanging from the trees of the orchard, the alienated servants (Firs), and a vagrant who is '*going somewhere*'.

But this reading is then challenged by a series of 'external' intertexts: *Monty Python, Hellraiser, Waiting for Godot, King Lear.* These intertexts seem to convey to the students, as further comments indicated, a number of inactive 'moods': absurd comedy, fear, existential angst, tragedy. In this way intertexts – prompted in part by the deep Act II acting spaces that Griffiths didn't want ('it's three minutes while he walks up the path and says this') – colluded with the canonical reading of Chekhov to derail the discussion of those students who did seem to be tending towards articulating Griffiths' Act II sub-text. Thus, according to this intertextual reading the production 'misses the point' (of the canonical 'usual type of' Trofimov); and, conversely, where characters *are* introduced who promise active change, 'the production felt distinctly uncomfortable at that point ... He could have come on and said, "Oh sorry, wrong play!" and gone off again'.

The students do not read from within Griffiths' socialist/realist formation. Rather, as students of theatre, they appropriate their earlier critique of 'BBC' costume drama to read the 'uncomfortable' moments of the text as 'clumsy', 'badly done' or 'halfway' amalgams of theatre and television. Instead of taking up one student's conversational offer of a discussion about naturalism and the passive audience (quoted earlier), the group responds with a theatre-oriented critique.

'It's also that choice of whether they're filming something that is staged or they're filming something which is film .... And for me, at times when people wander out of shot you kind of think 'don't go half way, either make it something for TV or let us watch it live' – I can't stand watching something that's meant to be live on TV.'

'There's that bit with the windows, remember when you have this light and it all became ... an Ingmar Bergman movie with these profound profiles. And that was very set up, and then you had that bit where ... the tramp was coming. He's coming. Here he is now. He's here. And then, he's going. And you'd have edited that much more tightly, wouldn't you, for making TV.'

'You know, it did seem confused ... We have to get this difference between TV and a live event ...'

'You can sit and wait for those pauses in the theatre because you're there and you're watching those people and you don't mind if there's pauses. But if you're sitting here watching TV you really mind about those pauses.'

It may seem unfair to accuse a television production of being fixated with the stage, and then blame it for adopting filmic technique (e.g. the intertextual reference to Bergman). But this is to miss the point. Some students, at least, are contrasting the Griffiths of *Comedians* with the Griffiths of *The Cherry Orchard*, and complaining that the pretentiousness and 'profound profiles' of the 'Bergmanesque' Act I window scene (with its star emphasis on Judi Dench) represents the appropriation of the radical theatre playwright by 'BBC' television money and style. The students are focusing here on Howard King's most significant 'cube of light' transition in Act I:, the opening of the shutters. This moment represented the quintessence of the 'new technology' approach to television espoused by Richard Eyre, which, in actual production effort, imagination and time, worked at the expense of Griffiths' favoured Brechtian Act II. Griffiths' preferred mix of high naturalism and modernist 'alienation' does not seem to have come off in the view of even this highly Griffiths-sympathetic student audience.

Griffiths has always worked for critical readings in the interstices of texts, for small but significant subversions of canonical and formal convention. So one Loughborough student's reading of Griffiths' Chekhov is homologous with his own intention: 'It was still Chekhov, you know, undeniably at the end. But there *were* small differences to other productions I have seen, like little relationship differences [between Ranevskaya and Lopakhin in Act II], like "Oh, hello ... I didn't think of that being sexy like that before".'

The difficulty with this kind of response from Griffiths' point of view is not the 'small differences', but rather the lack of a coherent and critical reading formation (of gender and class) through which to interpret the 'little relationship differences'. *All* focus groups that we interviewed (whatever their discipline, their politics or their reading formation) noticed the more 'sexy than before' relationship between Ranevskaya and Lopakhin; and nearly all students liked this 'small difference'. But in most students' opinion, it was Gayev's earlier line (as adapted by Griffiths) about his sister's 'wanton' style of life that motivated the 'sexy' reading.

It also gave Judi Dench the opportunity for a star performance in Act II, as she was able to wring the other characters' (and the audiences') hearts with the mixture of emotion, happiness and pain, extravagance and pity, escapism and pragmatic sensualism that many students said they liked in the questionnaire survey. But that star performance by Dench (with her naturalistic range and density of emotions) sat uncomfortably with Griffiths' Brechtian intentions of Act II. Hence, the vagrant might, indeed, have said 'sorry, wrong play!', as too might Charlotta, Yepikhodov and the servants in the 'alienated' opening to Act II. The confusion in many students' discussion between wanting/not wanting stage/television techniques in fact replicated that deeper confusion in the BBC's *The Cherry Orchard* between 'quality', star-filled classics and formal/political innovation.

In the space of that confusion, a further tension – between the canonical Chekhov and the voice of Trevor Griffiths – was generated, even among his most sympathetic of audiences. Because one thing was especially noticeable across all the focus groups: whereas they all noted the more 'sexy' relationship between Ranevskaya and Lopakhin (which, Bill Paterson emphasised, they did not particularly play for or *perform*), at the same time *only one* of the focus groups noted Griffiths' changes to Trofimov's 'eternal student' lines in this production, *which were so important to the actors*. In other words, while students used Gayev's 'wanton' lines about his sister to justify (and thus like) the more 'flirtatious' Ranevskaya/Lopakhin interaction in Act II, no single student in any focus group drew on Trofimov's lines 'I'm still a student. And if the authorities have their way I suppose I will remain a student' to motivate or explain a more positive reading of the *student-in-the text* in Act II.

The one group which did laugh over these Trofimov lines contained Australian post-graduate Literature students. The screening and discussion of *The Cherry Orchard* took place at the time of major impending government cuts to university funding and student places; and asked why they laughed at Trofimov's 'if the authorities have their way' lines, a student said (to general approval), 'I merely thought if the authorities had their way now none of us would *be* students'.

Griffiths would have liked this contemporary re-working of his 'restored' Chekhovian line. But it hardly happened at all among student audiences in three countries.

Griffiths reviewed: the print media and *The Cherry Orchard, Through the Night, Country* and *Bill Brand*

4

> Griffiths's great strength (though critics, including myself, have some-times been slow to realise it and have categorised him as a doctrinaire propagandist) is his ability to dramatise his own conflicts. (Robert Cushman, *Radio Times*, November 1975)

Trevor Griffiths' reference in his *Through the Night* Preface to a tele-vision 'education that subverts' was talking as much about conventional genres as about politics. *Through the Night* directly engaged with existing hospital soap opera. *Country* critiqued the vastly popular country house genre. *The Cherry Orchard* challenged a British middle-class construction of 'Art' classics. *Bill Brand* attempted to pull the male-audience world of politics (Brunsdon 1981) into the realm of 'working-class idioms, speech patterns, behaviours', and, in so doing reach out via the popular series form to a less gendered audience (hence some reviewers referred to it as soap opera). As Jonathan Bignell noted (Chapter 1), Griffiths' pleasure in playing with mixed generic registers sometimes confused critics who preferred an overt 'political' signature. I want to take Bignell's obser-vation further in this chapter, which focuses on the construction of Griffiths in newspaper reviews.

Critics, genre, intertextuality and the fictional 'real'

Marvin Carlson has argued that the role of newspaper reviewers is often 'more powerful than any other single source in structuring the way that audiences will receive the performance within the theatre' (Carlson 1990, 23). Carlson draws on reader-response theorist Jaus to provide a useful map in foregrounding three reviewing factors that he sees as underpin-ning (as principles of restraint) an audience's 'horizon of expectations': (i) the familiar poetics of the genre (ii) the intertextual relationships to works in the literary-historical surroundings, and (iii) the opposition between fiction and reality presupposed by text/production. While TV reviewers, responding to the 'ephemerality' of television, have a different public temporality from theatre reviewers – as this chapter will show, usually responding with an on-the-day preview or a review the day after screening – these theoretical reviewer frames of generic poetics, intertextual references and opposed fiction/reality modalities make a useful starting point to look at the television reviewing of Griffiths.

Genre and the negotiation of interpretive communities

Carlson argues that after the French Revolution, a new community of spectators and readers appeared who were eager to participate in the cultural life of novels and theatre, but who lacked the traditional knowledge of how to do so. Reviewers stepped into 'the role of model reader and unquestionably [were] powerfully influential in the training of a whole generation of theatregoers' (p. 22). To do this, reviewers provided much of the kind of information which earlier generations of theatregoers already had as part of their cultural competence: knowledge of intertextual relationships with other works, acquaintance with the generic tradition, with the author and so on. As a result, even if spectators did not know what specific play was being performed at a certain theatre, in the nineteenth century they 'could predict with reasonable assurance the *type* of play offered there, with all the attendant generic expectations' (1996, 16). Hence, of course, the well-known first night disaster of Chekhov's *The Seagull* at the Emperor's Alexandrinsky Theatre in St. Petersburg, where a play presenting new forms of theatre was performed in a place where the site-expectation was for grand melodrama.

Television tends towards product differentiation in similar but also different ways. Here particular channels focus both on particular audiences, and at the same time seek to maximise audiences via generic strategies to lure 'floating' audiences away from other TV channels at key 'break' moments (Tulloch 1986, chapter 12) – and it is clear from many reviewers of Griffiths' *Bill Brand* that they were unconvinced that ITV would succeed in getting or keeping his preferred, large working-class audiences with his 'quality' productions. Indeed, much of the discourse of tabloid newspapers around early episodes of *Bill Brand* can be conceived as seeking to do just that.

Newspaper reviewers often still have a key role in establishing and changing audience perceptions of genre and channel. For example, even though the 'melancholic' Chekhov still lingers among some producers, actors and audiences, *reviewers* (following the tradition established by Michael Frayn, Trevor Griffiths and others on the British stage) have for some time been emphasising a generic shift from tragedy to comedy (or at least to tragi-comedy). Here, for example, are some reviewers of Adrian Noble's production of *The Cherry Orchard* at the Swan Theatre, Stratford-Upon-Avon in 1995: 'Ever since Michael Frayn started to produce his translations, it has become conventional to say that Chekhov is funnier than we think. Noble does all that he can to underline the point. (Robert Hewison, *Sunday Times*, 9.7.1995); 'Was there really a time when Chekhov was invisible behind the melancholy mists and autumnal hazes of the self-consciously atmospheric productions in which English directors shrouded him? After a revival as lucid and robust as this, it is hard to believe that sensitivity could be so crass. I can remember few *Cherry Orchards* that made me laugh so often (Benedict Nightingale, *The Times*, July 6, 1995)

Similarly, Jennifer Selway wrote in the *Observer* (October 11, 1981) on the Eyre/Griffiths BBC television *Cherry Orchard* that 'Griffiths' new English version ... has freshness and an ear for the comedy which can easily be lost in more brooding productions'; while Peter Fiddick commented in the *Guardian*, 'Away with melancholy, this new *Cherry Orchard* is in a different vein. Directed by Richard Eyre for BBC 1 in the same fresh and muscular version by Trevor Griffiths that he first commissioned for the theatre, it stands foursquare for progress' (Peter Fiddick, *Guardian*, October 14, 1981).

What is clear is that this negotiation with 'comedy' between reviewers and audiences takes place in relation to both genre and perceived authorship: Fiddick, for instance – drawing not only on the recent shift in reviewers' competences to think of Chekhov as comic, but also on a long-running emphasis among Griffiths' theatre and TV reviewers on his 'politics' – speaks, of his TV *Cherry Orchard* 'standing foursquare for progress'. Here was a reviewer, unlike those Bignell discussed, who could still readily see the 'Trevor Griffiths' he expected, and yet blend that with reviewers' new wisdom about a contemporary playing for comedy in Chekhov.

Intertextual relationships to familiar works of the literary-historical surroundings

Carlson notes that newspaper reviewers systematically foreground features of imaging and staging, often with a powerful intertextual referencing (1990, 23). It is clear that intertextual image reference is an important way of mobilising audience expectations generically by theatre professionals (Tulloch, forthcoming). Set designers frequently draw intertextually from the history of art. For Adrian Noble's 1995/6 RSC *Cherry Orchard*, designer Richard Hudson drew on the Scandinavian painter Hammershoi for his 'cool Northern light' interiors to support Noble's direction that this was not an 'anthropologically' Russian production (Tulloch 1999, 44). For the set of Ron Daniels' *The Cherry Orchard* at the American Repertory Theater, designer George Tsypin drew on the early twentieth century Russian avant-garde painter Kasimir Malevich. Whereas Noble kept his set design abstract, providing 'Russian feel' via the frenetic polka he directed into the ball sequence, Daniels – who felt his Boston audience had no political interest at that time in interpretations relating to the Russian Revolution – established his 'period feel' by way of the intertextuality of set design and costumes based on the Russian paintings of Malevich (Tulloch, Burvill and Hood 1999). Thus Malevich's 1928 painting, 'Red Cavalry' was used for the backcloth *without* the red cavalry which appears in the painting itself. That would have been too 'political'.

In contrast in the 1981 BBC television production of *The Cherry Orchard*, director Richard Eyre did want the 'political' interpretation of Griffiths, at least to the extent that it challenged the dominant English middle class generic reading of the play as lachrymose and melancholy. To assert a class/colonialist 'ownership' reading Eyre chose not a painting as such for his Act II staging, but a radical television *reading* of a painting. Eyre's imaging of the gentry on a single bench for Act II drew intertextually on John Berger's recent 'land ownership' reading of Gainsborough's *Mr and Mrs Andrews* in his TV series *Ways of Seeing*, where (in a further intertextuality) he had critiqued Sir Kenneth Clark's reading of the same painting in his *Civilisation* television series. In the same production, lighting director Howard King tried to reproduce the 'cube of light' indirect lighting effect of the Dutch nineteenth-century painter Josef Israels.

On television this play on visual intertexts can lead, as David Edgar has said in criticising Griffiths' notion of 'strategic penetration', to such a surfeit of naturalistic images that any political intervention simply gets drowned out, for newspaper critics and audiences alike. Arguably, this occurred in the most direct way for most reviewers in relation to the BBC *The Cherry Orchard*, which was screened in the same week as the first episodes of *two* hugely expensive historical/heritage series, *Brideshead Revisited* and *The Borgias*. Most reviewers seem to have missed seeing Griffiths' 'rediscovery' of Chekhov altogether amidst the imagistic glitz of these much bigger television events, which had their own melancholy ('Jeremy Irons is magnificently melancholy as Charles Ryder'), their own aristocratic charm ('Anthony Andrews charming as the daring devil

Sebastian'), and their own much higher production values ('loving shots of punting and picnicking in Oxford which contrast sharply with the gloom of army life or the dark oppressiveness of the Ryder home', Susie Cornfield, *Sunday Times*, 17.10.1981). Alternately, reviewers did get to see *The Cherry Orchard* but contextualised it *via* these intertexts. Thus *The Times* began its review of the Eyre/Griffiths production: 'Television resounds with history and drama this week. On Monday ITV's *Brideshead* blast-off; tonight the BBC's long journey into the Borgia labyrinth; and last night, Chekhov's *Cherry Orchard*, written within intellectual sighting of the eclipse of traditional Russian society' (14.10.1981).

Peter Fiddick's *Guardian* review focused more centrally on the Eyre/Griffiths play, yet in picking out a moment of Lopakhin's speech and Scottish accent as his particular memory of the production, he engaged yet another 'visual' intertext.

> The new men, rough-edged and only slightly regretful, are in the driving seat: Lopakhin, son of a serf, uneasy as he is written to be, yet positively trumpeting, 'This is the new master speaking', once the Ranevsky estate is his. There is no sense at all of that familiar Russian cadence common in stage translations ... But then, Richard Eyre's other perceptive move, skilfully brought off, pulls this production even nearer home: this is a Scottish cherry orchard. Madame Ranevsky, Anya, and the servant Yasha (David Rintoul, suave and sinister as Bogarde was in The Servant) are the Sassenach voices of a fashionable, distant metropolis being carried into the country where the very accents – of Lopakhin, Epikhodov, Firs, Dunyasha – give an instant reminder of different values, and of a bridge that cannot be recrossed. (*Guardian*, October 14, 1981)

Both *The Times* and the *Guardian* reviewers provide what Carlson calls a certain relevant intertextuality: *The Times* relating it to television's 'blast-off' with expensive new 'history and drama', and the *Guardian* foregrounding Dirk Bogarde's overturning of master/servant power relationships in the film *The Servant*. It is via this latter audio-visual intertext (and not the 'cadence common in stage productions') that the reviewer encourages us to read 'the new master speaking' in (as Eyre would wish) a colonialist setting; while in addition referring to the 'Dustin Hoffman version' of Yepikhodov, played by Timothy Spall, and the BBC TV current affairs 'Fyfe Robertson earnestness' of Bill Paterson's Lopakhin.

The Times reviewer also reached for a 'new colonial' reading of the BBC *Cherry Orchard* via a very different but contiguous television intertext.

> 'Looked at rationally', says Lopakhin at one point in the play, 'life is meaningless' – but rationality is not as common as we might think, nor compassion either, which Granada's three-part series Rich World, Poor

World invites. Last night's 'Business as Usual' focused on the trade ties between North and South, which benefit the former to an extent increasingly resented by the latter ... One of the issues was stated quite simply: one quarter of the world's population enjoy four-fifths of the wealth. The commodities the poorer nations sell ... the attempts to grow and sell cash crops marginalises their population and sacrifices land that should be supplying food. (*The Times*, October 14, 1981)

Yet the obvious connections between the Granada programme on neo-colonialism and the Eyre/Griffiths' colonial 'ownership of land' *Cherry Orchard* were not made by this reviewer. Lopakhin's 'meaningless' words were used simply as an intertextual programme bridge to *Rich World, Poor World*, whereas his words (so important to Griffiths) about *redistributing the land* and *changing* the rich world, poor world syndrome were not mentioned.

There were further connections that *The Times* and other reviewers might have made. The Eyre/Griffiths *Cherry Orchard* (emphasising Thatcherite conservatism) happened to be screened on Mrs Thatcher's birthday, and while the reviewer was marginally connecting *The Cherry Orchard* to *Rich World, Poor World*, *The Times* itself was featuring the 'Iron Lady' in its page 1 headline, kneeling to cut her birthday cake while announcing that she would never appear kneeling in a newspaper again. Meanwhile the *Observer* was calling for a Conservative U-turn on Thatcher's 'simplistic economic policies', and for her resignation because of the significantly increased unemployment in Britain among young black people and other underprivileged groups. Interestingly, just one reviewer made reference to this issue, Betka Zamoyska commenting in the *Sunday Times*, 'Trofimov (Anton Lesser) could have just emerged from the LSE. The contemporary aspects of the play come over most clearly, especially Trofimov's invectives against the inequalities of the social system' (17.10.1996).

But this was an isolated case. No reviewer commented on either the contemporary aspects of Bill Paterson's 'Thatcherism' performance as Lopakhin, or on his social/environmental speeches (indeed *The Times* review speaks of 'Bill Paterson's admirable, acquisitive peasant'). And yet the relationship between Chekhov's fiction and reality *is* a continuous preoccupation of reviewers. Although generic shifts into comedy are recognised (and sometimes negotiated) by reviewers as part of their 'quality' evaluation of the performance, and although intertextual (often imagistic) relationships to 'familiar works' are established, these are seldom defining aspects of the overall review. We are looking here for the mechanisms of limitation ('regimes of truth' in Foucault's sense) which are circulated by reviewers.

Juxtaposition of fiction and reality

As we saw (Chapter 3), Trevor Griffiths and Richard Eyre strongly
emphasised class relationships in their translation and productions
of *The Cherry Orchard*. The Eyre/Griffiths' emphases on progress, on
Lopakhin as change agent, on English/Scottish coloniality (as a 'bridge
that cannot be re-crossed') and 'away with melancholy' were all recir-
culated by Peter Fiddick's ten-column-inch review to readers of the
Guardian, but nowhere else. It would be easy to argue that this is a direct
effect of the *Guardian*'s liberal-left readership; and clearly, while Carlson
is right to emphasise the importance of reviewers in establishing horizons of expectations for audiences, this should not be homogenised and
seen in isolation either from aspects of production and performance,
or from newspapers' intended readerships. Carlson's map of theatre
reading formations tends to take each part of this process of 'productive
activations' as relatively discrete areas, as though interpretive commu-
nities, production values of practice, reviewing and audience reading
are not, in part, mutually constructed (Bennett and Woollacott 1987).
In Chapter 3 I looked at production values of practice and audience
reading, and in this chapter will look at newspapers reviewers' leading
of audiences in the 'juxtaposition of fiction and reality'. I focus here
on some key television texts of Griffiths that were ostensibly all about
current (or recent) reality, unlike *The Cherry Orchard*, and which were
often both highly popular with audiences and critically acclaimed. Two
things will be emphasised. First, though it is clearly the case, as Bignell
argues, that critics' competence in understanding Griffiths' authorial
signature as socialist can lead to a closure of interpretation, this needs
to be understood as mediated by newspaper reviewers in terms of their
negotiations with their perceived readers. Second, a popular television
series offers different possibilities of mediation to critics/readers than
a popular one-off play. I will start with reviewers' responses to two of
Griffiths' most successful one-off television plays.

The 'experience' of personal politics: the hospital and class systems of *Through the Night* and *Country*

The regular conjuncture in newspaper reviews between Griffiths'
Marxism and his 'quality' (defined in a variety of ways, according to the
particular media/readership economy) has tended to generate significant press discourse about 'the real' – the reality of Griffiths' representation of domestic life, of parliament, hospitals, the upper- and working-

classes, etc. Indeed, frequently it has been via this 'reality' that Griffiths' quality as a television writer came to be tested.

The genre and form of the works reviewed has been important, too. Most reviewers and audiences had some experiences of hospitals, and said so in their reviews or letters to the editor about Griffiths' *Through the Night*. But few knew the inner-workings of the House of Commons, except through other television, and few indeed had any experience of grand English country houses. In these cases, where experience gave reviewers little access to 'the real', alternative yardsticks would be employed: direct sources (e.g. drawing on detailed reviews by actual MPs like Dick Taverne in the case of *Bill Brand*), and intertextual sources (in the case of *Country*, this was generally *Brideshead Revisited*, in the case of *Bill Brand* usually *The Nearly Man*).

Trevor Griffith's *Through the Night*, strongly based on Jan Griffiths' hospital diary about her mastectomy, and with powerful performances by Alison Steadman as the female patient Christine Potts and Jack Shepherd as the only sympathetic doctor, was screened as a BBC1 *Play for Today* on Tuesday, December 2, 1975 at 9.25 p.m. It attracted not only an audience of 11 million, but in addition a highly visible letters campaign conducted by Marjorie Proops in the *Daily Mirror*.

The date of *Through the Night* in terms of the British TV hospital genre was important. It came *after* the 1950s and 1960s hospital soap operas which, as Jacobs says 'were respectful of the growing power and authority of the medical institution and took care to show that whatever the outcome of individual cases, medical progress was inexorable' (2001, 24). It came ten years *before* the 1980s *Casualty* which in one significant aspect it prefigured, in that *Casualty* represented medical staff 'as fragile workers caught before a rigid bureaucracy and the contingent violence of everyday life' (Jacobs, 2001, 25). And it came well before, and very much opposed, what Jacobs describes as the 1990s medicalisation of everyday life. '[R]egular health scares, the theorisation of the "risk society", the state promotion of "healthy living" as a moral as much as a medical imperative all contributed to a popular engagement with the fictional depiction of hospital life. At the same time, with the collapse of distinctions between Left and Right, and the narrowing of politics to a managerial role, any sense of social change became collapsed on to the body itself' (2001, 26). Griffiths' hospital drama countered in advance 'risk society' theorist Ulrich Beck's emphasis on the societal individualisation of the life project, and the cult of the body which, in Jacobs' view, replaced the 1990s loss of hope in progress.

In *Through the Night*, Christine Potts' body is just one signifier of the inarticulacy of working-class people in the face of the (often hidden) procedures of those with power. Her husband's meek 'doctors know best' response to the loss of her breast is another example. The senior specialists neither speak to nor look at her when discussing her body (as Garner notes, during the early consultation Christine is excluded from the camera view altogether), and the trajectory of the play is to blend Christine's subjective point-of-view shots with the hospital-critique of the junior doctor Pearce, who befriends her. But as well as being one of *Casualty's* 'fragile workers' caught between the violence of Christine's mastectomy and a rigid bureaucracy, Pearce is also agentive in repositioning the subjective voice of a working-class woman until at the end she forms part of a new, subversive community in a night-time drinks party in the ward. Garner describes this well: 'In an institution that operates through the enforced isolation of its patients, the makeshift party represents a coming together and the assertion of solidarity. To the extent that the exercise of institutional authority has also involved subtle and not-so-subtle gender hierarchies, the surreptitious gathering is also the achievement of a specifically female community ... [W]e are reminded here of the vision that has always stood at the centre of Griffiths' socialist ideal: the sense of spontaneous community, grounded in shared experience and mutual support' (1999, 118–19). In this sense it is extremely important that as with Griffiths' versions of *Sons and Lovers* and *The Cherry Orchard* – but this time in relation to hospital soap opera not classic authored texts – the subjective view of the patient-as-victim is de-centred and that *Through the Night* positions female working-class patients 'as subjects within the structures of their own lives' (Griffiths 1982, 11–12). Poole and Wyver make the related generic point in describing *Through the Night's* use of the visual style of soap operas like *General Hospital*. 'Ann Scott and Michael Lindsay-Hogg mounted the play in a studio, exploiting the look and feel of hospital series. This self-consciousness, together with a limited use of Christine's point-of-view shots, imparts an edge of non-naturalism to the rigidly naturalistic writing, and thereby certainly increases the work's impact' (1984, 118)

The previews and reviews of *Through the Night* were highly favourable, covering a number of main themes: Griffiths' wider societal scope for the production than simply hospitals (this was particularly emphasised in the *Radio Times* preview, which wondered whether the medical impact would be such that 'viewers will not look beyond it'); reviewers' personal experiences with opaque medical institutions; the BBC1 discussion between Griffiths and two medical professionals immediately after the screening; and the fact that the play 'hit a nerve' (in relation to the treatment of breast cancer) with very many women in Britain at that time.

Across the reviews of *Through the Night*, the tension between the known Marxist playwright writing parables for a broader societal critique, and a play strongly focused on an audience's very personal health fears could lead in two directions: either to a recognition that this blending of highly personal feeling with broadly ideological concepts was something that Griffiths always does (as Griffiths' quoted reference to Gramsci and *Occupations* in the *Time Out* review of *Through the Night* implied), or to a polarisation where the personal was so strongly embraced that the broader societal critique was lost within a 'could that have actually happened to me in our hospitals?' public debate.

Most newspaper reviewers led their readers into an emphasis on the 'personal' in response to *Through the Night*. Stanley Eveling, in *The Scotsman*, was typical in eschewing a broader political competence, arguing that 'it takes a talented eye to see in the structure of the hospital, with its hierarchies and its mystique of knowledge, the adequate image of a wider conspiracy' (*The Scotsman*, December 6, 1975); and preferring to emphasise his own personal hospital story. 'I remember going into a hospital to be looked at and over in an area normally concealed from the general eye. Passing innocently through a harmless-looking room to another where I was merely told there was a consultant I found myself in a glare of light and facing a hundred loutish, joking faces. Thereupon I was inclined on a plane and prodded and stretched like a lump of idiotic white meat' (December 6, 1975).

Nevertheless, Griffiths' quality of writing the highly personal into the social meant that many reviewers' personal memories were presented as also a systemic reflection on British hospital (if not wider societal) practice, and this broader approach did get something of a run in the weekly media reviews. Left academic Brian Winston, writing in *The Listener*, used *Through the Night* to lambast the media (and medical profession) for always pillorying ancillary personnel or power workers when they strike, while not revealing 'that the current hodge-podge of Health Service labour problems, caused by various grades of doctors, endangers patients just as much' (December 11, 1975). And a consultant haematologist at St George's Hospital, London, Michael Rose wrote in *World Medicine*, 'Trevor Griffiths' play *Through the Night* ... told everybody, in effect, that ... the institutionalisation of medical practice prohibits caring – even if once in a while producing a fellow graduate who still cares. I have no ... criticism on Griffiths' play – he said it all and I for one just watched, stunned by the shame of it all and just a little encouraged by the possibility of a new start' (*World Medicine*, January 14, 1976).

Through the Night received an extremely favourable critical and popular reaction, typical of which was the *Daily Mirror*'s 'Serious subject, handled with humour and optimism' (December 2, 1975). Even the *Daily Mail*, politically not a friend of Trevor Griffiths, spoke of 'a painful but important documentary drama which deserves more critical attention than it has so far received' (December 4, 1975). This was partly because the reviewer liked the personalised aspect of the play, and partly because it could be used to berate Labour's National Health Service. Overall, Griffiths' socialism was not seen by newspaper reviewers of *Through the Night* as the central problem it certainly became for reviewers of *Bill Brand* and *Country*, mainly because critics (and Marjorie Proops' readers) could respond via their own intuitive and experiential competence (aided by Griffiths' repositioning of Christine Potts' subjectivity), while specific newspaper reviewers could then elevate that experiential 'truth' into an ongoing critique of the Labour government.

During the three month screening of *Bill Brand* in 1976 (which I look at in the next section), the Tory press frequently complained that it was time to turn the focus of political drama away from the Left. Griffiths gave them their wish on 20 October 1981 with the screening of *Country* – again to rousing acclaim from both Right and Left. The *Daily Express* critic James Murray, thought that the 'BBC should repeat the play as soon as possible so that everybody who was watching *Brideshead Revisited* last night can get a chance to see it' (October 21, 1981). And while not being able to resist mentioning the 'monstrous Socialists' who defeated Churchill in 1946 or from describing in detail the 'radical sister's' speech in *Country* about hoping to see 'the people disembowelling' the capitalists 'in front of your children', the *Daily Express* critic could also be forgiving. 'Strong stuff, but Mr Griffiths is renowned for his strong feelings. It is not a play that would go down well in many quarters but he got meaty performances out of a superb cast including Leo McKern and Wendy Hiller as the senior Carlions, Penelope Wilton as the rebel sister and Jill Bennett as the dead heir's thwarted widow. The night, however, belonged to James Fox who made a spectacular return to the screen' (October 21, 1981). Even the *Daily Mail* was full of (almost) unalloyed praise for 'performances of very high skill' and 'a rare literacy', marred only by 'the besetting compulsion shared by all playwrights of the far Left to see the "ruling classes" as avaricious monsters and human dignity almost exclusively confined to those who work with their own calloused hands' (October 21, 1981). The *Daily Mail* critic, like many other reviewers, was obsessed by Virginia's words in *Country* about 'the people' disembowelling the social elite in front of their children. Still, Howard Kretzmer said, *Country*, despite its 'over-the-top bias, rang with the kind of passion rare on the box. It was very much a play about England, and our screens would be much poorer without this kind of steam' (October 21, 1981). Clearly, in the case of both *Through the Night* and *Country*, the prestige of the British single television play, with its critically accepted tendency to radical styles and subject matter (Creeber 2001, 13) created a positive environment for the reception of Griffiths' plays.

The Times reviewer, Michael Ratcliffe, for instance, noted the generic *performativity* of the production, not least the intertextual play with Griffiths' version of *The Cherry Orchard* screened in the same time-slot one week earlier, also directed by Richard Eyre. However, the relationship between this and *Country* was 'ill-defined', and the latter both 'failed to live down the writer's reductive economic view', and was itself threatened by the production's 'elegance and style, that becomes a pleasure, perhaps distracting, in itself' (October 21, 1981).

This 'elegant' and seductive lure of capitalism (encouraged by the innovative potential of the one-off play) became the theme of Kenneth O. Morgan's piece. 'Loving your class enemies' in *The Times Literary Supplement*. 'It is easy to see why this superbly paced production won such instant acclaim from television critics. The interaction of characters is quite gripping...The direction, concentrating on stylized conversation pieces of Chekhovian quality, is masterly in its control, while Nat Crosby's photography is haunting. It is clear, in fact, that producer, director and cameraman are enchanted by the class enemy. The disintegrating Carlions offer as beguiling a defence of the rotting world of the declining gentry as does *Brideshead* on the rival channel (October 30, 1981).

The *TLS* review comes close to a reviewers' theory of capitalist 'subversion' of the radical text. 'The Marxist playwright...is now in danger of becoming the licensed rebel of the establishment...No more enchanting vision of our late-capitalist society has been presented than by this socialist propagandist' (October 30, 1981). Sheila MacLeod in *The Times Education Supplement* took up a similar theme. '*Country* may have made the mistake, so rare in television, of overestimating its audience, as well as underestimating the fatally seductive power of the medium itself to render even the unspeakable acceptable, especially when used with the loving skill so evident throughout this production. Did the "tyranny of the technicians" render *Country* a self-defeating exercise?' (October 30, 1981).

Just a few reviewers took sides more clearly and vehemently. Philip Purser, writing his review 'The Class Bore', said 'Griffiths is a political dramatist (Marxist according to the *Radio Times*) ... The one member of the family, or families, the audience was invited to admire was the daughter Virginia, who turned up in time to serve the rest with a smug little notice of their fate when the revolution came .... [But the rich would hang on to their riches then as effortlessly as they will now elude Trevor Griffiths' sour attack.' At the Left-edge of the reviewer spectrum, Mike Poole, offered the reader a different competence, referred to the six-part series that *Country* was originally designed for, and constructed in the *New Statesman* a complex review which, referencing Eton choristers at the opening and closing of the play, established a sense of continuity about Tory politics that matched Griffiths' engagement with the Labour Party in *Bill Brand*.

> Entitled Tory Stories, the plays would have dealt with key moments in the post-War history of the Right ... Changes in the brewing industry – first keg, then lager, then multinational mergers – were to have served as a metaphor for the re-structuring of British capital. But beer was also chosen because of its importance within working-class culture, the area where consumerism, the multinationals and, eventually, monetarism were to wreak the profoundest changes of all. We got a hint of how the series might have worked towards the end of Country when workers drinking to a new Labour government are shown to be consuming Carlion beer. Their future appeared to be already in someone else's hands as chants of 'Roll out the Barrel' ominously modulated to an Eton choristers' version of the song and the closing titles went up. (*New Statesman*, October 30, 1981)

The differences among reviewers of the one-off plays *Through the Night* and *Country* can be clearly seen across the generic, intertextual and fiction/reality frames which Carlson maps. *Through the Night* reviews tended to ignore both generic and societal-realist critique, but by focusing on the experiential reality of the personal, did generate an extensive media campaign on behalf of women-as-victim and against the hospital 'system'. *Country* was praised with equivalent unanimity, but here the focus was predominantly intertextual, with Griffiths' 'ideological' version of reality being seen as symptomatic of the single play genre, yet absorbed by the 'sumptuous' visual style of 'heritage' television. Only Poole's review refused that 'past' association, insisting on the multinational contemporaneity and the possibilities for mini-series' stylistic innovation which had, in the end, to be cramped into one episode of 'Tory Stories'.

The 'lean and hungry' Left: the parliamentary system and 'Bill Brand'

Bill Brand ran weekly from June to August 1976, recording the hopes and frustration of a left-wing Labour MP who messily gives up his marriage for an affair with a feminist student (who then leaves him), and who finally relinquishes some of his anti-institutional politics by supporting a senior, Left-leaning minister who is beginning on the path to the compromises of Edward Waite in *All Good Men* by caucusing for party leadership as Prime Minister. Like Brand's affair, this endeavour fails, and the series ends with a swing to the Right in the Labour Party, while Brand pulls away to identify more loosely with a fringe political theatre group that evokes strong feminist, Chilean and Cuban political connections. Despite being dismissed by many as idealistic, this final multi-ethnic and cross-gendered solidarity is symptomatically worked for as Griffiths both maintains and de-centres (in terms of feminist discourse via his mistress, and via Last, the Labour minister who involves him in institutional leadership) Brand's political subjectivity.

An eleven-part series with a regular following of over 11 million viewers in Britain invoked special opportunities for reviewers. In particular, there was the possibility of *early rumours and warnings* around the upcoming series, followed by *imminent previews* (which could predict, could caution, could hope, could compare), and finally came the *summarising* of the reviewer's longer narrative relating whether the series had, in the end, 'come good'.

Early rumours and warnings: political gossip and police surveillance

More than *Through the Night* and *Country*, the long-running *Bill Brand* provoked longer-term and consciously generic newspaper coverage. The *Sun*'s January 17, 1976 first comment (five months ahead of transmission) indicates the conjoint construction of a future television series according to a variety of newspaper competences: of perceived readership, notions of quality authorship, genre, intertextuality and political 'reality'. As journalists do, reviewers loved punning on the name of the series, and the *Sun*'s review was no exception with the heading 'A firebrand chases power'.

> A hard-hitting young MP, hellbent on power, is heading your way. His name is Bill Brand. Like Granada Television's Nearly Man, he is a Labour MP. But there the resemblance ends. For Bill Brand is very different from the elegant intellectual Chris Colinson, portrayed by Tony Britton in The Nearly Man. Brand is 20 years younger, and a dedicated idealist, with a burning urge to set the nation to rights ... The plays are written by Trevor Griffiths, who once considered running for Parliament himself ... A Labour MP is advisor for the series. Thames Television will not say who he is. Shepherd says 'He has given us some incredible stories

about frustrated back-benchers like Brand. One Labour MP was so sick of trying to see a Minister that he finally grabbed the man in the corridor at Westminster, shoved him against the wall by his lapels and made him listen'. (*Sun*, Saturday, January 17, 1976)

Here the *Sun* emphasised Griffiths' socialism, but quickly converted it into its own tabloid come-hither to its readers: 'don't miss this, for unique political-insider gossip' (January 17, 1976). Briefly, there was a flurry of media interest (the *Daily Mirror* 3 February, *Variety* 10 February) in the rumour that this 'Labour MP advisor' might be no less than the Prime Minister, Sir Harold Wilson.

A very different take on Griffiths' socialism came from Judith Cook early previews (in both the *Guardian* and *Labour Weekly*), after Griffiths' opening of a series of lectures on British Theatre at the Institute for Contemporary Arts in London provided a new 'reality' hook for the coming series in the print media. Cook's *Guardian* piece 'A night in the life of the emergency powers' spoke of how she went to the Griffiths public lecture with her 'landlord, Roland Joffe, who is currently filming *Bill Brand*, Trevor's serial about a Labour MP', how after the lecture plain-clothes police arrested all three of them due to a supposedly stolen tax disc on Joffe's car, and how police at the station made sexual slurs against her (*Guardian* 20 February 1976). Her warning to her readers was about the recent Emergency Powers Act, which Griffiths was about to focus on in *Bill Brand*. Cook's *Labour Weekly* review (like another *Guardian* piece by Michael Billington) focused on Griffiths' comments about the importance of writing for television rather than theatre, but here Cook perceived a more specialist readership and quoted directly from Griffiths' lecture about the difficulties of popular socialism. 'He will qualify his Marxism to those who attack him and point out ... "You have to go back to the foundations, to what Marx and even Lenin had to say, to see that what has happened in most of Eastern Europe is a gross distortion of Socialism. But that doesn't mean you shouldn't work towards Socialism"' (*Labour Weekly*, February 27, 1976). For Cook, the reality of Griffiths' fiction was out there, in the ominous world of police surveillance and distorted socialism.

Imminent previews/early reviews: sex and politics

Bill Brand's first episode, covering his local electoral work, his apathetic family, and the death of his father, was screened on ITV at 9 p.m. June 7, 1976. The *News of the World* directly tied its June 6 preview into its readership. 'After ... letters from more than 12,000 readers [supporting the newspaper's campaign for better summer television] at last there's a new series I can thoroughly recommend ... The aspect of the series that will delight viewers – and probably upset MPs – is Brand's private life .... Writer Trevor Griffiths said 'His private life is a mess' ... Don't think that Brand is at all like the Labour MP played by Tony Britton in ITV's *The Nearly Man* ... Brand is uncompromising and hates the half-truths and deals that seem to be an essential part of today's political scene' (June 6, 1976).

A number of things are notable here. First is the way in which a 'campaigning' populist newspaper appropriated *Bill Brand* evaluatively on behalf of both its 12,000 letter-writing readership and its more general populist 'exposé' signature (especially of politicians). Second, we note the aspects of the Griffiths' interview that are used, relating the sexual ('soap opera') side of the text to the newspaper's world of exposé. Third, there is the newspaper's overt positioning of its readers as audience for *Bill Brand* ('The aspect of the series that will delight viewers'). Fourth, there is the preview's star focus: Shepherd is tipped for top acting awards of the year, and 'Arthur Lowe – Captain Main-waring from *Dad's Army* – as the Labour Prime Minister'. Fifth, – a feature that was to appear in all types of newspaper over the next couple of months – Griffiths' fictional 'reality' was emphasised. 'In fact it's so true-to-life that Mr Griffiths found he was writing history before it happened. The cast were rehearsing an episode in which the Prime Minister resigns when Sir Harold Wilson announced his own resignation'. Sixth there is the tabloid's profiling of 'authored' and 'quality' drama. This piece ends, 'Griffiths wrote BBC's *All Good Men* and *All Through the Night* [sic] and ITV's *Occupations*. All starred Shep-herd and all won wide praise. There is little doubt that Bill Brand will do the same'. But 'prestige' drama is more comfortably promoted if it seems to work seamlessly within a populist crusading mode: public exposé, a star-oriented intertextuality, and a self-consciously working-class profiling of the newspaper's constructed readership. Otherwise, such things risk being, the review says, 'upper-class intellectual', and 'dull and tedious' like *The Nearly Man*.

In contrast, the broadsheet *Sunday Times*, which previewed *Bill Brand* on the same day, said nothing of the sexual exposé aspect of the series, focusing instead on similarities in the real lives of the would-be Left-wing parliamentary candidate and his author. Yet the *Sunday Times* featured the same intertext, favourably comparing the 'painfully real' quality of *Bill Brand* with the 'windy speeches' Hopcraft gave his *The Nearly Man* characters. There was the first appearance here, too, of a critical theme which became a major one in reviews of the series: 'pain-fully real – though perhaps rather glummer on the day of an exciting by-election than they would be in reality' (*Sunday Times*, June 6, 1976).

The early reviews of episode 1 of *Bill Brand* were mixed. The *Guardian* television critic Nancy-Banks-Smith, spoke of Griffiths being 'fierce and funny about the backrooms and infighting of politics and the series promises very well', but 'Trevor Griffiths is not very good with women' (*Guardian*, June 8, 1976). The conservative broadsheet, the *Daily Telegraph* reached for high culture, Sean Day-Lewis comparing *Bill Brand* with the 'muted echoes of Ibsen's *Brand*', and finding in both 'a romantic idealist lacking in humour, passion or loving kindness, a dogmatic champion not of things as they are or could be made, but of things as he believed they ought to be' (June 8, 1976). This *Bill Brand* – in this conservative broadsheet – failed on the fiction/reality principle in comparison with Hopcraft's *The Nearly Man* since his 'miserable relationship with a mistress as well as a wife...does not have the articulate saving graces of that cynical and equally lonely social democrat'.

Similarly, Shaun Usher in the *Daily Mail* asked 'Is life really as rotten as this'. Usher led off with ironic observation on the series' title music evocation of 'some onward march to the sunny uplands of social justice', but judged that on the basis of 'its opening episode, Trevor Griffiths' saga of a Socialist MP with a mind of his own – political partisans may hail that as a fictional masterstroke in itself – will be short on optimism and happy endings' (June 8, 1976). Still, because Griffiths' by-election sequences were 'a powerful reproach to apathy', and it is a 'solid, caring production', Usher grudgingly intended 'to stay with it, but out of curiosity and duty rather than any great sense of pleasure'.

The naturalism of detail in Griffiths' work, which David Edgar had criticised, worked at this stage of episode 1 – the detailed family apathy, the death of his father, the local party-political workings – to keep the Conservative tabloids (just) on-side. The *Daily Mail*'s rival, the *Daily Express*, found in episode 1 a series 'too important to develop into a political soap opera', balking moralistically at a central character who 'has a passionate commitment to socialism, but the same kind of passion for his mistress' (June 8, 1976). The *Evening Standard* made no bones about its dislike of *Bill Brand* from the start, complaining that Thames Television 'have condemned us to spend the next 12 Monday nights living with Bill Brand's 'gloomy socialist conscience'. The lead actor, even in the moment of by-election victory, 'never stopped looking like a man on his way to be hanged', while his 'leftie social worker' girlfriend has principles which 'require her to go to bed in her denims'. We are then, said critic Max Hastings, stuck with banality, dreary, drab cynicism, and 'just another everyday story of Marxist folk' (June 7, 1976).

Not all early reviews were negative in the tabloids. The *Sun* took a populist tip from the *News of the World* in its first review, believing exposé was central to its audience's pleasures. 'Who can resist a peep through the keyhole of the faults and foibles of those in power? ... Maybe the real politicians will complain. But these 11 plays should arouse more interest in politics than a thousand party political broadcasts' (*Sun*, 8 June 1976). The discursive register was now set for most of the emerging weeks of debate that *Bill Brand* was to attract from the mainstream daily and evening press: the 'keyhole' exposé from some tabloids, the 'high-minded' but 'dour' and 'humourless' socialism, the intertextual contrast with *The Nearly Man*, the matter of 'Brand's women', the predictive naturalism of Griffiths' writing (about the resignation of a Labour P.M.), the physiognomy and 'lean and hungry' acting style of Jack Shepherd.

Publicly available discourses

Although similar reviewing frames of genre, intertext, authorship, readership, and 'reality' operate for single plays as for television series, as *unfolding* narratives newspaper and magazine reviews of *Bill Brand* constructed both a very wide range of registers and very clear idiolects around the series. These became the *publicly available discourses* about *Bill Brand* for television viewers at this time. In Britain, these available press discourses remained extremely wide ranging, and it is worth examining their complexity both synchronically (the reviews available to an 'ideal reader' at any one moment of the series) and diachronically (the reflexivity-factor in reviewing a series over time).

At any one time, the 'ideal reader' in Britain could have turned to a series of conflicts and inflections within different 'niche' readerships. For example, the specialist Left press factionalised over 'reality' in response to *Bill Brand*'s fiction, as between *International Socialist*'s, Tariq Ali who advised militants to be glued to their sets on Monday evenings and to organise political discussions around television's first real attempt to demystify Parliament and the labour movement for the masses, and the Communist Party's *Morning Star* reviewer, Stewart Lane who worried about the cumulative weight of the series in turning viewers away from alternatives available *within* parliamentary democracy. Lane noted in disappointment that 'marked throughout, and specifically in the "Fight to Work" campaign involving "thousands" and proud references to Spain and the International Brigade, has been the absence of any mention of the Communist Party and the significant role it has played in all recent mass actions and industrial struggles. An omission which, in my view, has to be deliberate.'

Aiming at a slightly wider readership, the broadsheets displayed their own differences. The *Observer*, which had begun negatively, adopted the rhetoric of personal idiolect, inflecting its subsequent praise for the series behind the ironically-raised eyebrow of Australian critic-humorist, Clive James. In an early piece that carried the flavour of his reviews throughout, James opined that *Bill Brand* 'looks like surviving well enough' the inevitable comparison with Hopcraft's *The Nearly Man*. This was partly because 'Jack Shepherd was ideal casting for the title role, since visages come no grimmer – possessing the only pair of sunken pop eyes in the business, he has always appeared to be just back from a long season in the Inferno'. The *Guardian* adopted a liberal-left 'in-depth' stance via a series of authorised interviews: Jack Shepherd outlining the differences between his and Griffiths' Left politics; Trevor Griffiths replying to MPs' complaints about the details of his Commons sequences ('Don't you find it curious that MPs go on about our getting it wrong? ... They work in more secrecy than the Curia. How the hell can you get into an MP's desk-room just to see what it looks like? I asked and was told it was not allowed', June 26, 1976); Joe Ashton MP describing the mix of derisory scoffing and heavy-breathing silences (as Cheri Lunghi disrobed yet again) in the packed House of Commons TV room (August 3, 1976). Noting the series' faults of detail (particularly Brand's 'unconvincing' relationship with his 'intimate ladies'), the *Guardian*'s Peter Fiddick nevertheless applauded *Bill Brand*'s huge public popularity, and called it 'the most interesting TV drama of the season' (August 3, 1976). Interesting enough, indeed, for the *Guardian* to devote an editorial to *Bill Brand*, noting that though 'intelligent', 'provoking', 'passionate' and realistic about the Left, the series also 'tilted the facts to a degree where credibility sometimes went under'. Who, the *Guardian* editorial said 'is to define reality? One man's reality is the crumbling of capitalism ... another's is yet one more loan from the IMF'. The 'real life' battles of the Labour Party are more 'cunningly' played out than in *Bill Brand*, which the *Guardian* says – in a precise reflection of its own political stance – 'is why many Labour MPs who share Brand's moments of disillusion continue to seek salvation through Westminster rather than like Bill Brand beneath the banners of movements which despair of the place altogether' (*Guardian*, August 18, 1976).

The daily tabloids were less wont than the specialist Left press to reduce the quality of *Bill Brand* so directly to the political persuasion of the paper, but here too there were readership-oriented differences. The Right-oriented *Daily Express*, for example, wrote of Griffiths' 'compassionate' authorship, even though his 'political background and his disillusion with the Labour Party spills out ... Author Trevor Griffiths is painting a very ugly picture of a half-baked spineless idealist which I sadly suspect is only too accurate ... Mr Griffiths' neat trick is to make it all splendidly entertaining too' (July 6, 1976). The *Daily Mail* followed its early comments on the Labour Party's '*Red Flag*' series (June 14, 1976), with its August 3 review 'This band of brotherly misery', where Shaun Usher said he forced himself to watch and not to 'wince when Brand compares terrorists with international money speculators'. Still, even the *Mail* grudgingly acknowledged quality: 'while jeering at Brand's dourness, I must also salute ITV for giving peak time to programmes whose basic coinage is serious ideas – not automatically popular or widely interesting at that' (August 3, 1976). The *Daily Mirror* soon also decided that there was 'Little Joy From Bill' (28 June, 1976), played by Jack Shepherd as a 'remorselessly graceless' man 'who believes life is one long battle'. Still, the newspaper's populist-Labour concerns were evident as Mary Malone wrote intertextually, 'Remember *The Nearly Man* ... Remember the worker politicians of *Days of Hope* and *The Stars Look Down*? If you're Labour, you're anguished and that's that. Only Tory MPs laugh. That's because they live in chintzy drawing rooms and rattle ice cubes in cut glass and the programme is called comedy, not drama!' (June 7, 1976). *The Sun* also supported the series, partly by focusing on the voyeuristic interest of Cheri Lunghi, the 'girl with the funny name', and partly via a tabloid version of the *Guardian*'s 'authentic interview' rhetoric, which involved not only tracking down Lunghi to Shakespeare's Stratford-on-Avon, but also Lynn Farleigh (who played Brand's wife), her lawyer boyfriend and their two young sons to their narrow boat 'in the most obscure and beautiful parts of the country' (June 21, 1976), and interviewing Winchester- and Oxford-educated actor Peter Howell, who 'looks and sounds like a frightfully well-spoken founder member of an exclusive Conservative Club', but is who is a 'very actively committed member of the Labour Party' (July 5, 1976).

A mark of the very widespread and accumulating profile of *Bill Brand* were the reviews in regional newspapers throughout Britain. These took up many of the same debates and refrains as the broadsheets and tabloids, varying, like the dailies, between, on one hand, *The Journal* (Newcastle-upon-Tyne) saying 'need [Brand] be so unhappy? Need we be treated to a slice of life with the assumption that life as an MP is thoroughly lousy' (10 June, 1976) and, on the other hand, its near-neighbour, the *South Shields Gazette*'s reference to 'gripping television...excellently portrayed by Jack Shepherd' (June 11, 1976). Griffiths' socialism was nearly always profiled in the evening regionals, ranging from the *Liverpool Daily Post* arguing that ITV had burned its fingers, because 'The great strength of *The Nearly Man* was its credibility. Against that *Bill Brand* is just a tract'

(June 26, 1976) and the *Evening News'* comment that 'Trevor Griffiths, the author, is, by his own admission, an extreme left-winger, and in this series is waving a banner for a complete Socialist State' (June 24, 1976), to the position of other conservative south English papers like the *Bournemouth Evening Echo* arguing that the series had 'rather too much unnecessary and unparliamentary language', but otherwise, 'the script is taut and informed', Jack Shepherd was portraying Brand 'admirably', and the series was making 'fascinating viewing' (June 21, 1976), and the *Exeter Express and Echo* which had found *The Nearly Man* 'verbose', whereas with '*Bill Brand*...everyone is where the action is....When it comes to the nitty-gritty of politics I do not want Brand X, but my voting cross would go to Bill Brand whether he be red, yellow or blue. His kind of truculent pig-headedness is irresistible' (June 26, 1976).

For newspapers of all styles, politics, locations and temporalities, the tension between quality, intertext, genre, the fictional/real and the author's socialism was an irresistible focus. What none of them did was to draw on the lead of a very few weeklies in exploring Griffiths' own reflexivity about the 'dour' male, working-class, former further-education teacher who has turned to politics and (with class-gendered difficulty) to feminism.

Narrative and summarising reviews

Unlike one-off television dramas like *Through the Night* and *Country*, a long series enables newspaper critics to be diachronic: that is to predict the narrative development, to alter or reflect upon their earlier view, and to summarise at the end. So, in this case, the issue of the relationship of Griffiths' political genre to intertexts about 'reality' could become a running, reflexive question.

It was the *Daily Telegraph* that sustained the most interesting interrogation of *Bill Brand* of this kind. Its TV critic Sean Day-Lewis developed a love/hate relationship with the series. After the first episode, he said that *Bill Brand*'s one saving grace was that 'Griffiths is too familiar with the British Left to write a drama that could be thought unequivocal in advancing its cause' (June 8, 1976). By the fourth episode he, like others, was criticising 'the unsmiling hero' and his 'women', notably his mistress, Alex, who celebrates Brand's wife's threat to sue him for divorce 'by taking off her denims and displaying all that is underneath'. However, Day-Lewis also admitted 'getting addicted to the proceedings'. On June 29, the reviewer said, the 'time has come in the interest of critical balance, to list the factors that are in its favour'. First, 'It is one of few drama series presently on any of our television channels which asks to be taken seriously'. Here was one critic, unlike Bignell's reviewers of *The Gulf Between Us*, who could handle mixed genres in Griffiths. Day-Lewis argued that the mix of the 'documentary precision of the background research' with 'the occasional moments of melodrama' (which Brian Winston had disliked in *Through the Night*) provided 'a properly shocking effect'. Secondly, 'Apart from the seething, introverted solemnity of Jack Shepherd's Brand', there were two memorable performances emerging. 'One is from Allan Surtees as the pungently canny constituency agent. The other is from Alan Badel, as the shaggy, Michael Footish, former "scourge of the right" who has realised that time is against him and he must work in the Cabinet now or never.' Third, and especially important, 'the series is looking realistically at a dilemma which sadly is of national importance. Has a Marxist Socialist any place in the Labour coalition, given power by an electorate that wants nothing of its revolution?' Day-Lewis was enjoying the series' self-lacerating reflexivity about the Labour Left. The 'fatal weakness', however, might be that 'Griffiths draws him with such insight ... because he shares [his] preoccupations [and] avoids everybody on the Right of his hero by dismissing them as caricatures' (June 29, 1976).

Like the *Observer*, the *Daily Telegraph* preferred *Bill Brand* as genre of 'political debate' rather than 'private life' soap opera. By the time of the *Daily Telegraph*'s 26 July review, however, the controversially 'political' episode 7 of *Bill Brand* had been televised, where Brand uses a parliamentary standing committee on anti-terrorism to berate the Labour government (and capitalists generally) for supporting high-financiers who 'kill by telephone'. This was a step too far for the *Telegraph* critic, who, while still noting that this was 'the most eloquent new drama series of the year', got stuck into both Brand's 'private life' and his 'politics'. 'To call them closet revolutionaries would be unkind. Yet Alex would surely find herself less dependent on men if fewer of her political meetings were conducted in a horizontal position beside one of them'. And as for Brand himself, 'such an assiduous activist should know that speeches made to such committees may receive still less publicity than those made between the sheets. This even applies to statements that capitalist captains of industry are as much "men of blood" as terrorist captains of the IRA'.

On August 2, however, Day-Lewis wrote that the ninth episode was 'The best yet. The script was written some time before Sir Harold Wilson's unexpected resignation and it does not precisely predict the election of Jim Callaghan in his place. On the other hand it gives a marvellous insight into the kind of tactics and jockeying, intrigue and horse-trading, that goes on whenever the Parliamentary Labour

Party is going through the process of picking a new leader.' There was continuing pleasure here over Left/Labour in-fighting, and by now Day-Lewis had come to the view that a one-sided political perspective was valuable in this writer. 'This proves to be a dramatic strength rather than a weakness, even though the other contenders, Venables or Roy Jenkins, Kearsley or Denis Healey, Wilkes or Jim Callaghan – are only seen from the outside'. For Day-Lewis, even though Griffiths picked the wrong winner in the Labour leadership spill, 'the tactics and intrigue of such an election, and the outwitting of Last, were so beautifully worked out and conveyed that they might have been the real thing' (August 3, 1976).

On 16 August, Day-Lewis introduced the last episode of *Bill Brand*, 'It is the people who choose'. Now was the time for final reflection and summary, and the *Daily Telegraph* TV critic was upfront why *Bill Brand* was popular with some of the conservative British press. 'If the aim of the series was really to produce "a critique of the Labour Party" it failed. On the other hand, Griffiths did maintain his claim to have been "honest to a Left, Socialist experience, to its illusory nature." ... It is precisely because Griffiths-Brand is so deeply committed to this struggle, needing to keep his delusions and illusions intact, that the series has really only produced a critique of the Labour Left'. Day-Lewis quoted Griffiths: 'I want people, when they have experienced a play by me, to think and feel'. Well, opined Day-Lewis, 'He has achieved this with me, at least to the point where I am now clearer about how the Griffiths-Brand position is reached, and deeply believed in, and why it is untenable'.

What becomes interesting when we look at the unfolding review-narratives about Griffiths' prime-time TV series is precisely what aspects of the *other* print media coverage of the series reviewers chose to pick up, and which they didn't. Day-Lewis is quoting Griffiths from the *Times Educational Supplement* review, when he says: 'Not, of course, that we of the despised middle-classes are the audience the author wanted...He backed the Thames fight for the highly desirable 9 p.m. slot because "my class, the people I want to talk to, don't watch from 10.30 p.m." Independent research on whether his class were impressed by the Brand gospel might be revealing.' Still, the reviewer conceded, 'There is no doubt that *Bill Brand* has had a critical success, with Labour MPs as much as television viewers ... It has predictably not pulled in a "top twenty" audience, but it has gripped a substantial middlebrow following'. And he agreed that Griffiths had 'filled in a lot of surrounding detail and often produced first-class drama', whereas Hopcraft's *The Nearly Man* only had an articulate hero 'surrounded by shadows'(July 16, 1976).

Despite his praise, Day-Lewis was extremely selective about what he chose from the *TES* review of June 25, 1976. This *TES* article featured an interview with Trevor Griffiths which did a lot to explore various media reviewers' early comments (e.g. Gilbert, *Time Out,* June 4–10 and Cook, *Labour Weekly,* June 11) about their pleasure in the episode 1 'reality' of Brand's family background, such as the death-bed talk with his father. In particular, Day-Lewis might have found in the *TES* piece Griffiths' reflexive response to his 'repressive tolerance' (typically he talks of 'beginning to read Marcuse at this time') in relation to his own domesticity, and his sense there of personal male/class contradictions.

Relating to the death of his own father, and Brand's visit to his father on election day in episode 1, Griffiths told the *TES,*

I lived in a culture that suppressed emotion. There were no caresses or fondlings. Being a boy or a man meant remaining impassive, suppressing all emotion in the face, the hands, the set of the body. My father ... worked colossally hard – he was a chemical process worker like Bill Brand's father. His frame, his constitution took terrible flack – he died of lung cancer at 54. I had this incredible love and admiration for him. But then came the need to assert myself, and I grew distant from him ... There was a historical explanation for every limitation in that man, and I had not understood that. Then, just at the time when relaxation and real contact were possible, he died – in very great pain at the end. So a lot of my writing is an attempt to fill up the experience that was denied during my early life ... I write about that because I think it's what a lot of people in our society have inside them, unexplored, in a way suppressed. (Griffiths, *TES,* June 25, 1976)

There was much for later newspaper reviewers of the series to pick up on here, most centrally the desire of Bill Brand to *speak* and not suppress his emotions, and to establish a directness 'very hard to find in...professional, middle-class life'. For example, what may appear (and did appear to some reviewers) as just another of Brand's 'dour' responses – when he goes to the home of the gynaecologist who is denying abortions to young, needy working-class women – could have been read very differently by Day-Lewis via this *TES* interview. The 'suppressing of all emotions in the face, the hands, the set of the body' might have been interpreted as being transferred textually from his father's class to that of the professional elite (played here by Robert Hardy), as all the etiquette, discrete, directionless humour, and *lack* of directness (as in *Through the Night*) of the doctor is punctured by Brand's *breaking* of his own professional image as 'nice young MP' (established earlier by the doctor's wife as she gives him a cup of tea). And this determination to be articulate – described by so many reviewers as rude, humourless and 'dour'- could have been read as itself articulated not only by Griffiths' personal attempt to achieve 'solidarity' with his past, but also his engagement with Brand's girlfriend Alex's feminism also, in the bedroom scenes which so many reviewers complained about but which were very important in Griffiths' emphasis on the links between 'private' and 'political', and in probing Brand's male inarticulacy. That 'personal' relationship with Alex was a central meaning behind Brand's last-second near-decision earlier in the episode to silently escape a young woman and her screaming babies, but then walking back into the political (and media-induced) turmoil of articulating on radio talkback his support for her abortion in a largely Catholic, working-class constituency.

Yet, the *only* aspect of this major interview with Griffiths in the *TES* which was drawn on in reviews over the next two months was Griffiths' argument that 'my class, the people I want to talk to, don't watch from 10.30 to 11.30, because they have to get up at half past six to go to work. Programme planners think more about size of audience than who you are talking to'. That statement could have been read, in the narrative context of this interview, as directly relating to his opening comment about his class background and the quest to speak. But it wasn't, anywhere in press reviews.

One feature, however, of *all* the reviews of *Bill Brand* (including the ironic Clive James) was their preoccupation with the *effect* of the series on the voters. *This* relationship between the modalities of fiction and democratic reality underpinned reviews from the *Daily Mail* to the *Morning Star*. Typically, Peter Lennon in *The Sunday Times*, bidding farewell to 'the most remarkable serial ever seen on the box', summarised 'Experts agree on its general political authenticity. Humanly it convinces too. But what effect is it likely to have had on the electorate? If there is already general apathy towards the established parties, Trevor Griffiths' serial will certainly have intensified the feeling' (August 15, 1976). In that context newspaper reviewers tended to a consensus of worry that the accumulation of this political genre with its preceding television inter-texts would lead to a real decline in democratic practice. Further, the depth of that worry was clearly related to the constitution of the Labour Party at that time, as the *Guardian* editorial, the *Daily Telegraph* reviews and a long review by Labour MP Dick Taverne in the *New Statesman* all emphasised, between a Right-revisionist and a Left/Trotskyite radicalism. This was what encouraged Griffiths' to write *Bill Brand* in the first place, and was a highly specific issue for reviewers and audiences of 1970s British political television.

Griffiths' key 'political' texts: *Country* and *Food for Ravens*

5

Griffiths's *Country* finally establishes him as a television writer to be placed in the highest pantheon beside Dennis Potter and David Mercer. Perhaps his metaphor of 'the people' knocking at the door is too obvious, maybe the revolutionary message of his 'Tory Story' is naïve, but the texture of the characters and their relationships is extraordinarily rich (Sean Day-Lewis, *Daily Telegraph*, 21 October 1981).

Country was originally conceived by Griffiths and the BBC as the first of six episodes of a 'Tory story', which would examine various key moments of recent Conservative Party history (the 1957 interest rate scandal, the Profumo scandal, Thatcher's rise to power, etc). In fact, for financial and other reasons only *Country* was made, and Griffiths speaks of packing his whole Tory history into this one-off play.

As Poole and Wyver indicate, *Country* as a television text in fact contains several intertextual histories: the history of the country house genre (and in particular the 1938 West End hit *Dear Octopus* on which significant aspects of the theme, characterisation and, in Griffiths' original writing, individual names were based); a history of recent plays and films commissioned and directed by *Country*'s director, Richard Eyre (*The Imitation Game, Brassneck, Touched* and *Clapperclaw*); Trevor Griffiths' own recent television histories, particularly *The Cherry Orchard*; the broader mythical history of British wartime class consensus that Griffiths was challenging through this play; and the history of the Conservative Party which initially the BBC had sketched out with Griffiths as 'Tory Stories' (Poole and Wyver 1984, 160–3, 165, 167). More loosely there was reference also to the recent history of cinema via the equation of the British ruling-class 'Family' with the mafia through the paralleling of names: the Carlion family in *Country* (pronounced Corlion) and the Corleones in *The Godfather*.

Country viewed via *The Cherry Orchard*

There are, then, a variety of intertextual ways of approaching the Eyre/
Griffiths *Country*, and the 'textual' analysis of this and the following
chapter will, necessarily, focus on intertexts. In the case of *Country*, I
want to be both reflexive and at the same time chronological in terms of
to-air screenings and viewings of Trevor Griffiths' works on television.
For British audiences (including myself as viewer), the closest Griffiths'
intertext, screened on the same television channel, BBC1, at the same
time and in the same scheduling slot just one week earlier, was the
Eyre/Griffiths' version of Chekhov's *The Cherry Orchard*.

Since this production of *The Cherry Orchard* was based on a new
Trevor Griffiths translation (with Helen Rappaport), Poole and Wyver
are right to note some of the key linkages (and differences) between the
two Griffiths pieces in terms of offering a class analysis of a society in
decline, each emblematised by the threat to a country estate, each briefly
encountering a hostile working class – but with the difference that in
Country home, business and social order are preserved.

Poole and Wyver's comparison of *The Cherry Orchard* and *Country*
rightly places *Country* in continuing line with Griffiths' central writing-
career intention of describing and analysing key moments of potential
societal change via his familiar mix of histories. As in *Absolute Beginners* (BBC1, April 1974) *Occupations* (Granada TV, September 1974) both
screened some years earlier than *Country*, and as in *The Party* (BBC1,
March 1988), *Hope In The Year Two* (1994) and *Food For Ravens* (BBC1
Wales, January 1997) screened after it, Griffiths spotlights in *The Cherry
Orchard* and *Country* a particular socio-political moment of massive
potential change. These various plays focused on the coming Russian
Revolution, the Turin metal-workers strike of 1920, the French Revolution, the potential for real socialism in a Labour Party had it been led
by Aneurin Bevan, and, in *Country*, that brief moment after World War
II in Britain when the Labour Party was given a massive mandate for
radical social change by the people's vote.

In many cases – Lenin in *Absolute Beginners*, Gramsci in *Occupations*, Danton in *Hope in the Year Two*, Aneurin Bevan in *Food For Ravens*
– Griffiths adopts Lukacian notions of a 'world historical figure' to
portray an era ripe for social change, to display major personae at the
cusp of it, and to examine the outcomes of the conflicting and conver-
gent discourses, pleasures and embodiments on which these changes
rested. The same is true in Griffiths' 'non-political' works (which are,
of course, always political) like his mini-series *The Last Place on Earth*,
which was centred around the 'world historical' characters (in terms

of their respective relevance in the 'new' Norway and the 'old' imperial Britain of 1911) Amundsen and Scott in their quest for the South Pole (Tulloch 1990). In the case of *Country*, the 'world historical figures' are not actual, but they are 'real' none the less. At the play's action centre (as in Griffiths' *The Cherry Orchard*) are the two major potential agents for change, Philip (gay, once a socialist, but becoming – from the perspective of the play's writing in 1979 – the new iron man of Conservative class renovation, foreshadowing the 'Iron Lady'), and Virginia (like Philip, a child of the Carlion family, but who became a lifelong socialist via her experiences fighting Fascism in Spain and the Nazis in France).

There is a key scene in *Country* between Philip and Virginia which leads to my second observation on Poole and Wyver's comparison of *Country* and *The Cherry Orchard*. In *Country*, shot like *The Cherry Orchard* by Richard Eyre entirely on film, and with a major stylistic emphasis on the dark interior chiaroscuro of expressionism (Eyre, cited in Poole and Wyver 1984, 164), this 'nursery' scene is notable for its brilliant 'day' lighting. Poole and Wyver note well the dominant expressionism of other scenes, for example one sequence in wide-shot in Sir Frederic's study. The tones are dark and suggestive of age and the frame is entirely dominated by two huge portraits of family ancestors – the past remaining in the present. Before the pictures Leo McKern's Sir Frederic bends over his desk, bowed down by the collapse of his world and by a realisation of who Virginia has become: 'She was my daughter'. Philip stands easy and erect by the window, aware of but relatively independent of 'the past'. Side-lighting picks out his profile, glamorising his mastery of the situation and illustrating the confidence which permits his easy irony of his description of the election result: 'I think it's what they call Letting the People Speak.' Sir Frederic's line is static, heavy, defeated: 'Everything passes.' Philip's is casual, relaxed, aware that this is not Armaggedon: 'It's possible' (Poole and Wyver 1984, 164).

'Everything passes' has been, of course, a familiar, conventional and nostalgic (affluent middle-class, in Griffiths' view) reading of Chekhov's *The Cherry Orchard*, and what Poole and Wyver do not notice is that this scene they describe in *Country* is immediately followed by one that replicates *The Cherry Orchard*'s nursery scene, and which continues the dark/light chiaroscuro *between* scenes. This is a highly contrasting, highly lit scene between Philip and Virginia in the old nursery. Unlike the chiaroscuro in Sir Frederic's study, this nursery scene is flooded with bright evening light through the open windows of the old house. There is a similarly lit scene in the Eyre/Griffiths *The Cherry Orchard* where, just post-dawn, it is the old landed gentry people, Madame Ranevskaya and her brother Gayev who stare out of their windows at the past of their orchard, while the production's two change agents are either in-scene in the background (Lopakhin), or out-of-scene and introduced immediately the window sequence ends (Trofimov).

But in *Country*, it is the two change agents themselves who engage as they stare out of the windows at the past and future of their 'country'. And, like so much of the key action of *The Cherry Orchard*, this scene is played out in the old nursery. Though Griffiths describes the nursery as now 'buried beneath the accumulated junk of many disused years', Eyre's camera features it from the start via a child's Kitchener mask, and with dolls' house and toys as background and objects for actors' business. It is as though both the family's past of Ranevskaya and Gayev (Griffiths' script instructions for the opening of the Virginia/Philip scene is that 'They share the laugh, easier in the past tense, wary about the present'), and the family's future of Lopakhin and Trofimov (who also commune sensitively in the nursery in Act IV of *The Cherry Orchard*) meet here.

Virginia has come to Kent to write a magazine article on 'the country', and we first see her in this scene photographing the potential future, the horses liberated and running free from Sir Frederic's stable, and the hop-pickers and their children who have invaded the stables and are beginning to set up camp, working and playing towards a new future. The voice-over that introduces the scene is the BBC newsreader announcing that the Labour Party, for the first time in its history, has been returned to power with a large majority. When we first see Philip in this scene he is humorously hiding behind a mask of the past, Lord Kitchener, saying 'Your country needs you', just as his father (and the version of 'country' he represents) in the previous scene described by Poole and Wyver desperately needs him to 'do something' (handing him his hunting rifle).

But in this day-lit nursery scene Virginia, not Sir Frederic, is the quiet interrogator. She, like the rest of the family but with different motives, wants to know what Philip will do about his father's request that he take over the Carlion brewing company so that 'things will go on as they have done'. In contrast to the scene in Sir Frederic's study, this 'nursery' Philip is less glamorised and confident, as the choreography has him and his sister pirouette around each other, exchanging windows as Virginia continues to probe his 'beliefs' and his intentions.

At the beginning of the scene brother and sister are intimate, in day-lit two-shot, clearly each still close to the other, engaged in meeting for the first time in a decade. These are, as Griffiths writes in the previous scene, 'old friends and allies from the past' and 'pleasure passes between them' now. Yet they *are* wary about their future. Virginia asks, 'What are you doing here anyway. I thought you'd *washed* your hands ... ', and Philip for the first of two occasions in this scene, but still in two-shot with her, wheels away with, 'Oh, yes. I just couldn't find the towel. Not you though, eh?' Still in two-shot, Philip begins to probe in his turn, about her past in Spain and the French underground during the War.

Virginia speaks of having just met her former husband and son downstairs, and says they didn't seem real to her. Brother and sister are now separated in a series of inter-cut close-ups as, all ironic flippancy gone, Philip (very seriously and feelingly) asks: '*Why* 'Gin? You left all this, your child, marriage, for what? A trench in Alicante? A cellar in Montmarte?' Virginia (equally seriously) responds: 'I was young and very romantic. I felt I needed to purge my guilt for all this. This *has* to end, Pip [over prolonged close-up of Philip, head turning down and away]. Not because I feel guilty about it, but because it really does stand in the way. I came back to help.'

> Philip [a little ironic again]: 'You were always a bit heroic, Froth, passionate.'
>
> Virginia [intently, but slightly whimsically]: 'I modelled myself on you.'

The series of close-ups ends with Philip's defensively amused 'hah!', and they remain in two shot for the rest of the scene as Philip approaches her again to say that he saw her near Fleet Street coming out of some office while he was on a bus, and (seriously again), 'I wish you'd called us, Froth'. For the only time in the sequence Virginia walks away into the two-windows, deep focus two-shot that will remain for the rest of the scene. From the near window he asks her why she came, she replies from the far window 'impulse ... perhaps a little love', and said she had remembered the Carlion annual gathering. Philip, closer to camera and looking out of his window, is back in flippant-casual mode. 'Did you hear about the people in the barn. Hop-pickers mostly, working Carlion farms. Perhaps this *is* the Millenium [chuckles]. Do you think? It would be nice to think we were making history [flippant]'. Virginia leaves her window, and still in two shot comes to camera to join him, sensing some hope still from his words.

> Virginia [looking at him closely, unblinking]: 'Would you object?'
>
> Philip: 'Object? Why would I do that?'
>
> Virginia: 'I don't know. I don't know what you believe any more.'
>
> Philip: 'Believe? Hmm. In the main I've come to believe that belief is really not my bag.'

He goes on to tell her that his 'crazed' father also wants him to believe, and to take over the company. In Griffiths' script, there is 'Silence. She goes on looking at him. He continues staring out of the window, fiddles a cigarette into his mouth', but, on the words about 'take over', 'He glances at her suddenly'.

> Virginia [still looking at him unblinkingly, hesitant with her tongue at her lips, but firm also]: 'No one can...make you do anything Pip. You're your own man.'
>
> Philip [distantly flippant]: 'I know'.
>
> Virginia [in her last appeal of the play to her brother]: 'Especially you Pip'.
>
> Philip [lethargically evasive]: 'Absolutely.'

Philip turns and there is a significant look of mutual recognition as to what their separate futures will be. And for the second time in the scene Philip walks away, still in two-shot, to look out of the other window. Virginia's unblinking eye-line engagement with him is broken at last, she lowers her gaze, blinks several times, and with a toss of the head that seems to indicate 'real' recognition, looks down and out of the window, thrown from her hopeful intimacy with her brother into some inner space, which she has to force herself out of to hear his comment about Blackie the former poacher being the butler now. The scene ends with them apart, looking out of their separate windows as he says he hates the country, and the newsreader's voice-over about Churchill's resignation at the Palace bridges the viewer to the next short scene (shot from Virginia's elevated eye-line) of three urchins throwing stones at the great house windows as the dark begins to set in. Griffiths' original script does not have the urchins. Instead, in 'Virginia's point of view we see a Carlion horse-drawn dray pulling up in the forecourt, a single keg of beer on the back, which the cart driver begins to unload'. But the effect of each character at the end staring out of their separate windows is the same. Griffiths writes, 'They stand at separate windows, seeing different things, as it were, back-to-back'. Virginia sees a working-class man. Philip, no doubt, sees the beer keg he has converted into the re-carbonated 'weasel piss' that he will introduce as his pièce-de-résistance in the final Act.

Raymond Williams spoke of people looking out of windows as a central visual motif in Chekhov's 'structure of feeling', representing an urge for something better, something yet unknown, something not yet articulated. For Griffiths' characters in *Country*, the future that is 'out there' is clearly indicated, but ambiguous and ambivalent in its agency. This scene between Virginia and Philip, two sensitive 'outsiders' to the family who once shared similar political ideals, is pivotal because it marks the moment of final coming together and parting, just as in the case of Lopakhin and Trofimov in Act IV of *The Cherry Orchard*. By then the future divergent paths of these two *Cherry Orchard* 'change agents' are already well marked out; and it is in this scene in the nursery-past of *Country* that Philip's and Virginia's different future paths are most clearly expressed, and for the first time, perhaps, mutually recognised.

I use the word 'expressed' rather than 'articulated' here, because their different paths are conveyed by fine acting, eye-lines, head-turns, choreography and film lighting rather than by language. Ted Braun has observed that, post-*Reds*, Griffiths undertakes 'a fundamental shift of stylistic direction' (1988, 22) with *Country*.

One has only to compare the script of *Country* with his earlier work to see the extent of the stylistic shift. While all the television plays from *All Good Men* onwards incorporate powerful visual imagery, it is used far more intermittently to concentrate or to modify verbally articulated meaning. The burden of the debate is carried by the characters ... In *Country*, the key to the style is Virginia, the disaffected elder daughter, stalking her sometime family with dispassionate camera ... Similarly, the lighting exercises an ironic effect, telling us much more about the characters than their clipped utterances convey. Lit and shot by Nat Crosby and designed by Geoff Powell, the film runs the gamut from the bleached exteriors of high-summer indolence to the ominous chiaroscuro of the grieving Sir Frederic alone in church or absorbing the impact of the election catastrophe in his study. The far reference point in this carefully calculated scheme is Philip, raffishly attired in 'unsuitable' lightweight suit – until, that is, he assumes the subfusc appropriate to his newly assumed authority as Chairman and Managing Director (1988, 24–5).

It is this film-lighting 'scheme' that is mobilised in the contrasting dark/light study/nursery scenes I have been describing. And in the nursery Penelope Wilton's extraordinarily long unblinking close-up stare into the face of the brother she loves and had believed to be a 'comrade' replaces for a moment her 'dispassionate camera'. Philip's acting motif in this scene is playing with props – Griffiths has him 'disturbed, crosses to the [child's] swing, sets it in movement'; the television play has him instead pick up and fiddle with a child's toy train carriage as he drops his head and turns away in recognition of both his sister's ongoing force and her structural difference from himself. The Philip we now see – with his 'disturbed', self-conscious laughter when she says she modelled herself on him, with his mix of unspeaking, prolonged glance and uncomfortable playing with props – is already in process from that 'unsuitable' lightweight suit to the gravitas of new Tory, pragmatic capitalist boss.

Poole and Wyver are wrong to say that it is simply recognising the new reality of the Labour election landslide which leads to Philip understanding 'where his duty lies and accedes to his father's wish' (1984, 160). In fact he had already been preparing the new re-carbonated beer before the Election, and he had been vetting Faith as the obligatory wife that his father demands before the results too. Now, as a marker of the separate paths he and Virginia are taking, the next scene after the nursery meeting with Virginia will show Philip pressing further his vetting of Faith, the manager of the house, as his future wife, while his mother gazes on them. The 'new Tory' Philip, unlike Lopakhin (whom actor Bill Paterson describes as the new Tory in *The Cherry Orchard*), *will* marry his Varya. And Blackie, the poacher turned 'gamekeeper' (as the butler Ashford), will replicate Firs' giving away of his 'Freedom' in *The Cherry Orchard*. In the script for *Country*, as Virginia is forced to 'retire' with the other women after hearing from Philip that the hop-pickers were 'persuaded to move on', and Blackie serves the port over which the future control of Carlions will be decided, Griffiths writes, 'Virginia stands eventually, nods, walks slowly out, looking at no-one, passing Ashford, shadowy by the door. They exchange a very brief look. Ashford looks back towards the table ... passes the port around. The atmosphere thickens, darkens, the women gone. Ashford, outside the light, stares impassively' (1988, 292–3).

The almost subliminal glance between Blackie and Virginia in the televised play stands in for the lengthy speeches about 'class betrayal' evident in a play like *All Good Men*, and so much is conveyed by camera, acting and lighting that an interaction like this one is frankly more 'readable' (for this viewer at least) *via* the Eyre/Griffiths *The Cherry Orchard* that many viewers had just seen. Blackie, in this other crucial (and chiaroscuro) scene in *Country*, is both Firs (as master butler) and Yasha with his tray of champagne glasses that he drinks himself in Act IV of *The Cherry Orchard* (Griffiths wrote a similar scene for *Country* which was not included where Blackie drinks the new beer).

Similarly, the relationship between Philip and Virginia, pivotal and determining in the nursery scene, matches structurally the 'sensitive' finale of Lopakhin and Trofimov in *The Cherry Orchard*. In both cases, the only two change agents in the play, new Tory and socialist, engage gently with each other before walking in their different directions. Later, in the port scene where Philip reveals the steel he has had all along to take over the company – a scene which Griffiths speaks of as 'where the nexus of families becomes class, and transposes into a class discourse' (personal interview 18/7/92) – Virginia includes him among her list of the condemned. Virginia, dressed in her coat to leave, returns briefly to the men, now drinking the new Carlion beer, to say (in words much repeated by newspaper reviewers, see Chapter 4):

> One day – soon I hope – there'll be a banging at your door. It will be the people. Because they'll be English, they'll probably give you a third-class rail ticket to Dover or Southampton, when they ask you to go. Frankly, I would not object if they followed the example of Spanish peasants and garrotted you in your beds. Because I feel that, were there a God, he would want you to suffer for the suffering you cause.

But Philip has already pre-empted her words with his own speech to his family/shareholder rivals about class resistance, where he too speaks of the threat of the landed class having to leave the country. Sir Frederic has asked his shareholder-family to support Philip as the next head of the company. There is some initial resistance from Philip's rivals, and Weldon asks, from a lawyer's position, what the motion is. Is Sir Frederic suggesting Philip as Managing Director or Chairman of Carlions? Sir Frederic hums and haws, at a loss. But Philip's voice captures instant and shocked attention as his words cut across his father's, and in parallel the camera cuts from the instantly attentive body-turn of his serried-rank rivals to Philip in close-up.

> Both .... It may not have entirely slipped your notice, gentleman, that today, Thursday the 26th of July, people of this country declared war on us. This whole discussion may already be obsolete. Before the year is out we may all be living in the West Indies on such capital as we've been able to muster from the expropriation of our possessions that the socialists have been elected to effect. The ship's sinking, gentlemen. That's water round your ankles. Now, if I'm to enlist, I shall need safeguards. Crucially I shall need to know that I have sole authority to chart the course ahead. Both, and now!

This is, symptomatically for Griffiths, the blending of history 'then' and 'now'. As Braun says of Philip's major rival, Harcourt's begrudging recognition that Philip is in fact their necessary new leader,

While the entire action is punctuated and determined by the radio reports of the Conservative rout of July 1945, Griffiths' eye is fixed as ever on the present day. The viewer is being warned never to underestimate the resilience of the new pragmatic Toryism, like Philip totally unconcerned with values and only with winning. Apart from the reference to the present being indicated by the occasional planted anachronism ('really not my bag', 'bachelor gay'), Harcourt's summary of the socialist threat is couched in terms that allude unmistakably to the radical aspirations of Tony Benn and the resurgent Labour Left in the early eighties (1988, 25).

The Conservative 'wets' (from Griffiths' 1979–81 perspective) crumble before Philip as they recognise that in the face of the socialists' 'thieves' charter' they need a different leadership. Philip's absolute pragmatism replaces Sir Frederic's gun, and the father looks well pleased with his son. When old Sir Piers mumbles, 'Great pity that young Pip didn't fight though' (in the War) Sir Frederic, now back in equilibrium, emphasises, 'He will. Peephole.Bank on it!'

Philip then, as Poole and Wyver indicate, introduces the men around the table to Carlion's future wealth-making project, re-carbonated keg beer. Poole and Wyver note that the history of working-class consumption of, and commoditisation by, 'weasel piss' beer – 'first keg, then lager, then multinational mergers' (Poole and Wyver 1984, 167) – was to have been a continuing theme of Griffiths' six-part 'Tory Stories'. It is this moment of Philip's triumph and re-grouping of his class that is interrupted by Virginia's entry, her pronouncement about their impending 'funeral' and her exit of the house, followed by Philip who appeals to her not to 'go like this. 'This is how we are, you know that.' Virginia exits into camera for the last time, saying she does know that.

Philip: 'You won't be friends?'

Virginia: 'Not while there's a war on.'

Virginia exits, and Philip's 'Varya', Faith, comes from inside to stand by him and shut the door on his sister and the world beyond.

Country begins to slow motion shots of public school boys being regimented in successive leaps from windows during a fire drill by Oliphant Jnr (as the prefect, bored, reads his *Financial Times*). This is counterpointed with the voice-over of Churchill's election speech about the people of 'Great Britain, the cradle of free democracy throughout the world' not liking to be 'regimented and ordered about and have every action of our lives prescribed for us'. As Poole and Wyver say, 'The ironic tone established here is crucial to the film which follows'.

Country ends with *Virginia's* British 'people' shambling away from camera, the sound of collective footsteps slowly obliterating the Eton choir boys' pristine voices over the end titles. These are the East End hop-pickers who in the final scene of the play are seen at night with bonfires, laughter and lots of Carlion kegs. The beer flows, people laugh, the golden flames cover the screen, and a black-garbed Eton dummy is also obliterated as it is thrown onto the fire. Sir Frederic, in a wheelchair after a stroke, is watching with Philip, and in a slurred voice asks, 'What is it? Is it a funeral?' But this is not quite the funeral Virginia predicted – or at least Philip doesn't think so, as his clipped, ironic upper-class voice gives the last lines of the play, 'I rather think it is, father. They have not yet noticed that the grave is empty.'

For Trevor Griffiths, *Country* is all about his growing recognition of the 'detachment' (represented by his visual style in this piece) of the ruling-class. 'I feel that I also discovered that one of the other extraordinary absences within that class is inner dialogue, or interior life ... For them there is precept, there is duty, there is opportunity, and there is power – these seem to occupy all the space within these people's lives ... In a sense they see themselves instrumentally' (Poole and Wyver 1984, 181 and Braun 1988, 24).

The nursery scene between Virginia and Philip was the last (only?) moment that a different *subjectivity* and 'interior life' was played for by two people who cared about each other. And their loss was conveyed not by dialogue in that scene so much as by eyes, lips, head movements, choreography, actors' business and lighting. Philip's distanced, ironic, fetishised and monosyllabic responses of 'I know' and 'Absolutely' to Virginia's appeal for new agency when she says 'No one can ... *make* you do anything, Pip. You're your own man ... Especially you, Pip' is the precursor of his final clipped words to his father, 'They have not yet noticed that the grave is empty'. The 'No one' in Virginia's 'No one can ... *make* you ... , Pip' now applies to the resurgent working-class community he sees before him, and which the next forty years of 'Tory Stories' will seek to smash in a totally different 'funeral'.

The workers' cheerful 'Roll out the barrel' in the last scene is, equivalently, replaced as the titles roll by the Eton schoolboys more formalised, aestheticised and ritualised version of the same song, which had also been heard at the play's beginning over the stylised shots of boys leaping in a fire drill. And so fire – being faked and put out at the beginning, real and potentially both able to extirpate and be absorbed by the ruling-class at the end – bookends this play. As in *The Cherry Orchard*, the working class is used by Griffiths as a formidable 'interruption', in *Country* breaking into the smooth process of the ruling-class renewing itself through Philip. Varya's talk of vagrants occupying the empty servants' quarters, followed up by the threatening vagrant who confronts the family in Act II of *The Cherry Orchard* is paralleled in *Country* by the hop-picker who bursts from the stable doors that Sir Frederic is banging on, and thrusts his large, calloused hands ('ripped away by years of hopping') forward as Sir Frederic, and the camera, momentarily backs away.

Hop-picker: 'See these. Eighteen years I've been coming down 'ere pickin' your hops and every year we have to ask you for a pair of bloody gloves to pick 'em in. We're through askin'. I'll tell you somethin'. It's the best place we've put our heads down inside a year. You treat your bloody horses better'n you treat us ...'

Sir Frederic: 'My horses have names' [raises his gun at hop-picker's head, Philip intervenes, taking the gun off his father].

Philip has already listened to the police inspector who advised them to have a little patience with the people in their stables, particularly as there were reporters around nosing out a story. 'Things are quite delicate just now ... There's a widespread feeling that people have earned the right to a decent roof over their heads .... So all in all we'd counsel patience and understanding for a day or two ... at least until the election's been declared and so on ... if you take my meaning, sir.' The election is now over, and the Conservatives have lost. But Philip, as pragmatist, knows that there are other ways of winning than via the older generation's gun. The ruling-class can kill, as Griffiths said in *Bill Brand*, just as readily via the stockbroker's and insurance executive's telephone.

Griffiths has said of the vagrant in Chekhov's *The Cherry Orchard* that he is the hard face of optimism. His is the energy and the pain from which change will emerge. He has, Griffiths says, to be *dealt* with and *reckoned* with. Lopakhin will employ him and Trofimov will organise him, but the vagrants will be the material out of which the future will come. Griffiths argues that it is a brilliant aspect of Chekhov to create that moment of terror. The play, he says suddenly becomes liquid beneath their feet, 'it's larval in its intensity' (Radio Nottingham interview, 1977). If the vagrant is played as a drunk, Griffiths argues, the threat is then perceived to be against the gentry's bodies only and to their status, not to their existence as a class. But if played frighteningly, as he is in the Griffiths version of *The Cherry Orchard*, 'He is a threat to everything they possess, to what they *are* in society' (Griffiths interview, Radio Nottingham, 1977).

Griffiths is attempting the same societal positioning of the Blitz-bombed East London hop-workers in *Country*. These are men who are young enough to have fought in the War, yet have given the Carlions 18 years of service also. Their reward is to be rejected at the end of the War from even the ruling-class stables ('My horses have *names*'). But their potential power is more directly conveyed by the 'distanced' Virginia, who reproduces them via her camera, than the vagrant class of Chekhov's Russia is represented by Trofimov. While Virginia identifies with 'the people', she also distances herself from the ruling-class, so that, as Poole and Wyver say, the loving camera identification with ruling-class lives and homes of *Brideshead Revisited* is avoided (though, as we have seen in Chapter 4, many reviewers would not have agreed).

Virginia is introduced taking photos of the Carlion estate, a device which establishes the idea of the families and their tribal rituals being dispassionately watched by the viewer ... As Griffiths says, there is 'the sense of real life being lived, real space being occupied and yet a very cool, detached and mobile camera seeing them from another point of view' (Poole and Wyver 1984, 163–4).

I have tried to indicate by focusing on the nursery scene between Virginia and Philip here, the way Griffiths used film lighting, chore-ography, extremely fine, nuanced acting from James Fox and Penelope Wilton, and a set of childhood memories to show (but not *say*) that even in their closest, most intimate and most lovingly, funnily nostalgic of moments, the British ruling-class were occupied by the aesthetic of the 'instrumental'. *Country* thus eschews the 'hybrid of traditional narrative romance form and heritage splendour' (Nelson 2001, 39) of other 'quality' country house television. 'Love' – whether of Philip for Faith, Philip for Virginia, or Philip for his father – is ultimately instru-mental.

Trevor Griffiths' script and the to-air text of 'Country'

In the context of his experience with other sympathetic directors like Ken Loach (Tulloch 1990, chapter 6), Griffiths' close collaboration with Richard Eyre on both *The Cherry Orchard* and *Country* is instructive. By comparing Griffiths' scripts for *Country* with the televised version, several things become clear.

First, Eyre (and the actors) in almost all cases followed Griffiths' script meticulously closely. This is true of actors' movements, eye-lines and glances (e.g. Philip/Virginia, and Virginia/Blackie in the scenes already mentioned), significant pauses, camera movements (for example, the camera taking Daisy at her birthday celebration 'in zoom focus – close up – from presentation table position'), Virginia's own intra-diegetic binocular/camera movement ('to pick up Philip ... as he stoops to pick something up from the ground'), bits of business (e.g. the police inspector speaking as he eyes Philip's gold cigarette case), precisely inter-cut noises of the horse in the entrance hall that pene-trate the billiard room business discussion, and even close-up details, as in the first scene between Faith and Sir Frederic, where Griffiths' instructions have Sir Frederic looking '*down at his left hand, which is balled into a tight fist. Opens it to reveal the two pills* [that Faith has given him]. *He shakes them off the palm, which is dappled with pigeon blood*' (1988, 242). In this way, minutely seen aspects of Griffiths' gender and class 'psychology', communication and narrative are conveyed visually in the transmitted text.

Secondly, with this degree of authorial inscription into the televised text, it becomes more interesting when Griffiths' writing was *not* followed. Many of these omissions were either overtly political (associations of the Oliphant family with Nazi Germany, comments by Sir James Blair about the need to attack the Russians, and thus save India, Greece and the East London of the hop-pickers from communism, Daisy and Alice's interchange about 'the Jew', Mr Joseph, which, once omitted, makes his later scene of discomfiture as he tries to leave the tight 'Family' circle redundant) or sexual (comments by Daisy and Alice relating to Philip's wearing scent, and only liking girls when they play *Peter Pan*, Daisy's 'instrumentalist' disagreement with Philip's emphasis on sexuality when he says that he can't take over Carlions because he has a male partner. 'No ... When I was nineteen and just married, I watched the fourth baronet, your father's father, do it to a sheepdog in the Orangery ... You only have to state your terms' (1988, 288).

Arguably, many of the socio-political statements being made in these elided scenes (for example, elaboration of Virginia's Spanish Civil War comments to Philip) were symptomatic of the 'old' Trevor Griffiths, making overt polemic and written speech work instead of the new 'filmic' resonances of *Country*'s politics. If this is so, Eyre's direction was taking the writer further in the direction he wanted to go. This is certainly the case with Daisy's scent reference and Alice's talk about *Peter Pan*. James Fox's walk, mannerisms, 'Noel Coward' intonations – not to mention his telephone call to his male lover – conveyed without further need for glossing his confident sexuality.

Missing also, though, are some of Griffiths' observations on the broader savagery of this British ruling-class, from mantraps at home to extermination of Jews and Communists (and Japanese civilians) abroad. On the day I was first drafting this chapter on *Country* in November 2002, Trevor Griffiths circulated by email a number of attributed statements by Winston Churchill, whose voice begins *Country*. In a different medium in 2002, Griffiths was re-inserting that 'Churchillian' savagery omitted from *Country* in 1981.

> This movement among the Jews is not new.... [T]his worldwide conspiracy for the overthrow of civilisation and for the reconstitution of society on the basis of arrested development, of envious malevolence, and impossible equality, has been steadily growing ... from the underworld of the great cities of Europe and America. (Churchill, *Illustrated Sunday Herald*, February 1920)

> I do not admit ... that a great wrong has been done to the Red Indians

of America, or the black people of Australia ... by the fact that a stronger race, a higher grade race...has come and taken its place. (Churchill to Palestine Royal Commission, 1937)

(We must rally against) ... an infected Russia of armed hordes not only smiting with bayonet and cannon, but accompanied and preceded by swarms of typhus-bearing vermin. (Churchill, quoted in the *Boston Review*, April/May 2001)

In the context of Churchill's quoted statements, Griffiths' (omitted) lines in *Country* for Jimmy Blair seem relatively mild. 'We can handle the Russians, provided the Americans don't welch on the thing ... They're our enemies ... and will be treated as such ... when the time comes' (1988, 265). It is this broader, global-fascist edge of Toryism that is mainly lost from *Country* via the cuts to Griffiths' text in production.

Food for Ravens: the 'ghosts' of Derrida

In Chapter 1 I indicated the way in which Garner reads the later television dramas and plays of Trevor Griffiths via the intertexts of postmodernism, in particular Derrida. He argues that 'At no point in *Food for Ravens* is the present's deconstructive slippage more directly and powerfully conveyed than in the film's concluding sequence' (1999, 270). This is the coda in which, after the dying Nye whispers to the grieving Jenny to take him home, the 'Boy is shown running ... "on down the years to Wales and home".' In a sequence inter-cut with scenes of Bevan's memorial procession, he passes moments of history: the photographing of a 1936 anti-fascist brigade on its way to Spain, a Miners' Band and demonstrators proclaiming the 1926 Lockout. While Nye's voice delivers segments of his political speeches, the Boy stands "rooted, watching, apart and part of, sniffing a future, some distance from the marchers"' (Garner 1999, 270).

Garner makes much here in his analysis of *Food for Ravens* of Derrida's account of the need to 'ghost' Marx. 'If it – learning to live – remains to be done, it can happen only between life and death...to live *with* ghosts ...And this being-with spectres would also be, not only but also, a *politics* of memory, of inheritance, and of generations' (Derrida, *Specters of Marx*, cited Garner 1999, 249). Garner argues that 'Griffiths' interest in the "ghosting" of history deepened' (1999, 264) in *Food for Ravens*, where 'the play's framing devices and its hierarchy of ontological levels are radically destabilised' (1999, 270).

Garner's is a lively and highly sensitive analysis of the play, and he has every right to use an 'academic' intertext like Derrida if it illuminates

Griffiths' work. However, I intend to use an entirely different kind of intertext in this chapter on 'author's significant texts'; preferring to Derrida Griffiths' own texts *Country* and *Food for Ravens*.

Country and *Food for Ravens*

What is my rationale for choosing *Country* as an intertext for the following analysis, apart from the fact that Griffiths himself nominated these two among his chosen plays for this chapter? There are three textual reasons.

First, *Country* chooses as its focusing history the moment when the Attlee government was elected in 1945 with a large socialist mandate, and examines the landed ruling-class' fears and actions in relation to that unexpected mandate. Aneurin Bevan, as Minister of Health and Housing, was not only the youngest minister in the new Labour Cabinet, but its most powerfully placed socialist advocate. It was his wartime speeches and dreams that the Labour Party would betray, as under the leadership of Hugh Gaitskell, it moved to the Right, thus confirming Philip's observation about Right-wing resurgence at the end of *Country* that the celebrating 'people' had not yet noticed the ruling-class grave was empty.

Secondly, there is a major speech at the heart of both plays that links the Spanish Civil War and the wish by the main socialist protagonists – Virginia in *Country* and Nye Bevan in *Food For Ravens* – for the people to 'return' to throw out the Tories and ruling-class. Virginia, as we have seen, speaks of the people following 'the example of Spanish peasants and garrott[ing] you in your beds. Because I feel that, were there a God, he would want you to suffer for the suffering you cause'. Nye Bevan makes one of his most impassioned speeches as a dying man in his cow barn, replicating his earlier speech in Parliament attacking the Tory's Means Test Bill second reading, and arguing that it will destroy the family comradeship which is at the very centre of poor people's lives. As Tories laugh at him, he says he knows he will not convince them with words or pity. He continues, in tight, close-up chiaroscuro.

> There's only one thing left, and that is hate. I believe in hate more than pity itself. Hundreds of young men faced with these conditions you have created are leaving to fight Fascism in Spain. Thousands more are now joining the Army and the Air Force to learn to defend the country that has given them these conditions ... Let not Honourable Members be so complacent. The time may come when these young men, remembering what you have done, may need to give you a lesson in return. I hope you

will remember what you are doing now to the millions of defenceless people in this country. And I hope when the opportunity comes those same people will take advantage of it. And I hope I will be there to see your faces. [Over this last line, the mumbled outrage of Tory parliamentarians has given way to silence and the muted cry of ravens].

Virginia was a privileged woman who went to fight for the Republicans in Spain and with the French Resistance in the Second World War, and returned, appropriately, to haunt her own class with predictions of hate. But this haunting is not of a Derridean ghost. Virginia has behind and before her the majority of the British population. And the same is true of Nye Bevan's 'hate' speech, with the difference that while Virginia distances herself stylistically as much from the working class as from her family via her camera, Bevan is linked directly to his working-class background both experientially (via memory) and potentially via the Boy's young-faced honesty and an innocent determination that replicates Nye's own. The *Boy*, then, is the crucial 'alienating' and de-centring device that challenges other parts of the text's naturalism.

Thirdly, the Boy is a continuing reminder of both experiential memory and class renewal in the face of the death of a class leader, just as, but in a very different way, Philip is in the face of his dying father in *Country*. As Griffiths has intimated, the renewal of the ruling-class Right is so much simpler than that of the working-class Left, partly because they have the power (which includes the power of articulation, through education, the media and so on), partly because they act purely instrumentally, without the self-doubt of inner dialogue. Consequently, Philip's 'change' is purely cosmetic – of suits, geographical locality and partner. Philip had the will to power from the beginning, and his ironic posture will remain unchanged. In *Country* it was only Virginia's demand for the intimacy of comradeship that unsettled him. It was only then that he walked away.

But for Griffiths working-class renewal is so much more complex and reflexive. He had remarked of the rich elite in *Country* on the 'extraordinary absences within that class [of] inner dialogue, or interior life'. In *Food for Ravens*, Nye Bevan, at the moment of his death, returns to that interior life of his class. So the play *has to be* dialogic, not instrumental, and therefore more about the 'mystery' of comradely agreement than about the 'outcomes' of Tory instrumentalism. This is captured beautifully by the opening (monochrome) scene of *Food for Ravens* as the young Nye carries his stool across the mountain and recites his poem for his loved one. '"Come to me my lovely and await the better days" ... She never came'. As Nye says near the end to the Boy, 'Once, your age in dreams, I set out alone and finding myself in some future world not yet my own. Talking with strangers ... searching for I knew not which'.

Working-class renewal is much harder, more unknown *because* comradeship must be the result of talking with both strangers and loved ones. First, there will always be profound differences of view not only about what is to be attained but how to attain it, hence the well-known 'tension' throughout Trevor Griffiths' work (no less in *Food for Ravens* than in *Occupations* or *Comedians*) between 'hard' hate and 'soft' love.

Second, there is the uncertainty as to what success *constitutes* (it is much more complex than taking over a brewing company and re-electing a Conservative government). Hence the conversation between Nye and the Boy (also called 'Nye') about 'Toff's' pleasures – wealth, big houses, art, literature, music, health – which had become also Aneurin Bevan's (and Trevor Griffiths') pleasures. A marked linguistic feature of *Food for Ravens* is the textual *return* of dialogue that is both self-reflexively real and tormentingly guilt-revealing. So, initially, when the Boy asks him why he has a big house and so on, Nye says he may well ask and he cannot fault his view that this is 'Toff's turf'. 'Well, that's your truth, and I can't say you're wrong'. Later, though, Nye returns to it, and argues that if you cede all these good things in life to the Toffs, you have lost the battle for happiness before you even start. These 'goods' should be shared by all, just as long as the working class insists on the truth that 'everything comes from the point of a pick'.

Thirdly, the Left's history is a history of defeats, whereas the Tory's history is of largely non-interrogated success. Indeed, re-imagining, re-imaging, re-articulating and, above all, re-historicising those defeats are a mark of Griffiths' unique authorship. Yet here, at 60 years of age, sharing a sickness with Bevan, Griffiths had to face his own success and failure in the context of his own mortality. *Food for Ravens* is perhaps the most 'personal' of all of Griffiths' plays that deal with Left failure. For a writer who has always refused to be 'terminal, like Beckett', he was now observing, through Bevan, a terminus that none of us can avoid. Hence, I believe, the extraordinary power of personal *and* historical lyricism in this piece that Griffiths directed as well as wrote. The fusing of love poetry and the future in the opening scene is then conveyed as an *acting* motif through the play via Sinead Cusack's agonised smile (as his wife Jennie Lee) in support of the terminally ill Nye, and via his almost-but-not-quite asking of Jen whether his 'ulcer' is in fact something worse. The reason for his not asking, and her not telling, is clearly stated in Nye's response to the Boy's open-faced honesty when he does ask about it. 'We live in hope Jenny and me. Always have done ... Got to keep going ... in the right direction'.

To admit to the death of the Labour Party's only hope of a socialist leadership would be to betray that 'living in hope'. Nye says to his doctor, 'I need another five years, man. If I'm around in a couple of years I could be leading this bloody party. Gaitskell's a loser. It's in his eyes, in his voice. You can't lead this Party from the Right. Not yet anyway, not *this* Party ... In three bloody years I could be leading this country. I'm not for dying just yet!' That 'You can't lead this Party from the Right. *Not yet anyway*' (my italics) is, of course, a mark of Griffiths' moment of writing, in the time of Tony Blair's leadership of New Labour. And Nye's invention of the Boy (who is *all* the things that Nye and critics have suggested – the young Nye, the son he always wanted, *and* the angel of death) is his gift of hope back to Jenny and the Party as he dies.

This is not just a gift of hope in the simple sense of Bevan as 'giant' of the Labour Party that Neil Kinnock speaks about in the television lead up to *Food for Ravens'* initial screening on BBC1 Wales: 'The word giant is probably too often applied to people of distinction. In Bevan's case the word can accurately be used. In terms of his ideas, in terms of his courage, in terms of the breadth of his vision, in terms of his qualities, he was a giant' (Kinnock, BBC Wales, November 1997). Nor is it only in the sense of the power of articulation that Tony Benn describes in the same programme opening: 'He did illuminate the landscape. He would fire a pyrotechnic into the sky and for a fraction of a second you could see the lie of the land' (Benn, BBC Wales, November 1997). But more profoundly, the gift of hope lies in the insistence that the socialist dream *must be dialogic*, hence the play's structure around Nye and the Boy talking, in challenge of each other – as Nye says, the Boy is 'bright as a pin, staring me down'. And it lies, also, in the recognition that that talking has a clear, material aim – not Derrida's ghosts and spectres, but in (as Nye says in his last words to the Boy) 'Not the cause but the bloody cure'.

The Boy, structurally and thematically in *Food for Ravens*, is also Philip in *Country*: the hoped-for-future of a dying father. Yet, visually and performatively he is so different. Philip, for all his will-to-action, is always restrained, repressed beneath his upper-class irony, and unable to retain eye-to-eye contact with Virginia, walking away from *her* will to intimacy-as-comrades. But the Boy is transparently open, is not fazed by the great celebrity Aneurin Bevan, because he, too, has the potential of his mentor (as he makes clear over the miner's lamp award), and he reproduces the Nye Bevan honesty and courage to ask the great man the most obvious but frequently unasked questions. Why the great house? Are you dying? Why the failure of Nye and Jen to talk about his death?

So, for the adult Nye Bevan who, Jen has always said, was 'born full-grown' with his belief in the 'mystery' of a future utopia and yet the near

impossibility of earlier dreams (the footstool carried across the mountain to the girl who never comes), there is also, as Jen recognises at his
funeral, the man who died a boy – the boy with the clear face engaging
innocently (with the camera, and with Nye) with the ongoing harshness
of life, but who has the strength given by youth and life to begin from
the bottom again. He *will* win that miners' lamp award that Nye's says
he won't, and he has the *time* (that Nye has not) to both experience past
history/defeats (hence his observation of the Spanish Civil War volun-
teers and the 1926 miners at the end) and whatever struggles the future
holds. As Nye has told him about the National Health Service that, as
socialist politician Bevan has fought to establish, 'There's no such thing
as forever, Boy. It'll last as long as there are folk left with the faith to fight
for it'. *Behind* Nye Bevan, as he recognises, there is 'the long history of
class action ... stretching back to the Chartists'. But *beyond* him, in the
face and will of this Boy, there is a resilient will to a future, whether it
resides in the resistance of class in Britain or Arabs in Palestine and Iraq
(as in *The Gulf Between Us*).

As the *director* of *Food for Ravens*, Trevor Griffiths opens this television piece with the black-and-white lyricism of a Welsh boy chasing
his dreams carrying a stool across a mountain. He ends the play with
a savage cut, as the Boy, on his first day down the pit, drops sharply
out of sight in the miners' cage. The material conditions for struggle
continue.

Like the hero of the seventh-century Aneurin's poem which ends the
play and gives it its title, the Boy is both fresh-faced and experienced-to-
death. 'Food for Ravens', yes; but the 'food' – whether Welsh working
class or (in other Griffiths' pieces) Middle-East Arabs – is *alive*, growing,
'eaten' again and again, but re-growing separate from Monsanto's
'terminator gene'. Far from being about the 'ghosts' of Marxism and
other 'grand narratives', *Food for Ravens* is about *living*, and living
dialogically with love, comradeship, and lack of 'dulce-eyed' moralising.
These, in their combination, are the 'happiness' which may one day
grow from the current 'mystery at the heart of things'. Rather than
Philip's ironically distanced instrumentalism ('They haven't yet noticed
the grave is empty', to his father at the end of *Country*), the language of
Food for Ravens is based on a dialectic of uncertainty (Bevan's stammer,
which Robin Day comments on in the introduction) and a clarity of
articulation. This tension and this politics of language are pointed to
by Nye Bevan when he says to the Boy (who also stutters), 'Between the
stammer and *le mot juste*, Boy, we can learn to word the future'.

Style beyond reality: Griffiths as writer/director

Trevor Griffiths has often spoken of how, from the time of writing *Country*, and partly out of his experience of film-making, he was moving beyond realism. Garner speaks of Griffiths as director of his own film for the first time in *Food for Ravens*, giving 'an attention to form and visual composition more generally associated with Continental films. Underscoring the film's reflexivity and its conception of realism as something plastic, self-transforming, Griffiths told his production crew that what he wanted in *Food for Ravens* was 'a painting, not a photo-graph' (1999, 266).

Following Derrida, Garner speaks of the 'deconstructive slippage' (1999, 270) in which 'past, present and future exist – in and for one another – as competing horizons of meaning' (1999, 270). Speaking of scenes where Bevan and the Boy discuss being a 'toff' and the use of language, Garner interprets the sequence as one where 'On the threshold of death the past assumes virtual life, and memory confronts itself in an impossible space both inside and outside of time ... The self is subject to these thresholds and divergences, and in the exercise of memory the subject encounters a principle of difference at the heart of identity' (1999, 269,269). It is this which underpins Garner's inter-pretation from Derrida that *Food for Ravens* 'unhinges' living meaning, deconstructing it via this *'non-contemporaneity with itself of the living present'* (Derrida, *Spectres of Marx*, xix, cited in Garner 1999, 270).

However, I want to select the same scenes of Nye and the Boy and interpret them differently, via Griffiths' own intertexts. It is certainly the case that when the sequence Garner is describing opens, it is re-presenting European film. As Bevan enters the 'natural' landscape scene, drinking at a spring from a stark earthy bank silhouetted harshly under his big hat, the lighting, the tilted 'wall', the angled trees and figure, and the gnarled tree roots immediately evoke (even though in colour) German Expressionist films like *The Cabinet of Dr Caligari*. This is augmented by starkly contrasting camera angles, from the front of Nye as he sits small against the Romantic (pictured) landscape, yet also dramatically downward on him from some bird's eye.

Yet this contrasting camera angle is then immediately 'explained' in wide-shot, as we see that Nye has dreamed the Boy on to a tree branch, so that it is the Boy's eye-line we share looking down at Nye, who in turn looks up with us at an angle from the front. The camera style thus adopts predominantly the classic naturalism of establishing shot followed by shot/reverse shot sequencing. So although the visual expressionism continues (especially in the lighting), it is dialogic debate and especially

Nye Bevan's *rhetorical* response to the Boy's accusation about him being a 'toff' which profiles this sequence as formally 'different' from Griffiths' earlier works like *All Good Men* (where similar debates about radical labour ideas and well-heeled Party leadership occur).

The Boy asks, 'How do you get to be a toff then?', and Nye responds by saying that's the Boy's 'truth' with which he wouldn't argue, and anyway it would take him too long to do so. The Boy then asks what he is reading, and Nye says it's Dylan Thomas, and they speak about Welsh poetry in English (Thomas) and Welsh (by the Boy's dad). Nye calls the Boy an 'old soul', they talk of evolution in nature and politics, and the Boy comes back, as is his wont, to ask, 'What is an old soul?' Nye replies, 'One who carries the past of the tribe in his being. Like a Revelation. Like an. Illumination. Arabs use it of their hakawati, story-tellers, poets of the people ... Old souls'. The link is clear with the 'old soul' Arab narrator in *The Gulf between Us*. Nye shuts his eyes, and the Boy asks if he will sleep. Nye shakes his head, opens his eyes on to a different cornfield-type landscape and begins himself to tell stories from the inside of his tribe.

The rhetorical signifier of this Nye Bevan as 'poet of the people' is his beginning each disparate 'tale' with the story-telling marker, 'Once ...' The Boy listens without speaking.

> 'Once, when I was young, your age, I carried a stool across a mountain. I'd written a poem, had it in my pocket. "Your eyes are green as valleys/ Your hair like corn gone wrong".'

> 'Once I was the youngest union deputy in all Wales. 19'. Then he was youngest councillor, youngest M.P., youngest Cabinet Minister – but now he's sixty and that 'may have to be enough.'

> 'Once I got drunk in the George with Dylan Thomas.'

> 'Once we had a check weighman who knew on sight the cutting signature of every face-man in the pit ... "Coal's not just bloody dug, he'd say, it's bloody well crafted".'

> 'Once I swam in Lord Beaverbrook's pool with young starlets, lunched on lobster and Bollinger in the Savoy, 'stuffed doctors' mouths with gold' for putting 'people's health before class poverty.'

> 'Once I set out to seek the source of power' – unions, council chambers, Party, Parliament, Cabinet rooms, and 'everywhere I came on that journey I found that power had just that morning moved on. Black taxi at dawn. No forwarding address.'

> 'Once I asked a simple question, "What do we put in place of fear?"'

Having spoken as *hakawati*, Nye can at last respond to the Boy's 'toff' question. 'If we let ourselves believe that reading and writing and painting and song and play and pleasuring and imagining, good food, good wine, good clothes, and good health are the toff's turf Boy, haven't we lost the battle already? They're our human birthright.'

The Boy says that he, too, can be a toff then, and Nye replies yes, as long as he remembers it all comes from the labour of a pick. Then he closes his eyes on to his one last 'Once ...' story, as the camera leaves the field to reflect tree-tops shimmering in a pool and then, to the word 'strangers', it images a reflection of the Boy in the pool. 'Once, your age, in dreams, I set out on these long walks on my own. And found myself in some future world, not yet my own. Walking. Weighing. Talking to strangers I felt I somehow knew. Searching for something. Never sure which.'

The Boy vanishes to a beat of wings, asking whether he's ever heard an 'old soul' with a stammer; and the camera tracks Nye walking painfully, bent with his stick through trees, cutting to a very distant, then closer long-shot of him alone in a farmed field. Over these shots, his voice-over bridges changes of camera shot and style:

> Between the seer and the seen, between subject and object, beyond reason and science lurks a mystery we call reality. Reason and science shows us the real in all its material unshiftability. But it's only language lets us grasp it not simply as something material to be endured but as something living to be worked. When all's said that can be, Bach, it's language not ripeness is all.

The camera focus is blurring in and out to the words 'unshiftability' and 'living to be worked' until the image fades into an extreme close-up of a record turning. And the image of the Columbia record now evokes a new camera style, of Hollywood silent movie melodrama of young love, a shepherdess on a plinth in a wild garden beckoning the Boy (as young Nye) to her in black and white. This bleeds slowly into partial colour (roses, arms, hair, faces) as they circle, dance and hug to a *La Traviata* aria, 'Di Provenza il mar', a song about home and memory, and a father's love for his son. Nye's voice is out of synch with the music, until the camera blurs out of that 'Hollywood' past and into the 'natural' country of the old 'father' Nye, bent, kneeling and exhausted in a country lane next to a graveyard. Now, again late – and again after a 'Once ...' story – the older Nye, in voice-over, answers the Boy's last question. 'Between the stammer and *le mot juste*, Bach, we learn to word the future.'

Dreams and memories are, as in *Country*, the key to both class nostalgia and future action. But whereas in *Country*, Griffiths tends to foreground a distancing 'alienation' technique via Virginia's camera, in *Food For Ravens* there is an almost vertiginous interplay between filmic styles, as between camera, sound, colour, lighting, dialogue and (different kinds of) performativity. This sequence is all about Nye Bevan as story-teller and Trevor Griffiths as film language-maker, stumbling between 'stammer' and '*le mot juste*' in learning to 'word the future'.

Yet this sequence also directly precedes the barn scene where Bevan delivers his speech of 'hate' against the ruling-class, and this is by way of a precise combination of *mot juste* and stutter, leading to a ruthlessly clear condemnation of the Tories who laugh at his performance. 'This infamous Bill, and all infamous Bills that will follow it as surely as death follows pestilence will eat like acid into the homes of the poor. In their small rooms and around their meagre tables, hells of personal acrimony and w- (stutters) w-wounded vanities will arise.'

As a Tory laughs at his prediction of the death of the working-class family as a result of this Means Test Bill, Bevan says that this Tory may well laugh since he is unaffected by such a Bill. 'He and his family have thriven on the proceeds of banditry for *centuries*'. Off-stage on this occasion – literally off-stage since in the expressionistically-lit barn scene the Tory lords are surrealistically represented by a ring of 'idle' hay bags – are the personae of *Country*, but their ironic laughter is heard; and, as in *Country*, it is the laughter of these lords that evokes the 'revenge' speeches of Virginia and Nye in both plays.

In contrast, then, to the distancing style of *Country*, it is important to recognise this dialogic 'poet of the people' attempt by Griffiths to achieve the 'inner dialogue, or interior life' of his class. Moving rapidly between Nye's personal sense of failure as socialist politician and the terminal breakdown of his body, it is these dialogues (with the Boy) as 'story-teller' which give *Food for Ravens* its particular power and form.

As a final example, we can 'read back' from the sequence I have been describing to an earlier sequence, beginning with the camera roaming Nye's bed, books, Party posters and other objects from a lifetime as his voice-over presents his controversial Party Conference speech where he describes the motion for unilateral nuclear disarmament as a 'spasm' rather than statesmanship. The Boy is trying to play the piano, and Nye takes over singing two very different songs, interspersed by the Boy asking him if he is a film star ('No ... just a celebrity ... Nine day wonder'), and if he is going to die. Nye's two sung 'poems of the people' are very different.

The first is a hymn, sung in fine tenor voice.

Thank God for coal, God bless the men
Who work in cheerless gloom.

And when their day of toil is done,
God bring them safely home.

The second is a more sombre and surreal tale, still linking though
with the 'black bodies' of miners.

Sudden trees, bear a strange fruit.
Blood on the leaves, blood at the root
Black bodies swing in the sun dreams.
Strange fruit hanging from the poplar trees.

Most of this is shot in harsh chiaroscuro close-up of Nye, head down
over the keyboard. But at the words 'black bodies', just as to the word
'strangers' in the later sequence, we see the same pool-inverted shot of
the Boy, but on this occasion black, among the trees. The sequence ends
with Nye's minder, Jack massaging his neck, while Nye tells him to 'Go
back to your life, while you still have it'.

Nye Bevan is dying, much too soon for his socialist cause, and he
knows it. The Boy is indeed the 'Angel of Death' Nye asks about in this
scene. But he is also both the future hope of the Party (as is the 'life'
of the younger Jack) and the 'black bodies' of the workers on which
both hope and oppression are still focused. As the pool-imaged reflection of the Boy shifts back and forward between darkly 'surreal' chiaroscuro and bright 'natural' daylight, so do the 'poems' of Nye Bevan. It
is the best he (and his author) can do to 'word the future' and bring the
workers 'safely home'.

Griffiths' television 'histories':
The Last Place on Earth and
Hope in the Year Two   6

When we come to Scott ... still taught in schools ... we are talking about a
piece of the country's history that has become mythologized into a time-
less presence ... The spirit of Scott is with us today. Palpable, breathing,
in the way that we perceive the world, the way we seek to change it or
retain it ... The central aim of the project as I perceived it...was the nature
and genesis of historical distortion. (Trevor Giffiths interviewed by Misha
Glenny, 1985)

Trevor Griffiths always engages with history, whether old or new, residual or emergent, via the contemporary. Thus *The Last Place on Earth*
was a comment on the late-imperialism of Thatcher's Falklands War
at the same time as a demystification of the early-century 'Scott of the
Antarctic' imperial myth (Tulloch 1990, chapter 5). And *Hope in the Year
Two* related to the recent fall of the Soviet Union, while seeking new
revolutionary potential in the old agencies of the French Revolution.

In each case, Griffiths was engaging with both personal and formal
possibilities at the moment of production: *The Last Place on Earth* as a
major mini-series on commercial television transmitted at peak viewing
time; *Hope in the Year Two* (1994), a two-hander, one-off play that marked
not only Griffiths' increasing political pessimism, but also his inability
(unlike in the 1970s and early 1980s) to get his works produced on television as a result of what he describes as the 'Kulturkampf' waged by
Thatcher. In the case of *Hope in the Year Two* the work did get produced,
but he was annoyed by cuts both to the script of the television play and
to the *Kaleidoscope* Radio 4 review of his later stage version of the work,
Who Shall Be Happy ...?

Both of these histories – of substantive theme (the era of Antarctic
exploration, the French Revolution), and of television access – were then
relevant to the dialogue of form and theory I described in Chapter 2, as
Griffiths wove within and between various radical-theoretical mentors
(Lukacs, Goldmann, Brecht, Benjamin) in constructing the generic-
formal markers of his television works. In this chapter I will analyse

The Last Place on Earth and *Hope in the Year Two* as overt histories (i.e. overtly set 'in the past') structured around the head-to-head 'collision' of two male characters, thus raising again questions that feminists have asked about gender and 'Trevor Griffiths' (Chapters 1, 2, 4).

The Last Place on Earth

Griffiths situated his Scott/Amundsen mini-series in terms of the two rival state nationalisms of Britain and Norway at the beginning of the twentieth century. In the case of Scott, a declining but still rampant British imperialist power, a class-based/ career nexus which drove Scott to seek Navy preferment via Polar exploration after he failed as a battleship captain, an hegemonic ideology of ruling-class 'amateurism' and Romantic manhood (drawing on nearly a century of Romantic images of males pitting themselves against nature), and the particular gender-personality of Robert Falcon Scott himself generated the continuous series of mistakes that led the expedition to disaster and its leader to his death (Tulloch 1990, chapter5).

In the case of Amundsen, a 'new nation' public relations profiling of Norway for its sporting and exploration success, and a competitive professionalism within this profile which on one hand looked to understand local conditions and cultures (Amundsen, for example, learned much from Eskimos about extreme cold and ice conditions before attempting his journey to the South Pole), and on the other hand established a comradeship between skilled professionals (whether world ski champion or local carpenter) in the Norwegian team, led to them 'taking the Pole'.

Yet, in Griffiths' original screenplay, these different national identities are *both* underpinned by one dominant economic force. In Norway, Amundsen's change of plans, to go south after the North Pole is 'taken' by someone else, is connected with 'the press barons and the industrialists and the politicians' who 'want a coup' before they will fund his serious explorations in the north. 'So we'll give them one ... We ... take the South Pole' (Griffiths 1986, 64–5). In Britain, Scott's supposed interest in scientific exploration is given economic underpinning as he tells financing Liverpool manufacturers 'of precious industrial ore discoveries (pitchblend for radium) that would restore British industrial pre-eminence' (Griffiths 1986, 68). And in both countries, money is being found for polar expeditions while 'there are people dying of cold and hunger in our capital city ...Thousands living in squalid and miserable shacks and we say there is nothing we can do to help. Sick people waiting for medical care, the needs of the old and the impaired ignored' (Griffiths 1986, 59). In Manchester's Free Trade Hall where Scott addresses the capitalists, *'a large picket of militant trade unionists blocks the exit. Banners proclaim their cause: Jobs not Glory. Why go to the South Pole, there's a wasteland on your doorstep called Lancashire. Not a Penny for the Pole; Send an expedition to Manchester and discover Poverty'* (Griffiths 1986, 68)

Within the format of a popular action-drama mini-series which has time to pause and linger in building up the characterisation of the large team of men (and their partners), as well as that of the donor-capitalists who fund and support their work, Griffiths adopts the Lukacian device (Chapter 2) of Scott and Amundsen as world-historical individuals, the 'whole idea of a character working as a confluence of important social and political and moral forces within society, in real historical time' (Griffiths 1982, 39). Thus the television drama mini-series amalgam-ates Lukacs' notion of 'the social collision [of Scott and Amundsen], as the centre of drama' (Lukacs 1969, 119), with the mini-series' potential to amass detail conveying something too of Lukacs' notion of the novelistic 'totality of objects' where human actions, ambition, pain and greed are embedded in daily routines and rituals.

Amidst the balls, official dinners, daily politics, family quarrels, births and love affairs in Britain and Norway, and the daily jokes, competitive-ness, bitching, bathhouses, football, painting and letter-writing of the men in Antarctica, this formal mini-series mix of 'totality of objects' and 'totality of collision' between world-historical types led, in the produc-tion of *The Last Place on Earth* to a 'flatness' of performance by Martin Shaw as Scott and of Sverre Anker Ousdal as Amundsen, whereby Scott is something of a loser, whinging about the bad weather and his men's failings in his Antarctic tent, while predictably authoritarian in interper-sonal relations as the 'owner' of his expeditionary team, an 'essentially little man' (Griffiths 1991) bolstered up and driven on by the towering personality of Kathleen Scott and the imperial legacy of British ruling-class 'manhood'. At the same time, Amundsen, deprived in the trans-mitted television text of the dream sequences Griffiths wrote for him, becomes more visual Viking (Griffiths' description of the first view the British Expeditionary Force have of him) than conveyor of the mix of intimacy and leadership required of a comrade who is also a leader.

Some of this adheres to the specifics of acting interpretation: Martin Shaw, who became close to the Scott family, clearly reworked Scott's characterisation by Griffiths (Tulloch 1990, 138), while Ousdal's struggle with his English perhaps led to a similar lack of nuance in performance that Romy Clark describes of Drittermann's father in *Fatherland*. But some of it is the result of the Lukacian typicality concept, where Scott and Amundsen 'represent' grand historical forces which tend to get played out and nuanced in *other* characters and images that surround them. The mini-series' tendency to cumulative multi-narrative story-lines (Creeber 2001, 36) encouraged this kind of characterisation, as did Griffiths' long-term commitment to de-centre familiarised characters (as in *Sons and Lovers* and *The Cherry Orchard*) to foreground other subjectivities.

This is particularly the case with Susan Wooldridge's portrayal of Kathleen Scott. What interested Griffiths was less the revelation by Roland Huntford's book *Scott and Amundsen* (which he reworked for his screenplay, see Tulloch 1990, chapter 5) of a supposed affair between Kathleen Scott and the greatest Norwegian explorer, Nansen, while Scott was away at the Pole. Certainly, Griffiths' screenplay, *Judgment over the Dead* contained this affair, as another example of the mobilisation of gender within international power politics (Nansen was Norwegian Ambassador to Britain at the time). But much more interesting in Griffiths' construction of Kathleen Scott is the representation of a powerful female identity which, at the same time, is culturally and historically situated, rather than stereotyped psychologically.

Kathleen Scott (née Bruce), an artist 'vagabond' embedded in the aesthetic and literary community of Beardsley, Beerbohm, Thesiger, J.M. Barrie, Henry James and her friend Isadora Duncan, dominates Scott visually, sexually and politically from the moment we first see her staring down at him from a staircase at Mabel Beardsley's salon. In their first scene together, she also dominates visually, initially shot as in a picture frame, legs spread apart, calves 'generously revealed', and allowing him to take her home rather than going to a pre-arranged supper party. Once at her apartment, Kathleen quickly rejects his caution to protect her reputation by not entering her rooms. 'Captain, I lived in Paris for five years as a student. I have fended for myself since the age of seventeen, and am *absolutely* my own woman. I would *like* you to see my room.' When Scott responds that she is an 'extraordinary woman', Kathleen replies, 'Because I know my own mind? If I were a man I would be very ordinary indeed.'

Positioned above Scott, her face highlighted within a sombre black/white studio *mise-en-scène*, Kathleen pronounces with near-mystical artistic reverence, 'Will you get there Captain, the Pole? You will. I knew it the first time we met'. There are intimations here of Futurism's contemporary celebration of the power and destiny of male polar explorers. When Scott responds by talking about the financial difficulties of organising an expedition, she says, 'It's not details I talk, it's destiny', and she then physically descends to his level in intimate two-shot to take the lead sexually. 'I don't believe sleeping together would be a particularly good idea. Myself, I am reluctant to risk more complications in an already complicated life' (we see her later make meaningful eye contact with Shackleton, and may remember her earlier line to Scott that she meets so many great and famous explorers that she has difficulty in telling them apart). Having taken the lead in determining their initial degree of intimacy, Kathleen now kneels before Scott to announce, 'I love your *modesty* – it's so English, you're like a foreigner', thus allowing the camera to elevate Scott as we look up at him, but *only* from her own positioning eye-line.

Soon after, meeting Scott's sister at his mother's house, Kathleen responds to Grace's awkward demand that she should continue to respect the close bond between Scott and his mother, with 'I'm not even sure I can cope with being his wife. I certainly have no desire to become his *mother*'. In the next scene with Scott, we watch her swimming naked in the sea from Scott's position on the cliff, and then she 'endows' him with her body. They have made love for the first time the previous night, and the implication is that his virility has deserted him. Despite Kathleen's words that she is not judging him in competition, Scott asks her desperately to 'Teach me to be like you. Free, bold, your own self ... I have never found the world trustworthy. To me it has always been implacable, hostile, against me at every step. Life drives me ahead of itself. I have no say in the matter.' Railing bitterly against his humiliation by the Navy in being sacked for incompetence as a captain, and angry over Shackleton's greater public visibility as an explorer, Scott says that now he has her he may retire and write books. Kathleen's response is to expose her leg for him to kiss, and then to his timorous request as to how he can keep her, she tells him from her dominating physical position,

> I want your son. Nothing else will make me happy. Nothing. Oh Con, my destiny, I've known it since the age of fifteen, is to bear a special son to a special father, just as yours is to prove itself to a hostile world, a man above other men ... It means shaking off all this talk of writing books and retiring and leaving the field open .... I chose you because you have greatness in you and I want some of it in me.

But this is no 'mere wife' role either. When Mrs Evans says she does not actually want her husband going on another risky expedition but that she has come to endure it, Kathleen says, 'The only thing that makes me unhappy Mrs Evans is that I'm not allowed to go with them. Nothing in a woman's life can ever compensate for not being born a man. Men do, women don't. And I should despise myself if I learnt to bear it.' Checking the provisions on the ship and ordering P.O. Evans about before the departure, she responds to 'Birdie' Bowers' comment that he wished she were going with them: 'I'm not allowed to. I'd go on this thing any day. Travelling with the wives isn't my cup of tea, I'm afraid.' And when she takes the advance mail packet to Australia (to avoid 'the wives') and boards Scott's boat there, Bowers' comment 'It's The Captain's lady' is capped by Oates' 'More like the Lady Captain'.

Earlier, in Switzerland, and beginning to establish a friendly relationship with Nansen, Kathleen is impressed with the Norwegian's deliberate set-up of an incident where one of his skiers offers to get Scott a spare part for his (already) broken-down Polar tractor. Kathleen dominates Scott into agreeing to send the skier for the part, and as he leaves Griffiths' script has 'Nansen seek Kathleen's eyes: a covert understanding between them, across Scott's blank stare after the disappearing Gran' (Griffiths 1986, 86). On Gran's return with the part, Kathleen then colludes pleasurably ('*Finding his eyes; Intimate*') with Nansen in persuading Scott that it is now his own idea to add the young man as a ski-instructor for the Polar expedition.

When we see Kathleen going through painful labour pains, she leaves the nurse helpless as she growls and scrambles around the bed in agony, but willing her son out, forcing her abdomen down via the bed frame. Soon after, as she tells Scott that they will name the baby Peter Markham Scott to bind the great and famous to them with 'hoops of steel' (Lord Markham is their major sponsor), she sees Scott holding the baby with tears in his eyes. We may be reminded of this at a later scene in New Zealand, when Scott apologises over his anger with her after Evans' wife has run hysterically from her during Scott's press conference. Kathleen tells Scott in reply that she will not be there to see them leave for Antarctica the next morning. 'I don't want the men to see their leader upset. Leaders must be above such things.' She looks long at Scott and drops her eyes. Earlier she had told Scott that she would confine her looks to him alone as long as he was going forward. She already has Nansen's private address at the time that Scott receives Amundsen's ominous telegramme, 'Going south'. Her affair with the greatest explorer of the era, Nansen, is not far off.

Scott leaves on his quest for the Pole, and succumbs to becoming the embittered, 'essentially little man' which is Griffiths' description of him. This is the leader, who as Meers the huskie handler bitterly complains, 'sits in his tent in Antarctica and whines about the weather'. Antarctica dwarfs this man and his 'heroic' British team, but it is also a tabula rasa in its implacable whiteness representing yet one more space where Scott, as lower-upper-class British male, aspires to elite status. Antarctica is in this sense simply an extension of the British socio-economic system, driving Scott beyond himself. Britain/Antarctica is the historical-spatial 'structure' that determines 'Scott of the Antarctic', and *Kathleen* is his personal 'agency'. But both agent and structure, working together, belittle and destroy Scott. This is his (Lukacian) typicality.

As Scott and his party struggle to the Pole to find that Amundsen has been there already, Griffiths' screenplay (but not the television mini-series) has one last scene between Nansen and Kathleen Scott. It is in a hotel room in Berlin. Nansen is telling of his dream in which Kathleen Scott in Antarctica, 'strong and bold and full of the future', speaks to Nansen in his coffin.

> Nansen: 'You said: Each age is a dream that is dying. Or one that is coming to birth.'
>
> Woman: (OOS) 'See, Fridtjof.'
>
> Nansen turns slowly. In the shadow, his eyes gleam, burn. Kathleen Scott stands naked in the bathroom doorway, lit from behind. They stare at each other across the dark room.
>
> Kathleen (low, intense) 'Tonight you must talk of life, Fridtjof. No dreams of dying.'
>
> Slow mix begins as he crosses the large room to lift her into his arms and carry her to the bed (Griffiths 1986, 249)

Act II, 'A Dream That is Dying', is prefaced by the Shaughnessy lines, 'Each age is a dream that is dying. Or one that is coming to birth'. There it is linked, via the narrative of Act I, to the 'old' British imperial dream and the 'new' Norwegian enterprise. But the opening shots of Act II are of Kathleen's determined birth scene, so that the dream 'that is coming to birth' is linked directly with her, as it is in Nansen's dream later.

So, at the same time that Griffiths' Lukacian 'typicality' makes of Scott a reactive role, this approach to the mini-series drama generates the potential for nuances and performative variation: as in the historically and personally specific representation of women's liberation in Kathleen Scott. Rather than a 'liberated' stereotype, Kathleen is positioned in her artistic milieu and her historical time, at best appropriating greatness through her painting and then through her sexual control of men. Scott, Shackleton (we may assume) and Nansen also (as an explorer on the point of retiring) will all fail this 'remarkable woman', so that, subtextually, it is not male heroes at all who triumph (there are a number of allusions to Amundsen's sexual impotence also). In Griffiths' text, it is the dream of a 'new woman', Kathleen Scott which is born and Scott's which dies.

However, the commercial claims of the mini-series worked against Griffiths' intent.

> Since ... TV drama series are implacably about narrative, about action, about carrying the story on, a lot of the stuff that I wrote e.g. the dream sequences, the social and historical context of imperial Britain at the beginning of [the twentieth] century, certain relationships within the text, Kathleen Scott and Nansen, for example, these things tended to represent areas of provocation and danger, or areas of massive resource use, expenditure. They disappeared without trace. (Griffiths, cited in Tulloch 1990, 129)

The failure of this series to take up key areas of his script for the 'more complex ideas and stylistic innovation' (Creeber 2001, 38) that authored mini-series can offer was a disappointment to Griffiths. On the other hand, much of his Brechtian challenge to the naturalistic *facticity* of conventional television histories via the series' reflexive narrativisation of British imperial myths did go to air (Tulloch 1990, chapter 3), focusing on the active construction of heroic 'myths of dying' via Scott's diaries, and later on their editing and censoring as his published journal of the expedition.

'Hope in the Year Two'

There are no main women characters in *Hope in the Year Two*. When women appear at all, it is as part of flashback, memory or dream sequence, as in the case of Danton's second wife, Louise.

Danton is living his last night before execution on 16 Germinal in Year Two of the Free Republic. He is incarcerated in a cage within a grand, decaying and locked room at the Luxembourg Palace, his only companion a young guard, Henry, whom he tries to convince that he is not the true Danton but an impersonator also imprisoned in the Palace to confuse would-be rescuers (Griffiths prefers to leave his status as Danton open, calling him only the Prisoner). While Henry is absent (Danton has tried to persuade him to send a message out to his followers in the guise of a letter to his wife), he picks the lock of his cage with part of the razor, and slips out. He says, 'One road to freedom opened.'

Jack Shepherd as Danton now stands in front of a severely cracked mirror, which fragments his image into several parts. He adds, 'And here's another [road to freedom]' as he opens the razor, pauses it next to his throat and then opens a superficial cut across it. There follows a complex sequence of images and sound – and several different Danton voices.

Sound/image: thunder/whiteness flashing like 'sheet' lightning.

Danton 2 (voice-over): 'April.'

Image: Tree branches from below, a few dark leaves.

Danton 1 (the prisoner with razor, laboriously, puzzling): 'Who shall ...?'

Danton 2: 'How will I tell them?'

Danton 1: 'Be happy?'

Danton 2: 'Seed time.'

Image: Rain on water.

Danton: 1 Who ... shall ... be ... ?

Image: Young red-headed woman walking in spring daylight, left to right.

Danton 2: 'Ah! Yes, yes. Girl'.

Danton 1: 'Happy, if...if...if ...Who shall...be happy if...?

Danton 2: 'Yes, yes, my girl bride.'

Image: Young woman turns slowly to stare into the camera.

Danton 1: 'Who shall be happy if what? If what?

Young woman: 'Wet.'

Danton 3 (as lover): 'Yet.'

Image: Lovemaking, woman beneath looking up, and at him, eyes closing, enjoying.

Young woman: 'Again.'

Danton 3: 'When?'

Young woman: 'Now.'

Danton 2: 'Kissing a son on the mouth, knowing my mother eats. Horse sweat. Cheesecake and cider at the Procope. Wood-smoke. Swimming in the Seine. My new bride's sweet cunny in my nostrils, all day long. Frost. Men's laughter.'

Danton 1: 'Who?'

Danton 4 (as orator, dressed officially, with busts behind): 'The future lies in an alley, its throat's slit.'

Danton 1: 'Shall ...?'

Danton 4: 'Even as we've been new-minting the coins of hope.'

Danton 1: 'Be ...?'

Danton 4: 'We've been yet busier re-issuing the banknotes of despair.'

Danton 1: 'Happy ...?'

Danton 4: 'Twin legacies bequeathed to all who come after.'

Danton 1: 'Happy what? Who shall be happy what? Happy what?'

Image: Robespierre (played by Jack Shepherd).

Danton 1: (in Luxembourg room, holding his razor-nicked neck): 'Ah, Robespierre! What will you miss when your turn comes? The Committee? Podium? The Terror? The Instruments of Rule? How sad to leave this earth so ... untouched by it. How sad the man who's never embraced commonness, never dared to be ordinary.'

Image: Danton 1 jigging to a revolutionary song, 'Ça ira', prodding at Henry's cards laid on a table with his open razor. Singing:

'A hero is honoured no longer
Than it pays to have him about
We reap the fruits of his labour
And then we sling him out
This may not seem fair play
But it is the people's way
In a Re Re Re
In a pub pub pub
In a Re-a pub-a Republic.'

Danton 1: 'The song that toppled a King. August '92. The Champ de Mars again. This time we meant business. This time we would re-make the world. Re-invent it. Year 1 of the new Republic. There was even a play.'

And Danton 1 describes how this play was planned for presentation at the next Festival of the Nation. But that it was never performed, probably because it was called Danton saves France.

Danton 1: 'Never mind, there'll be others'.

There are several ways of approaching this sequence.

    1. *Intertextually*, we could read this sequence via the sex scene (also out in the open) between Scott and Kathleen in *The Last Place on Earth*. In both (in Griffiths' screenplays) young women first swim naked, before (in *Hope in the Year Two*) '*a shadow falls across his face. His point of view: directly above him, naked, glistening, his new wife LOUISE, almost sixteen, the pool beyond. The blocked sun silvers her outline, blackens the rest: unreal*'. In *The Last Place on Earth*, Scott is also lying down as, the naked '*Kathleen stands over him, the blood-orange sun at her back. He sees her dark shimmering mass as in a vision*'.

    In the multi-narrative mini-series *The Last Place on Earth*, the sexual scene is part of at least two trajectories. One is Griffiths' anti-imperialist narrative as he deconstructs the chauvinist 'Scott of the Antarctic' mythology. A second is the slow build-up of the mini-series narrative as Kathleen Scott sets the conditions of her husband's 'greatness' and of her sexual loyalty to him. As the series continues, and the episodes unfold, Kathleen's eyes and glance will tell us that her conditions are not being met, presaging her move to her next 'great explorer'. It is this conjuncture of narratives (historical and generic) which gives a space in the text for Kathleen as 'strong woman', contextualised through her art, her 'free' sexuality and her feminism. But even in the outdoor sex scene, Kathleen, dominant, *'kisses his brow, a mother with her child'*, before initiating the sex *'gently, then more sensually'* in order to bear the 'special son of a special father' (in Griffiths' screenplay the scene ends with Kathleen telling Scott to take note of her 'most fertile days' to 'help me achieve *my* end').

In *Hope in the Year Two*, unlike Kathleen, Danton's partner Louise is silent apart from those few words, 'Wet', 'Again', 'Now'. But they are words of ordinary sensuality and time – of now and the close future. As such, as well as being part of the pleasures of the ordinary which is one meaning of this play, they are words that are spoken out to the future audience that is reflexively inscribed in Griffiths' text.

As we have seen, there is some similarity between the scenes in *Last Place on Earth* and Griffiths' screenplay for *Hope in the Year Two* (which was cut in the television play). But in *Hope* Kathleen's 'Art' embodiment (as in performing the naked 'Isadora Duncan') is replaced by the *everyday* pleasures of sexual intimacy, as Griffiths writes (also cut) the lines: '*She gestures him to feel. His hand moves gently up between her spread thighs. The fingers reach her, slowly sink into the black ... She moans, moves on her heels. He sits up to lay his face at her lower belly. Her hands draw him in.*'

2. *Narratively*, the sequence is introduced by a shot of Robespierre (again played by Jack Shepherd, thus increasing the fragmentation of Danton's identity that is central to the scene). Robespierre compares modest virtues with excessive vices. 'Vices are surrounded by riches, carouse in the arms of pleasure and debauch in the halls of perfidy'. We may see in this the sexual excess of Danton, and yet Robespierre also writes to Danton in sorrow, empathy and 'love ... better than ever; and till death' after Danton's first wife Gabrielle has died in childbirth. As Danton later admits, he stayed in Belgium for politics and whores when he knew Gabrielle was about to give birth, knowing that she might die of it. Thus his talk now of digging up and hugging her corpse is complicit with Robespierre's death-charge of 'excess'.

Yet Danton's excess also includes the sexual companionship with Louise that we see him enjoying, and which he says that Robespierre in his 'virtuous cot' will never encounter. Robespierre's 'moderation' (which Danton likens to chastity) includes the political rationalism of a revolutionary leader that has no time for the everyday pleasures of wood-smoke, cheesecake and cider, men's laughter, or outdoor sex.

Near the end of the sequence, Danton walks to the locked prison door and, urinating against it, says, 'Historians of a sentimental cast may want to read this as the deep desire in all of us to say "Hello, well met" to those we cannot otherwise touch. The rest of you [as he looks directly into camera] will know better.' 'Historians' might interpret Danton pissing against the door behind which he can see his sleeping guards as a 'two fingers to fate' response. The 'rest of you' (as audience) are encouraged by the earlier narrative of sensuous pleasures to understand his pissing as another of the 'embracing commonness' things that Danton enjoys, but Robespierre cannot.

Yet, as he walks away from his pissing and his gaolers, Danton says 'The letter is already history', indicating that *his* history (via his attempted ruse with Henry) is probably also almost over. The sequence closes with Danton, having locked himself back into his cage, staring straight into camera: 'It's not escape I seek, it's rescue. It's not life I ask, it's meaning.' But if Danton's life history is almost over, and neither 'excess' nor 'moderation' in life and politics is sufficient, where is meaning to be found among this post-modern fragmentation of Dantons? We should remember the insistent, hesitant refrain throughout the sequence (and the play), 'Who shall be happy if ...?

3. *Theoretically*, the play is, as Garner notes constructed across a multiplicity of Dantons. 'Rather than select a single Danton from the divergent historical accounts, Griffiths makes this undecidability the cornerstone of his dramatic representation. Coherence and consistence are rather the domain of Robespierre – "a system on legs" (in Danton's words) who "has outlawed doubt. Doubleness. / All blur, haze and hover" ... With Danton, Griffiths marshals the results of his own research to maintain a multiple, contradictory characteridation. "The whole piece is about the nature of identity", [Griffiths] notes. "What I found was that there were as many as six Dantons"' (Garner 1995, 337).

As Garner says, this undecidability is not only conveyed by narrative theme (the 'real' and 'imposter' Dantons) and by casting (Jack Shepherd is a slight man, not the big man everybody 'knows' Danton to have been). Undecidability is also conveyed intertextually by Griffiths' conscious engagement with many other literary and dramatic Dantons (for example, as constructed by Buchner, Weiss and Wajda). In particular Griffiths was engaging with Buchner's *Danton's Death* as 'deeply wrong because it's hugely romantic' (cited in Garner 1995, 335).

As Danton 1 says in this sequence, 'Never mind' that *Danton Saves France* was not produced, 'there'll be others' – and there are many others in Griffiths' play alone. The emphasis here, and throughout the play, is thus on *performativity* (of the post-modern) rather than the linear, modernist 'scientific' drive of exploration (and modernity) that we see structuring *The Last Place on Earth*.

4. *Formally*, the breaking of the narrative characterisation of Danton into multiple parts in this short television play foregrounds a performativity inhering both in 'great leaders' (in contrast to the 'flatness' of both Scott and Amundsen in *The Last Place On Earth*) and in the writing of plays. Janelle Reinelt has argued for a post-Brechtian (and post-Lukacian) aspect to Griffiths' later work, which is undeniable. There is a strong sense, too, of Goldmann's emphasis on formal innovation beyond Lukac's 'realism', conveyed via a 'homology of structures' between time then (the Enlightenment Revolution) and the post-modern fragmentation of world order. But whereas in plays like *The Cherry Orchard* Griffiths limited himself to an 'alienating' Act II which (in his screenplay at least) challenged the 'big house naturalism' of the other Acts, and whereas in *The Last Place on Earth*, the Brechtian *use* of histories (in contrast to the Lukacian *reflection* of history via his concept of world historical individuals) is mainly confined to section titles and the juxtaposition of 'great' British failures (Scott and Gallipoli in a film-insert sequence that was omitted in production), *Hope in the Year Two* is far more thoroughly Brechtian in its continuing reference to the theatricality and performativity of the play.

In particular, this is conveyed via the raising of theatre safety curtains, by the multiple personae and performativity of Danton, and by the reflexivity of direct audience address. After staring into the camera to say 'It's not life I ask. It's meaning', Danton again discovers the audience as he conducts his final ablutions on the morning of the execution. This audience might be perceived to be voyeuristically contemplating the half-naked man, until Danton catches them at it. 'Still there? Aye, I see ye. Little white faces in the dark. The future we are hatching here'. As Garner says, 'Danton's introspective monologue is conducted as a form of address to this invisible audience, a technique underscored by the character's frequent direct stare at the camera lens ("Still there?"). Historical subject confronts the future's historical regard in an exchange of gazes, and history becomes the site of doubled interpretive scrutiny' (Garner 1995, 336).

But this is not a happy encounter. As Danton says to his future audience,

> 'Looking back's all that's left ye, you spent what was left of the future long since, you have nowhere else to look save back, do ye, poor sods ...'
> (Looks at lens, smiles).

5. *Ideologically*, this play (and the sequence I have looked at – 'the letter's history') is taken by some to be the most pessimistic of Griffiths' works. With the fall of the 'Socialist' world to contemplate, and after a decade of Thatcherism in Britain, the play, says Garner, is 'easily Griffiths' darkest work, charged with disillusionment and agonised self-questioning. Griffiths himself has described the play's composition as "a terminally bleak experience. I went into a space inside me I shan't return to in a hurry. I might not come out next time".' Garner adds, 'In its spareness and brooding retrospect, its stretches of monologue taped and spoken, Griffiths' portrayal of Danton's final hours has, at moments, an almost Beckettian feel' (Garner 1995, 335).

Yet Griffiths has always rejected the sense of the 'terminal' in Beckett, and Garner himself notes that not only was Griffiths not upset by the fall of the Soviet Union, but as opening out new revolutionary horizons. Garner quotes Griffiths: 'What it actually means is that the full agenda of the French Revolution has now resurfaced. The Russian Revolution was meant to transcend it, which it singularly failed to do. And now those three elements [liberty, equality, and fraternity] are back at the forefront' (cited in Garner 1995, 334).

Griffiths was inevitably depressed by the military imperialism of the 'New World Order' (headed by Bush, father and son), and he had already produced a play, *The Gulf between Us* (1992) which, like the 'Poles Apart' titling of episode I of *The Last Place on Earth*, indicated the gap between 'old' historical cultures (in this case Iraqi) and the 'new' (U.S./British) military-imperialist cultures.

This depression clearly informs Danton's words to the 'poor sods', his future audience. But we should not forget the insistent, slow, obdurate, puzzled build-up of the question-refrain of *Hope in the Year Two*: 'Who shall be happy if not everyone?' It is in that slow-witted refusal to give up that Danton – performative, excessive, quick and witty in every other aspect – merges identity with his young gaoler, Henry. Whereas in *The Last Place on Earth* we are confronted with two 'world-historical' leaders, and at least one is found wanting, in *Hope* there is ostensibly only one leader, though Danton also doubles as Robespierre and Marat, and is splintered into many parts himself. But *his* competitor is not the 'Viking' Amundsen.

There is no 'Pole' to gain. There is only survival (set against the 'performance' of leadership), and the small, everyday pleasures that survival may still allow. As part of his trick to get a message out, Danton advises Henry to roll the letter down his musket barrel to pass the thirteen check-points at the Luxembourg Palace, and when the younger man asks what he will do if they want to check his musket too, Danton quick-wittedly says he should 'accidently' fire it to destroy the evidence. Quick wit, rhetoric, performativity, 'leadership' are all part of Danton's style, and his gaoler frequently asks him to perform for him.

But *survival* is one man's alone – and this man, Henry, as Danton himself says, 'is but the first fruiting. The new citizen, the new man'. Having progressively stripped Danton of his money, his watch and his best clothes as a bribe to get the letter out of the prison, we see Henry return to the Luxembourg room after Danton has been taken to his execution. Henry sits with some pleasure to light his pipe, and to do so he extracts the letter, which has in fact never left the muzzle of his gun, and lights it. Thus he does destroy the evidence, but for the purpose of simple pleasures.

His lit pipe is one of the 'ordinary' pleasures – of horse sweat, wood smoke, swimming in the Seine, frost, men's laughter, sex – that Danton counters to Robespierre's ruthless revolutionary 'system on legs'. But it is the young gaoler who has 'embraced commonness' and 'dared to be ordinary', having little other choice. He too enjoys performance – he likes telling 'funny' stories and admires another working man's impromptu dramatic impressions of 'great men' (including Danton, which made him wise to whom he in fact had in his cage). But Henry cannot perform well or for long. He just *endures* – like Blackie's glass of beer in toast to the empty table, 'a hard little smile on his face', in Griffiths' *Country* script.

Undoubtedly there is pessimism in *Hope in the Year Two*. Near the end, Danton addresses his watching audience directly.

You are in my hands. Here, now. I feel you. We are the same flesh. Composed of the same atoms. Everything we have thought, everything we have tried or imagined, everything dreamt and whispered, designed, done ... you will develop and perfect. Such a dish of worms we've served ye and ye'll eat 'em, every one. The free dance of capital, the human imperative. The sovereign people, the all-seeing, all-saying state. Owner, worker. Nation and war, people and peace. The power of the machine, the machinery of power. Me, all. The impossible and the necessary dream. The road to freedom, mined every step of the way. (Griffiths 1994, 33)

Yet even here there is a 'road to freedom', and despite his bleak view of it, Garner does in fact recognise Griffiths' residual optimism in the play. One meaning that Danton is seeking is completely dystopic. As he says, 'You have filled me with such fear for the future ... How will I tell you, as I scan your tiny faces in the gloom, you are yourselves already dead, immured inside the dungeon walls of cant and lies and language this revolution has all the while and under our noses been a-building?'. But there *is* another meaning, as Garner says. This lies in the 'the love and natural sensuality between Danton and his second wife ...; the interactions between Danton and Henry and their guarded, failed search for trust; the recollection of life's ordinary pleasures ... 'Who shall be happy, if not everyone?' Hope and a question – they may not seem much against the failure of revolutions then and now. But in the apparent setback of the socialist project in Year Two (and on the eve of the year 2000), they stand, for Griffiths, as seeds in time, the opportunity for new beginnings that history – across the space of mutual scrutiny – offers the present' (Garner 1995, 340).

As Danton says to his watching future-audience, 'Like me tonight, you cannot live but in hope. Liberty may wither, Fraternity evaporate, Equality rot on the vine, Hope's a survivor, and will not die'. But in quoting this, Garner does not recognise enough the importance of Henry, the gaoler. He emphasises Danton's and Henry's 'guarded, failed search for trust' as one of the grounds for reclamation of the Revolution's 'transformative project'. But there *could* be no trust between the leader-performer and his gaoler-citizen. Danton's lived-life as leader, before and during the revolution, had – as he emphasises in the play – been at the expense and death of thousands of Henrys. And Henry betrays him over the letter in return. As Danton's song says, 'It is the people's way' to throw out old heroes. Hope in the transformative project cannot be in *their* mutuality because they share an exploitative history, and nor can there be any singular and authoritative trust in a post-modern society of multiple identities and performativity.

The only trust to be shared in this play is between past revolutionary principles and future audiences, and it resides in the residual nature of hope, when all principles and promises have been betrayed, again and yet again. As Danton says early in the play, 'I play this game for hope; without it, what are we if not already dead?'

If we read *Hope in the Year Two* intertextually, by way of *The Last Place on Earth*, we can see that Henry is, after all, that other 'leader'. But he is a leader only in the sense that – and reading *Hope* intertextually this time via Griffiths' 1990 play, *Piano* – ordinary people take the lead in refusing their consent to fatalism and exploitation. Quoting the peasant Radish's lines in *Piano*, Reinelt says:

'Grass dies. Iron rusts. Lies eat the soul ... Everything's possible.' This odd little epigram is the central core of the play. In fact, things change; those who are exploiters are truly eaten by their own sins; someone may come after. It is in some ways a perverse message of hope to those of us who live through postmodern times in a state of nausea and confusion, pointing to historical process as a hopeful attitude to life (Reinelt, 163, 164).

If that sounds somewhat 'Chekhovian', it is a Chekhov who has been a Trevor Griffiths project too. In his version of *The Cherry Orchard*, Griffiths found in the vagrant a representative (already in 1977, prior to the collapse of the Soviet Union) of the enlightenment project released by the liberty, fraternity and equality of the French Revolution. But in *The Cherry Orchard*, the vagrant is a brief if 'massive disruption', at the end of Act II. The future is thematically *secured* through the 'world-historical individuals', Lopakhin and Trofimov. By the time of *Hope in the Year Two*, the world historical types of *The Cherry Orchard* and *The Last Place on Earth* have stepped from the stage, replaced by the performative, multi-identitied 'leader' (Danton) and the minimal-identitied 'citizen' Henry. In an important sense it is that play between the performative post-modern of fracture (Danton 1's mirror) and the residual 'real' of the ordinary-everyday which marks the continuing optimism of *Hope*.

In an interview about *Who Shall Be Happy?* (the stage version of *Hope in the Year Two*), Griffiths acknowledges his debt to Chekhov in the play, via his own *Piano*. 'The great work that Chekhov did wasn't, I think, in theatre. His great work was this body of stories that he wrote, especially the stories about peasant men and women which are absolutely fucking extraordinary'. *Piano*'s Radish with his 'Grass dies. Iron rusts. Lies eat the soul. Everything's possible' is, Griffiths says, 'a character born from a short story, though not the central character. He's really bottomed, if you know what I mean. Chekhov knew what he was talking about' (1996, 11).

Henry in *Hope*, like Radish in *Piano*, is a 'bottomed' out anti-leader-as-citizen. As in Griffiths' text for *The Last Place on Earth*, old heroes (Shackleton, Scott, Nansen, Danton) are 'thrown out'. But whereas in the mini-series the forceful winner is the 'new woman', here the resilient winner is the 'new citizen'. It is in that quiet pipe which Henry smokes at the end of the play, all performance over, all tricks converted, that hope for the future resides.

Garner is right to note that in its combining a very cinematic, roving, active camera and a reflexively signified stage setting, *Hope* indicates Griffiths' 'deepening interest in the relationships between cinematic and theatrical techniques and between film and the cinema as representational mediums' (Garner 1995, 338). Yet Garner's conclusion, that Griffiths in *Hope* has a 'more fundamental conception of the play or film as an act of production, a specifically *made* object of cultural intervention' (1995, 338) is wrong. Griffiths has always had this understanding of 'writing fictions' (Tulloch 1990, chapter6). Two comments Griffiths made about *The Last Place on Earth* are revealing in this respect.

For too long, any view of Amundsen and the Norwegians was one of banal professional hacks. Spoilsports, liars, cheats, freebooters. Nothing could be further from the truth. These people believed in doing things well, and not losing their minds in vainglorious, rhetorical gestures ... The way they turned back, for instance, was a democratically arrived at decision because they had started too early, because it was too cold, and because it was no fun anymore. Compare that with the absolutely autocratic power wielded by ... Scott. (cited in Tulloch 1990, 101–2)

Professionalism here means the openness of Amundsen and his comrades to the environment and to the everyday knowledge of simple people – which is why Griffiths has Amundsen sitting with Eskimos in his very first scene 'learning to live the life of the people in ice and snow' (Griffiths, cited in Tulloch 1990, 104). But the past history is important too. Amundsen, as Griffiths says, was not a Socialist, and his 'democracy' could never be more than 'seeds of the future', entangled (via the omitted dreams and sexual encounters that were in Griffiths' screenplay) with an impotence of his own in the face of world-power national competitiveness.

But professionlism also means to Griffiths – and always has – the working with television and theatre colleagues in the 'here/now' of history-making. He said of the production of *The Last Place on Earth*, 'what one looks for is a working process which involves everybody who works on a piece and involves them totally, so we are not just talking about a director's response to the text on which he bases his creative interpretation. We are also talking about actors and craftsmen of all kinds, researchers, costume people and wigging and make-up. This is a huge conglomerate of different sorts of craft skills and talents and histories' (cited in Tulloch 1990, 109), just like the different craft talents of Amundsen's team in the snow and ice. The sense of 'fellow workers as comrades' is, in Griffiths' intention at least, transferred from the snow to the TV industry itself, and we should understand Griffiths' recent concern for 'film as theatre' and 'theatre as film' as his response to the greater difficulty of getting his plays produced on television, rather than any Derrida-inspired 'ghost' of the dead Marx, as Garner suggests.

Griffiths *engages* with Marx, not with his ghost. In the case of *The Last Place on Earth*, introducing his scene between Amundsen and the Eskimos, Griffiths says 'Marxists' ... whole notion of rural idiocy, of ... the life of people at a very simple level ... as quaint and charming and passé, overtaken by history ... that electrification, organisation and industrialization will eliminate ... is deeply troubled ... As a Marxist I don't do that' (cited in Tulloch 1990, 104).

But this is not a romantic nostalgia, any more than his screenplay's concert-ending of *Fatherland* with 20,000 young 'Faces gleam[ing] at the future from the darkness' (*Fatherland*, first draft) is simplistically utopian. Rather, like Gethin Price's act in the face of the commercial entertainment structure in *Comedians*, it is a refusal of consent to the inevitability of state and economic power. 'So that while ... all the elements of state surveillance, state control...objective suppression of the individual as the agent of his or her own destiny ... are set intellectually in place in *Fatherland*, we still find these spaces for ... something oppositional to emerge that may carry a seed of the future ... There is an innocence, an *unschuldig* quality, *un*-guilty' (Griffiths, cited in Tulloch 1990, 112).

For Griffiths, it is the 'desire of the text' that 'in the absence of comradeship ... we invent them' (Griffiths, cited in Tulloch 1990, 109). We should remember Griffiths' rejection of simple folk's 'idiocy' and his invention of the 'un-guilty' when we hear Danton's words about 'plain people' like Henry in *Hope in the Year Two*: 'to hope is to be human ... Like me tonight, you too [to the audience] cannot but live in hope .... Hope's a survivor and will not die'.

Danton's interaction with his audience as 'Little white faces in the dark' should be compared with *Fatherland*'s 'Faces [that] gleam at the future from the darkness', not uni-dimensionally as a sign of growing despair, but as also part of Griffiths' ongoing engagement with Gramsci's 'pessimism of the intellect, optimism of the will', and his continuous play between history 'then', 'now' and 'future'. As with Griffiths' comments on *Fatherland* about 'all the elements of state surveillance', so too with Danton's dream about the dead Marat (as painted by David) in *Hope*. Here, state surveillance is seen as part of a performatively new 'Empire of Images' which 'must colonise not just the minds ... but the very *lives* of the people', and despite all the horrors we see being committed by the revolutionaries, hope still remains. As we watch the tethered middle-class people being systematically drowned and shot by the 'Marat Company' playing at being soldiers in Danton's dream, a voice-over (Danton 2) says, 'Did Danton do this? Did any of us? For what? To make the world a better place for our class of people'. And again, he describes the dual potential of 'The Empire of Images. Virtue and Terror. Hope, despair. Love, hate. Kind, vicious. Hot. Cold. This is the inheritance, pale tiny faces in the gloom. Who shall be happy if not ... ? Not! Not!'

'Not!' for Danton at his death, certainly. But at the moment of being taken, hooded to his execution, Danton *at last* remembers the question a beggar once asked him to convey to the King: 'Who shall be happy, if not everyone?' Danton exits, leaving behind him Henry who is not 'of our class', and is thus 'innocent' ('*unschuldig*') of his crimes. Henry, though, has in his possession Danton's watch, coat, ring and money – and Danton's hope of finding 'meaning' via the letter appealing for 'rescue'. Henry burns the letter (and with it Danton's meaning, Robespierre's meaning, Marat's meaning) on behalf of his own meaning, which is to survive with his small pleasures until the next Revolutionary prisoner arrives.

> I relish the sense of conflict in an audience ... I've always believed that
> audiences of whatever kind actually do constitute a very important part
> of the meaning of the play. (Trevor Griffiths 2000)

Even if we look at his early production of *Comedians* (Tulloch 1990,
267–71) at a time when Griffiths already preferred working in television, there clearly were important aspects of his work – particularly
those confronting a live audience *in performance* – that he thought were
realised better on stage than on television. In February 1976, Griffiths'
play *Comedians* was running at Wyndham's Theatre in London's West
End after being produced at Nottingham Playhouse, and Judith Cook,
reviewing for *Labour Weekly*, quoted Griffiths. 'Once you've taken away
that fourth wall, which is the conventional function of an audience
and that audience finds it is also playing a part – as the audience in
the working men's club – then they find it worrying although just how
they enter into the spirit of the thing varies tremendously from night to
night' (Cook, *Labour Weekly*, 27 February 1976).

There have been no 'actual audience' studies of Trevor Griffiths'
television work, though Tulloch and Burvill conducted extensive after-
the-event student-audience analyses of Griffiths' *The Cherry Orchard*
(Tulloch, forthcoming). There are otherwise only some indirect audience studies (as reported in Bignell's analysis of young audiences for *Oi
For England*, see Chapter 1).

There were no Trevor Griffiths television plays being broadcast during
the writing of this book, but in October 2000 I conducted empirical
audience research around the production of Griffiths' *Comedians* at the
Northcott Theatre, Exeter. *Comedians*, no less than *The Cherry Orchard*,
illustrates the highly interactive relationship in Griffiths' work (as in his
thinking) between theatre and television, since it responded indirectly
to a Granada TV series *The Comedians* (Garner 1999, 129), yet generated upfront issues about audiences, 'liveness' and change. Focusing

on Griffiths' theatre production of *Comedians* also provided the opportunity to examine currently Michael Billington's *Guardian* response to Griffiths' emphasis on television in his 1976 ICA lecture (see Chapter 3) that theatre can offer a more dynamic forum for social debate.

The *Comedians* audience

The Oxford Stage Company, in association with Northcott Theatre Exeter, revived Trevor Griffiths' *Comedians* in October 2000, the play running first for ten days at Exeter, and then at the Oxford Playhouse from 16–20 October. Dominic Dromgoole was Artistic Director, and the cast included Ron Moody as Eddie Waters, David Tennant at Gethin Price, George Layton as Bert Challenor, Stephen Kennedy, Vincenzo Nicoli, Martin Freeman, Nicolas Tennant, Billy Carter, Kish Sharma and Richard Simpson.

Trevor Griffiths wrote a theatre programme Introduction to the new production, drawing attention to the fact that it was the hit 1970s television series, *The Comedians*, which was an important generic source for his play. 'So you had your racist jokes, your sexist jokes and enough homophobia to run a testosterone factory for a year' (Griffiths 2000, 10). In contrast, Griffiths looked for 'the existence of another kind of humour ... which was quite hard-edged (that's what I see Eddie Waters as being), but had goals which were much more humane, much more healing, much more (as Eddie calls it) personal' (Griffiths 2000, 10, 13).

The interactive *event* of live comedy was an important part of Griffiths' thinking here. In particular, Griffiths, who emphasises the importance that comedy should not 'close things down' and wants its discourse 'to be as full and potent as it can be', ponders in his programme notes the case of comedian Bernard Manning. He is completely against 'banning Bernard Manning' for his 'pretty rancorous and ugly' jokes. But on the other hand, comedians like Manning and Frank Randle (whom Griffiths has long planned a play about) themselves had their own genius for closing an audience down. '[T]he way each of them plays (in all senses of that word) with the audience is very exciting. And the sense of closure between an audience's experiences being dealt with in the comedy is so total it's almost religious.' But this is because Manning

> does know about poverty. He does know about the politics of coping. And those are still central to our lives. There are fifteen million people living at or below poverty level. It was five million in 1979. And somebody has got to be articulating that in the comic mode ... Somebody has got to be letting people know that their problem is known and shared. (Griffiths 2000, 15)

Hence for Griffiths a rerun of his 1976 play *Comedians* was appropriate in 2000 for the same reason that his television serialisation of *Sons and Lovers* was appropriate in 1981: massive unemployment in the U.K. He is aware that *Comedians* – now as when first performed – will create strong audience responses, hence Griffiths' comments quoted at the head of the chapter.

> Audience reaction to the play has been extraordinarily varied across the years. You cannot guarantee that you will get a politically correct audience and indeed, who's interested in one? What you get is an audience that isn't yet an audience – it has to turn itself into an audience for the play. And frequently what you get is a part of your audience that finds the reactionary comedy within the first act ... funny ... What's interesting is that another part of the audience will take issue with that reception ... I relish the sense of conflict in an audience. I relish the notion that an audience doesn't immediately observe the convention of theatre, which is readily to become an agglomerated mass of receptive tissue for the piece that's being played. (2000, 13–15)

Audience 'conflict' – *within* an individual audience member who 'laughs and is punished for it' (Griffiths 2000, 14), and *between* different parts of an audience – is clearly a central focus of the theatrical event of *Comedians*.

Audiences and theatrical event research

When Griffiths says that 'a play is very much determined by our own cultural shaping and understandings ... it has to be completed by the specific audience on the night in the city or town, in the country, in the language, inside the history of that place', he is knowingly adopting a cultural studies approach to his texts and performances. Here is an author who is, deeply and determinedly, aware of the embedding of both himself and his audiences – like the comedians he describes – in historical discourse and culture that is both local and global.

And yet M/C studies have not responded much to Griffiths' culturally contextualised interest in the theatre audience. Despite over two decades of research in the 'active audience' tradition, there has been little focus on the audience for live events like theatre – which is a pity because, as Auslander rightly insists, 'liveness' is always performed in the context of a 'mediatised' culture (Auslander 1999, Tulloch forthcoming). Meanwhile, theatre audience research has tended to remain bogged down in empiricism and head counting. Susan Bennett notes that the dominance of research of this kind has confirmed what we knew already: that our theatre audiences tend to be 'elite' white, ageing and middle-class (which is one reason, of course, why cultural studies has shown little interest in theatre audiences, and why Griffiths aimed his 'strategic penetration' more at television) – and so what more is there to say?

There is a lot to say; and various theatre theorists have begun to say it. Theatre theory is reaching beyond media studies audience work by advising the analysis of theatre 'as a culturally constructed product, *signalled to its audiences by the idea of the event*' (Bennett 1997, 106, my italics). Bennett's emphasis on *situated* research that explores 'the audiences' experiences of the event itself' (Bennett 1997, 106) is helping generate a new phase of 'theatrical event' audience research which promises to both incorporate performativity theory and extend it by emphasising the performance/audience relationship within very specific contexts. Indeed, overtures are now out for the kind of research which examines Griffiths' 'specific audience on the night in the city or town, in the country, in the language, inside the history of that place'.

This is a new way, theoretically, to approach Griffiths' TV/theatre problematic, at a time when the new technologies of satellite and cable have divided up the 'broad church' of the mass TV audience he used to speak about in the 1970s and 1980s. The focus here (picking up Griffiths' point about liveness, the audience and 'conflict') is on the localised, cultural *event*.

To get beyond the kind of quantitative, empiricist theatre audience research that Bennett criticises, I was interested in addressing some of these questions – from a situated audiences' point of view. Consequently, I combined quantitative and qualitative methods. If the quantitative method did (yet again) reveal that the theatre audience is ageing and middle-class, I could nevertheless take this further to ask 'what does this mean in terms of the theatrical event?' And how does this determine the meanings of *Comedians* via 'our own cultural shapings and understandings' (Griffiths)? Are the older theatre-goers, for example, the more conservative ones in relation to Griffiths' self-proclaimed 'ideological genesis' for the play, as so much of the talk about theatre as an ageing, elite cultural form has implied?

Do young audiences, in contrast, avoid being immersed in the 'theatrical event' of *Comedians*, used as they are to the different time spans and demands of film, television and the Web? How do *they* 'read' Griffiths' ideology (in relation to mass unemployment etc), if at all, in an era that seems loath to *speak* of ideology (even in cultural studies)? To what extent do these young people, brought up in what Auslander calls a 'mediatic system' find *anything* in 'the value of "liveness" ... the "energy" that ... exists between performers and spectators in a live event, and the "community" that live performance is often said to create among performers and spectators' (Auslander 1999, 2) – given that Auslander himself is extremely dubious about these 'clichés and mystifications' voiced by theatre fans and theorists? And do the older audience members find *these* qualities (or mystifications) in Trevor Griffiths' plays too? How do audiences of all age groups cope with Griffiths' determination to leave them in some kind of conflict? What does this mean to them? Do different age groups and genders react differently in liking or disliking Griffiths' work, and do they give what he calls *Comedians'* 'partial meanings' their own different closures and completions?

The *Comedians* audience study

Television audience studies tended between the late 1960s and 1990s to shift from either the individually-oriented (and quantitative) social-psychological uses-and-gratifications approach or the textualist (Marxist, semiotic and psychoanalytic inspired) screen-theory approach that dominated in the 1970s to a much more qualitative/ethnographic methodology by the 1990s (Morley 1980, Lewis 1991). There were a number of stages in this development. The breakthrough against purely textualist analysis began with focus-group interview approaches to TV current affairs audiences where groups were nominated in advance as particularly significant for the study. Thus Morley (1980) chose bankers, trade union shop stewards, as well as black further education students and predominantly middle-class university students to respond to current affairs coverage of the Budget. Feminist audience research challenged both this subject area (shifting from male-discursive news and current affairs to female-discursive soap operas, Brunsdon 1981) and this methodological focus, becoming increasingly interested in the embedding of television-watching in everyday, local lives (Hobson 1982, Gillespie 1993). By the 1990s M/C studies' increasing interest in popular television also generated a strand of science fiction fan-oriented studies which began to visit fan clubs and conventions for their audiences (Jenkins 1992, Tulloch and Jenkins 1995).

Griffiths' emphasis on the *live* audience for *Comedians* focuses on the special event of theatre, rather than the 'everyday life' routines and rituals of much current TV audience research. However fan audience research (coupled with M/C studies' refusal to see high and popular cultural responses as qualitatively different) does have something to offer, if we treat theatre and convention-going as comparable 'live' events, at least for initial heuristic purposes. Further, 'theatrical event' research has extended the boundaries of performance-oriented research to live spectacles and festivals, which necessarily brings to the forefront of analysis not only 'actual audiences', but the social, economic and symbolic aspects of these very visible public activities and events. The global/local (socio-economic) *situating* of these events becomes a key focus (Cremona *et al* 2004).

At one level, my research on *Comedians'* audiences at the Northcott Theatre, Exeter indicated the relevance of fan approaches to theatre audiences. Many of the Northcott audiences *were* fans of theatre, 38% of them visiting theatre 12 or more times a year (and several spoke of going to theatre as many as *25 to 40 times* per year). Related to this kind of quantitative data were qualitative (as well as multiple-choice quantitative) questions which teased out if anything was special – as *event* – about this play, theatre, production company, actors etc, and what was the particular reason for this particular audience member to go to this play on this day. The *live event in the audience member's everyday life* thus became a key focus of the methodology.

With the help of the Northcott Theatre Exeter, approximately 800 questionnaires were sent out to all people who had attended *Comedians* at that theatre. There was a 40% response rate. Simple demographic data confirmed 'what we know' about theatre audiences.

Age: Over 75% were above 45 in age, with only 3% in the 26–35 age-group. The significant numbers of A-level students studying *Comedians* took up most of the 9% of 11–17 year-olds. The Northcott's Marketing Officer Laura Hartley confirmed that these data 'match the average for most of our shows, sadly' – despite the efforts of this university campus-based professional theatre to reach a younger audience.

Gender: 58% respondents were female, 42% male. These data, together with the 'on the night' impressions of the theatre marketing director, tend to indicate that the mainstream theatre audience is not predominantly '*male* white middle-class', as Bennett says it is.

Educational background: The higher educational brackets were strongly represented; with

39% educated to postgraduate level (mainly professional: teachers, nurses, social workers, local government and civil service administrators, doctors, academics);

21% educated to undergraduate level;

26% secondary educated; and

4% non-respondents.

Occupation: Respondents' occupations were overwhelmingly professional and/or in the arts: with 16% teachers, 9% college/university students, 7% university lecturers, 5% civil servants and local government officers, and 4% medical professionals. Respondents in the commercial sector were less numerous, but still significant, with 3% private consultants and 3% company directors. There were very few indeed of Griffiths' 'fifteen million people living at or below poverty level'. Manual semi-skilled were represented by one machinist, a sewage mechanic, a carpet cleaner, and two gardener/handymen. There was also one policeman, one security officer and one unemployed (postgraduate-educated) man. However, the largest category of all was *retired* (25%); and this would have been larger if 'retired teacher', 'retired physician' etc had been included in this category rather than under occupation.

The tendency for audiences to cluster most strongly in the older age-categories, with almost no-show in the 26–35 category (which was rescued to some extent by the younger A-level contingents) reflects marketing directors' strategies and observations at many theatre companies within post-1980s 'liberalised' economies. As the Northcott's Press and Public Relations Manager, Andrew Sinclair put it, 'My personal view ... is that the best way to get younger people to the theatre is to leave it a few years until their kids are grown up and they've paid off their mortgage, and then they'll come ... We are extraordinarily successful here with the school and college (A-level) age group ... If you can catch them at that age with a good production that they come to see in a school group, I am convinced that stays with them in later life' (personal interview, 2000).

The Northcott's policy is to provide school matinees for appropriate productions, offer heavily discounted group ticket prices, compile a special mailing list, provide schools with information about their plays, put on special workshops, take account of current A-level texts, and, especially important, give the schools the time they need to arrange excursions. Hence, Marketing Officer Laura Hartley emphasised, the theatre tries to schedule some plays months ahead and provides schools with advance notice, well before the general public in certain cases.

Schools are, then, both an important current and 'futures' target audience for the Northcott Theatre as part of their earned income. Crucial 'unearned income' came from Arts subsidies from various regional bodies. About 50/60% of the theatre's working money had been coming from these subsidies, though, with better times upon them, the proportion of 'unearned income' had fallen to below 50% (a new major injection promised by the Arts Council as a result of a recent round of funding policy was predicted to change that percentage again over the next three years).

The Northcott had worked hard over the previous three years to re-establish a 'core' or 'base audience', which had earlier been slipping away. With this audience regained, the theatre could afford to be more adventurous with plays that were 'definitely a risk with our base audiences', like Churchill's *Top Girls*, Griffiths' *Comedians* and a forthcoming Australian Aboriginal play, each ringing the changes on the 'fan-base that loves Jane Austen adaptations' (Laura Hartley, personal interview). But these 'risky' plays could be packaged. *Comedians* was part of a three-for-two subscription that included a costume drama and an adaptation of Hardy's *Hard Times*.

Asked what the profile of their core audience is, Hartley and Sinclair responded:

> They are definitely people in the older generation, people with disposable income.

> We say 'core audience', but when you see them here in the evening they are not as old as we sometimes think ...

> Not all reactionary types from Budleigh Salterton who demand Jane Austen and 'normal plays'.

Andrew Sinclair set great store by the 'real theatre goers' who come to a first night's subscription series at 'a fiver a head. 'The first night crowd are very receptive ... I would prefer to think that our core audience is almost as receptive as that.'

A more interesting approach to the audience data, then, is to examine Sinclair's beliefs about audience profile. We can start with a correlation between age groups and 'liking/disliking' *Comedians*. Overall, *75% respondents liked this production*, with perhaps some predictable age-related responses (though no significant gender differences: 76% women and 73% men liked the play). Thus whereas 96% teenagers and 100% 18–25s liked this 'risky' play, only 68% of the 55+ group did. This latter had the lowest 'liking' percentage, compared with 81% of 46–55s, 71% 36–45s, and 88% 26–35s. In addition, the qualitative comments as to why 32% of the oldest group *disliked* it offered some predictable results. 'Language and sexual connotations were not to our taste.' 'Did not enjoy this play at all – it was sordid – blasphemous in part and had nothing to recommend it – left in the second interval.' 'A far too liberal use of expletives – one began to feel soiled by having to listen.'

There is plenty here to confirm M/C studies critics in their prejudices about middle-class theatre audiences, disturbed and angered as these respondents were by 'bad', 'obscene', even 'blasphemous' language; and not 'comfortable' with 'coarse' people and 'thick' dialects. Many critics of *Comedians* emphasised the high quality of its acting and sets, and some commented that they were sorry for the actors having to perform in such a play. Others felt that:

The play is so dated. Yeah, we know comedians used to be racist/sexist and everything else-ist. So what? It is preachy and unfunny. Cf Zadie Smith's White Teeth for how these points can be made effectively and wittily.

Dated. Clichéd. Time has really moved on – Time it was filed away.

At the end of the questionnaire there was an 'Any other comments?' space, and many of the negative respondents took the opportunity here to praise the Northcott Theatre's professionalism and its policy of ensuring a variety of plays in its seasons. It was just that the theatre had made a mistake this time (a very few respondents took a harder line and threatened to stop their subscriptions if any further plays like this were performed there).

One of the problems here was that many of the negative respondents had expected *Comedians* to be 'funny'. As the *only* negative teenager put it, 'The play was advertised as being funny, but I did not find it very funny. This left me feeling short-changed.'

This hints at an ambiguity in the theatre's marketing strategy. A problem, as Hartley and Sinclair pointed out, was that at the time of the marketing brochures and the poster being printed, the Oxford Stage Company had not *cast* the play. Consequently, the poster displayed 'a white sheet with figures in suits and dicky-bird ties and people thought it was a row of stand-up comics' (Hartley). Sinclair pointed out that they did emphasise in the season's brochure that it was a *drama*, viz a theatrical production and not actual stand-up comedians. But (as with the warning in the brochure about bad language which the Northcott people had added to the Oxford Playhouse blurb), not everyone seems to have taken notice, and thus some came to the play with false expectations – an example of what Carlson calls 'a radical disjuncture between the horizon of expectations assumed by the production and that actually brought to the theatre' (1990, 21).

Trevor Griffiths did not see the play this way. For him it is not a play about comedy as such, and so the appearance of the new alternative comedians over the last decade or so does *not* date it. '[T]his play is not ... about comedy really, but about opportunity, about the conditions facing the relatively disadvantaged in their efforts to change the condition of their lives. I wish I could say, twenty-five years on, that progress had been made in these things. But when I look at this blighted space we call Britain, I have to say I don't see it' (Griffiths 2000, 7).

Griffiths' negative respondents clearly disagreed with his take on contemporary Britain – which could, of course, have been a matter of their own 'Budleigh Salterton' world view. But we shouldn't rely too much on a simple 'conservative ideological reading' of 'dated' interpretations.

For example, a (head of faculty and English teacher) respondent who gave as her main reason for going to *Comedians* that she 'likes seeing Trevor Griffiths' plays', commented that she did not like the production because, 'The issues in the play hadn't been updated to be relevant to a modern audience and it ended up being a period piece of the 1970s'. Her own critical paradigm (which admittedly was probably very different from the company directors and consultant physicians who also found it 'dated') made it clear what exactly it was she thought *was* dated. In response to a 'how did you feel in Act II' question (when the theatre audience becomes the intra-diegetic club audience), she said 'it worked as theatre', and 'having the real audience as the stage audience did work – but the message was lost because our post-modern, ironic stance on racist/sexist jokes creates a different mood to what must have been the original impact of the play'.

Similarly, in response to a question citing Griffiths' emphasis on audience 'conflict', she wrote, 'An excellent viewpoint – and the use of the real audience as stage audience added in this sense. Yet the problem resides in the difference between a year 2001 audience and a 1970s audience: is conflict too strong a word for us now?' This respondent also attached to her questionnaire her own Internet review of the play. There she said:

> The play needs reinterpreting in light of the past 25 years, but Holme's production only succeeds as a period piece. Its fundamental flaw is to take a retrospective stance, as a result of which the audience can safely fail to engage with its ideas. Those of us who remember the 1970s can enjoy a sense of nostalgia, but in doing so, an exciting and innovative play loses its cutting edge (Wills 2001, 1).

By following at some length the *narrative* of one audience member's qualitative responses as to why *Comedians* at the Northcott Theatre was 'dated' we can see clearly why this kind of methodology is so necessary to expand on and elucidate quantitative material, especially in trying to trace what may make a particular work an *event* in theatre or television in one decade and not in another for some audiences. Wills, in fact, was a great supporter of the original play, and criticised the *production* of it in 2001 – a point Griffiths would probably agree with, since he commented to me that he found the production too slavishly 'celebratory' of his original text.

Still, many of the Northcott's positive respondents *did not agree with either of them*. The following is a sample of 'why I liked it' responses, which are typical of the considerable enthusiasm the majority of the audience felt for this production.

Representative of general working lifestyle in today's society. (55+)

It made me think about stereotypes, about what makes me laugh and what doesn't, and about what lies behind the comedian's performance. (46–55)

Though written a few decades ago, it still had relevance to current problems. Made me think about Comedy'. (36–45)

I had never seen Comedians before. It didn't seem dated (Very strange!) and I was surprised how relevant (in a strange sort of way) it was to the modern age. An excellent production of an excellent play. (46–55)

Husband and I worked in tertiary education in Manchester (University and College of Education) – familiar ambience. (55+)

Great dialogue and well staged + I liked Act 2 (the opportunity to switch our role in the audience). (46–55)

Good ensemble acting plus 2 or 3 stand-out performances; terrific play – still relevant things to say about social control, conformity, racism, etc. ... ; wonderful design and production. (46–55)

Certain words and phrases recurred persistently through these positive responses: 'thought-provoking', 'different', 'unexpected', 'original', 'funny but moving', 'funny, sad and very true to life', 'made one confront one's perception of truth and prejudice', 'clever set, excellent cast, challenging script', 'hidden depths which came out as the play unfolded'. Many of the positive responses of the kind above came from the 55+ age group, and they came equally from both genders. Andrew Sinclair's belief seems confirmed that the 'core audience' at Exeter was mainly 'as receptive' as their first-nighters; and looking, as Laura Hartley says, 'for a challenge, not just entertainment'. Further, unlike the reviewers of *Through the Night* we encountered in Chapter 4, they seemed well able to understand Griffiths' broader societal meanings.

Some responses had local experiential inflections. The A-level students (virtually all of whom liked the play a lot) regularly spoke of the relationship of this performance to *their* situation in the classroom. 'The play was really well acted and has helped greatly with the study of it'; 'The actors really suited the different characters and brought out different elements of their characteristics which I had previously missed while reading the play'. It was teachers, in contrast, who commented on the 'perfectly dingy classroom set' which had been part of their daily-life experiences (and there was the occasional comment from a social worker about how this reflected priorities in recent/contemporary Britain).

There were significant differences in age response within this highly polarised set of audiences. We should not let the 'excessive bad language' responses (and the physical *visibility* to the researchers of those audience members who chose to get up and leave) disguise from us the sustained pleasures that most of the oldest age group found in this play. It is worth following through the whole-questionnaire response of some of these older (55+) respondents to see what 'sustained pleasure' means here. But in profiling these qualitative responses, we can let them also 'cue' some of the quantitative and/or production data where this seems relevant, since this helps place them in a more generalised context.

Three respondents' narratives – and some data

(1) K.F. was a 55+ retired British Council officer who gave as his reason for coming 'Haven't seen this play – wanted to catch up on it' and found *Comedians* 'outstanding' in its performances, with an 'excellent script' and 'V.G. production'. 'It worked as theatre' for him because 'of the multiple levels of perception offered the audience – the surface that mixed funny/banal, the subtext compelling and painful'. Responding to what *Comedians* was 'about', he said, 'How our culture can, unperceived by us, unless we raise our awareness & analysis, present us with an entire programme (or *program*) of opinions, prejudices, stereotypes, approved/ disapproved attitudes and ultimately values which we accept into our ownership without realising how little free will or discrimination we have exercised. It is an impassioned plea and exhortation to resistance, to accept responsibility – and also to empathise with human fallibility.'

The British Council man was inflecting his reading of Griffiths with that double use (one of them American) of 'program'. For him, this British 'play stands brilliantly on its own' without any need for Griffiths' own programme interpretation, and he worries about American 'cultural imperialism'. Matching his 'what is it about' meaning quoted above, and also his pleasure in 'outstanding central performances' and 'excellent script', his 'particular memorable moments' in the play were the 'scenes between the teacher & the brilliant but painfully unfunny "comedian", Price'. Asked if there 'is ever anything "special" about going to the theatre for you', he commented 'Live is always better than dead' (American TV?); and he confirmed that for him *Comedians* was a special event in this 'live' way. Finally, in his 'any other comments' response, K.F. said that 'The range and variety of the theatre's annual programme make it a main element in the cultural life of the city. Production standards are high, and in fact its existence was an element in my family's decision to move to Exeter in 1997.'

Many of the Northcott respondents (including those negative about *Comedians*) made this kind of concluding comment about the 'freshness' and 'variety' of the theatre's fare. But here was one who showed how idiosyncratic yet systematic choices about his everyday life – where he would retire, bring his family's activities, and have leisure time – were deeply embedded in the kinds of 'live is always better than dead' theatrical event at the Northcott Theatre, Exeter. But K.F. was also *typical* of the mass of respondents in that he was a fan of theatre as a leisure form. Like most of the respondents, he was a regular subscriber to the Northcott, and went to other theatres as well. Indeed 27% of the sample went, like K.F., 8–11 times per year, and a bigger proportion much more than that.

This 'theatre/fan' finding was supported by responses to the question 'why did you personally come to see Trevor Griffiths' *Comedians*?', and to a multiple choice question about what attracted them to the play, results for which were very similar. It was theatre-going generally rather than Trevor Griffiths particularly that was the main reason for most people going to the Northcott to see *Comedians*. The multiple choice responses were:

52% 'It was part of the subscription package.'
48% 'Really like going to this theatre.'
22% 'Haven't seen this play – wanted to catch up on it.'
16% 'Star actors in the cast.'
16% 'Attracted by the production company.'
12% 'Read good reviews in the paper.'
12% 'The poster/leaflet attracted me.'
8%   'I'm studying the play for A-level.'
6%   'Like seeing Trevor Griffiths plays.'
5%   'Just chance.'
2%   'Friends saw it – said I should go.'
1%   'It was a special day out (Birthday, anniversary etc.).'
10% 'Other reasons.'

About half of the 10% 'other reasons' given related to having closely engaged with Trevor Griffiths' play before, often the TV version. 'Saw the play on TV many years ago. So wanted to see it on stage' (36–45); 'Saw original [theatre] production with Jimmy Jewel in lead – was very impressed' (55+); 'I remembered seeing it on TV many years ago and being impressed' (55+); 'I have taught the text for A-level Theatre Studies – it's a brilliant and *relevant* play' (55+).

Interestingly – and *unlike* K.F. who was unstinting in his use of 'brilliant' and 'outstanding' in response to *Comedians* – while most of these close engagers with the Griffiths text said the new production 'reinforced what a good play it is' and was 'faithful to the spirit of the original text', their personal long-term experience with the *play* (as compared with theatre *fans* like K.F.) did lead them to a number of criticisms of the 2001 version. 'Moody badly miscast and playing differently from Tennant and others (newer, more Americanized filmic style). Student comedians very good, however; also Patel' (46–55); 'A criticism of this production rather than play. Ron Moody – although he is a fine actor was unsuited to the part – far too stiff – had obviously not studied the "looseness of limits", which most stand-up comedians adopt' (55+). Different fandoms (of theatre generally, of a particular production company or star, or of Griffiths himself clearly have different sets of discriminations (Tulloch forthcoming).

(2) M.P. was a 55+ consultant who went to *Comedians* primarily because it was in the subscription package, but also because of 'some star actors in the cast'. Unlike bigger budget theatres like Theatre Royal Plymouth and Theatre Royal Bath, the Northcott Theatre does not first and foremost promote a 'star' policy. As Andrew Sinclair pointed out, 'We don't go for stars. In the case of *Comedians*, with a touring company like Oxford Playhouse, you will have recognisable actors, and we exploit that in our publicity. But it is a bonus when it happens. It is not something we deliberately do.'

The Plymouth and Bath theatres would, Sinclair said, put their star faces on their posters, and that cost them 'lots of money, with big corporate support'. In contrast, the identity of the Northcott Theatre was an 'emphasis on the product, on the quality, on the telling of the story, on the show'. It was this 'quality product' emphasis that attracted M.P., despite his interest in the 'stars' of *Comedians*. He liked the production because 'Believable. Excellent set. Empathised with them.' It 'worked as theatre' for him and was 'challenging' at the same time: 'made me think about what I laugh at myself sometimes'. Asked what it was 'about', he said, 'Hope – unfulfilled desires to escape their society/condition. The nature of humour.' Responding to the Griffiths' 'conflict' quotation, M.P. said, 'That may be the case in most audiences but the Northcott audiences (students apart) are mostly of one type – OAP and politically incorrect.' For him, the 'particular memorable moments' were 'Act 2 generally and the ending with the return of Mr Patel'. In his final comments, he remarked, 'Came away thinking what a strong cast it was. Northcott productions – less broad range than Plymouth but you do not have a studio theatre nor are able to accommodate the big productions. As far as the theatre – I could write an essay.'

Several people came close to doing just that. For example, A.T., a 46–55 year-old teacher who liked *Comedians* ('Well-paced, challenging. Great construction of "reality"'), and went primarily because he was a fan of Trevor Griffiths, wrote in some frustration at the end, 'I do often feel the Northcott aims at a too narrow audience – the Grey Dawn members. Thus its programming is too safe and predictable. How many Ayckbourns can a human take in a lifetime? Austen? Dickens? They were bloody novelists. Let's climb into the twentieth century (for a start) ... at least. *Comedians* has a radical programme (even 20 years on!).'

The fact that it was recent productions of Ayckbourn, Austen and particularly Dickens that older audience members who felt 'soiled' by *Comedians* wanted more of, indicates the problem for the marketing director. As we have seen, the packaging of *Comedians* with Dickens and a costume drama was a careful strategy aimed at retaining a core audience while allowing something more challenging. And there was certainly no need to be quite as pessimistic about the 'Grey Dawn' core audience as A.T. was. Here is another of this older group.

(3) 'Anon' was a 55+ Educational Consultant. She went to *Comedians* because it was part of the subscription package, and liked it a lot. 'Excellent balance in cast. Spellbinding tension between the tutor and anti-hero. Professional, hilarious and pathetic – the contrasts were strong.'

She said she was 'creatively disturbed' by the production, and when asked what it was about, said, 'Anger of the anti-hero who might yet win through and the patience and wisdom of his tutor. Misplaced ambition throughout – in the students, the tutor, the assessor, the night-club owner and even the caretaker (*still* hoping to find the building empty at night). An echo on how *paltry* is our expenditure on education – the tatty schoolroom, the likely poor pay of the tutor'.

This educational consultant had a very job-specific social focus here on the meaning of *Comedians*. She was pleased with Griffiths' remarks about the need for audience conflict, adding 'I relish the thought that my own confusions, prejudices and belly laughs might help to create a living atmosphere for the players to work in'. Both the overall dialogic theme of *Comedians* and tiny aspects of acting business were among the memorable moments that she remembered, including: 'Most encounters between tutor and anti-hero. Also the benevolent other student who absent-mindedly collected up rubbish and binned it – an unexpected piece of nurturing set against the violence, the shouting and the second rate.' Responding to the 'is theatre special?' question, she said 'Look forward to challenge, variety and "moments", as above. A sign of weekend wind down from work (there has to be something – we drive a round trip of 60 miles)'; and in response to *Comedians* as 'special', she capitalised, 'YES, VERY'.

Here was a 'Grey Dawn' respondent (and there were plenty of others like her), who wanted much more of the kind of 'challenging' but also 'audience-confusing' play that she saw in *Comedians*, and which Andrew

Sinclair was hoping that the Northcott was producing. As Sinclair saw it, lacking the big production profiles of Plymouth, Bath and Bristol, the Northcott Theatre at Exeter was in the business of reaching for its audience in the very large hinterland between those cities. 'There is a context of travel in Devon – people are car-based ... driving somewhere to do something, and not relying on public transport .... Devon has the greatest density of road networks in England by miles, and it is very much the case that the rural community is used to getting into their cars.'

'Anon' was one of the Northcott's car-based fans; and, reminding us that theatre-going itself is not exempt from the whole range of everyday routines, she commented finally that the theatre 'Badly needs refurbishment. Looks *TIRED*. *Ladies* Loos – *Awful* – 4 cubicles and long queues. Good balance in programme overall. OFTEN FEEL IT DESERVES BETTER (+ YOUNGER) AUDIENCES.'

This sense of the *local* theatre as public space was very strong indeed in respondents' summarising comments, and is something methodologies in recent 'live event' audience research is more equipped to expose than recent television audience research. The intimacy of the theatre was central to responses about *why* theatre was 'special' to so many of them. Nearly all respondents (98%) found that going to theatre could be special if it was the right production/play; and a majority of respondents (66%) thought *Comedians* was a special event. But special in what way?

'Anon' didn't tell us. But of those who did, 'theatre as special event' responses were post-coded into a number of generic categories, with the following results.

- 38% found the special event in the 'live atmosphere', 'live performance in intimate space', 'audience interaction with actors', 'audience/audience community and talk afterwards'.
- 18% found it in 'night (day) out, fun and entertainment', 'dressing up for evening', 'escape from ordinary life', 'relaxing after hard day's work', 'escape from life into a good play'.
- 14% liked to 'exercise critical faculties', 'thinking in a different way', 'getting into another world/culture'.
- 7% wanted 'to think *and* laugh', 'the whole (intellectual/emotional) experience'.
- 7% were in 'awe of the actors' craft', and loved their 'professional identity'.
- 5% found the 'special event' quality in the 'uplifting sympathy that is aroused in character via language and fine acting of a great play'.
- 5% found their special 'pleasure of putting all the parts together – sets, lighting, costumes, plots, acting'.

- 2% found it 'magic'.
- 2% had 'been to theatre all my life'.

Obviously, there may be overlap between some of these 'special event' categories. For example, in other theatre audience research (Tulloch forthcoming) where I have used long interviews to probe these 'special event' survey responses, 'magic' has been associated with the 'liveness', 'interaction' and 'intimacy' of the theatre; and the response 'I've been to theatre all my life' may well signify the same set of pleasures. Still, in all of the 'live event' audience research I have conducted, there has been enough difference between the major 'special event' responses to begin to make significant distinctions. For example, there was quantitatively a *significant* tendency for those who strongly disliked *Comedians* to be in the 'night (day) out, fun and entertainment', 'like dressing up for evening', escape from ordinary life' category.

Thus a respondent who found *Comedians* 'coarse, vulgar and without any appeal', said what was 'special' about theatre was 'to have a pleasant, entertaining evening'. Another who disliked *Comedians* for its 'bad language which unnerved me', wanted 'special' theatre to give her 'a good laugh, especially in good language'. Another who 'left in mid-performance' wanted 'special' theatre to be 'an evening out of entertainment – *relaxation*'.

Other statistically significant correlations between responses to different questions included the fact that the majority of people who disliked *Comedians*, said (unsurprisingly) that they were 'confronted and annoyed by the performance', and either found no special moments in the play whatsoever, or commented that their special moment was when the final curtain went down. However, overall responses to the 'how did you feel about the play?' question did not support this view. For 65% 'it worked as theatre'; for 30% it 'made me think about what I laugh at sometimes'; 29% 'felt creatively disturbed'; and 19% 'were emotionally involved with a particular character'. Only 14% 'were confronted and annoyed by the performance'. Not just 'theatre', but 'this play *as* theatre' was a special live event for most of its audience members.

Trevor Griffiths and positioning the audience

Marvin Carlson has remarked that the 'on-site availability of ... authorised readings ... provides a contribution to reading formation highly unusual in the modern theatre, one which would surely repay modern study' (1990, 24). Carlson is mainly referring here to theatre displays of newspaper reviews. But in the theatre programme, the playwright can often function like a TV or theatre reviewer, in interpreting for a future audience his own play. During the actual theatrical event of the *Comedians* at the Northcott Theatre Exeter, Trevor Griffiths had *two* direct ways of reaching the audience with his 'meanings'. The first, chronologically speaking, was via his programme notes. The second was via his attempt to induce audience 'conflict' and positive interaction via the live performance itself.

(i) *Griffiths' programme notes*. Of those who responded (N = 304), most (58%) said they read the programme notes, though more read them *after* than before the performance, mainly for time reasons. Of those that read the notes, 62% were positive about them 'helping them with the production', 29% were negative, and others did not answer or did not know. Symptomatic positive reasons given were:

Put play in 1970s context, and also issue of poverty.

Good to see TG's intention. But the director didn't concentrate on underlying concerns – social deprivation.

Yes, I warmed to the play, felt included.

TG said how the idea of play came from him watching men's clubs, watching The Comedians doing their turns on TV. I could relate to this, so knew there would be quite a few different styles, delivery, alternative turns.

I concentrated very hard on the script and production as a result.

The negative responses to Griffiths' notes tended to be more pithy: 'Pretentious', 'Gobbledegook', 'Pseudo-psychological verbiage', 'Just confused me', 'Confirmed my view that the playwright felt superior to his audience', 'Got basic plot but didn't give warning on swearing', 'It didn't help the fact that the play has dated badly'.

(ii) *'I relish the sense of conflict in an audience'*. Predictably, many of those who disliked the play a lot, responded to this question with 'If he wanted conflict, he got it – we walked out'; and one respondent said 'The only "conflict" I felt was whether to slip out for a pint of Guinness!' This group tended to regard Griffiths' reflexivity as aggression rather than conflict, or argued: 'I don't agree you need conflict within audiences – we are there to be entertained not make political points' (55+), 'I don't like conflict – there's enough in real life. Theatre for me is escapism and art' (46–55).

There were a number of comments like this, mostly from the 55+ or 46–55 age-groups, women as well as men. But there were many more countervailing views from among these age groups too. 'I agree that the audience is important to the atmosphere in the theatre and I quite liked the feeling of confusion about whether to laugh or not' (55+). 'I absolutely agree with Griffiths' sentiment. Theatre should not always be "comfortable" – but produce a shift – however slight in one's attitudes, beliefs, feelings or prejudices' (55+). 'Agree with Griffiths' statement. Certainly I did feel conflict personally when watching' (36–45). 'I was *very* aware of what people were laughing at, and the conflict it created within myself' (46–55). 'Yes – especially where we laughed at one kind of comedy only to have this turned on its axis and laugh at another. But this is good – makes us ask what really is behind our laughter' (55+).

Some respondents agreed strongly with Griffiths, but were somewhat patronising about the *Northcott audience*: 'a play of this kind really has the power to get people thinking. All the old ladies walking out were perfect examples of the fact that we as a nation cannot criticise ourselves' (20–25). Other respondents were obviously facing these kinds of issues for the first time, and were genuinely negotiating with what they had seen. 'This "play" knew it would shock – I didn't until the vituperation started. People behind us walked out – but I wanted to see the play to its conclusion. I did find it disturbing – antisocial – something really I couldn't handle particularly. I wouldn't go to see it again, though the acting was admirable and believable' (55+). 'The group of people I went with argued about the work for a long time during and after the play. I became aware of how different people in the audience received things differently although at times we all consciously shared the discomfort' (36–45). Responses like these show how important the live, special event audience is, and why Griffiths places so much emphasis on this play as *theatre* rather than television.

There was plenty of support for Griffiths' view that audiences should 'take issue' with each other in *becoming* an audience. Respondents of all ages emphasised the role of the club scene in making them reflexive – sometimes for the first time – *as* audience. 'The author used the audience in the club scene to good effect, once he overcame our initial middle-class tendency not to participate' (55+). 'This [conflict] was shown when the audience became part of the play at the sports and social club. This is clever use of the audience and got us involved in the play' (36–45).

Some respondents (usually the younger ones) took this observation further to argue that, in a sense, this made *Comedians* a play *about* its own audience. 'In some ways this play was about the audience's reaction to what they saw' (11–19). 'The fact that some members of the audience didn't return to their seats after the interval was, I believe, a sign of this very real "conflict" generated in the audience. Griffiths' use of swear words and anti-social mannerisms was intellectually justifiable, but "too much" for some people and this was very much a "part" of the play' (26–35).

One respondent, as we saw, felt that this stage/audience reflexive conflict may have worked in earlier days, but it was no longer valid in a post-modern context and that this was an important part of the play being dated. Another applied a New Age *ideology* to Griffiths' 'partial meanings'. 'Yes! The interplay of conflicts inner and outer and how we resolve them is essential to life. If we do not address the balance and accept them – we are lost in the see-saw for ever! Torn between extremes Bush(Blair)/Bin Laden, Lab/Con, Yin/Yang. The dance (Tai-Chi) comes from the acceptance and balance of opposites' (36–45).

Some audience members remained *unrepentantly* conservative, even though they had enjoyed the play. 'I wasn't forced to feel uncomfortable about my earlier laughter as Griffiths had hoped' (55+). Others (lest we fetishise 'age' too easily and simplistically here) were of a generation where they believed there was real (class) conflict only in a lost past. 'Conflict within the Audience? ... The play ... about "Deprivation" ... could have been about miners or shipyard workers in the thirties and could have then had something I could relate to' (55+).

Young audiences, too, were well able to discuss and agree with *Comedians*' ideology, especially if – like the Loughborough University students (see Chapter 3) – they had already read this play. *Comedians* was enormously popular with these Northcott students: 93% found it a special event: 'undoubtedly *Comedians* transfixed the audience'; 'it made me internally argue with myself'; 'it was full of energy and very *live*'; 'the audience participation was a big part of the experience'.

The question 'say in 3 to 6 sentences what *Comedians* was "about"' pointed to the students' understandings of Griffiths' ideological themes. The following were typical responses.

> Comedians is about humour: what it is, what it does and what it can lead to. Using stereotypes in humour can be an extremely damaging activity, as humour links people to each other ... Comedians is also about desperation, people trying to find a way out of the situation they're in. It says what stage stand-up comedy was at when this was written and there was a great amount of conflict.

> The play Comedians follows the ambitions of the comedians as they all prepare for their big debut. While this is happening, however, the play successfully deals with serious issues behind much of what comedy is based upon, e.g. stereotypes (Irish, blacks etc) and also our class system which is dealt with very well in Price's act.

Clearly, these students do have some understanding of Griffiths' own sense of 'what is *Comedians* about?' – viz 'the conditions facing the disadvantaged in their efforts to change the conditions of their lives'. And they also understand the crucial part audiences – themselves *as* audiences – play in confronting and in trying to change what Eddie in the play calls 'pellets to a final solution'.

Conclusion

Laura Hartley pointed out that Griffiths' *Comedians* was not a sell-out at the Northcott, but 'it did well ... We did actually go out of our way with *Comedians* to try that bit harder, because we knew it was a good show and we knew that the cast was worth marketing.' Andrew Sinclair added that 'You hook a few more people in when you say Ron Moody is in it, because he is almost a brand with [his leading role in] *Oliver*'. Sinclair didn't promote 'Trevor Griffiths', but he did advertise the fact 'that it was the Oxford Stage Company because this was their fourth recent production at Exeter, and the other three had all done well'. Though, as Hartley pointed out, the earlier Oxford Playhouse products had been Noel Coward and Somerset Maugham, so even here they were taking a new direction with *Comedians*.

Putting on *Comedians* was, as this chapter has indicated, always a matter of particular places and particular agencies – and of a particular theatre located in its own history. This history included, cumulatively: rivalry with the Theatre Royal Plymouth over the past 20 years; the new artistic direction at the Northcott Theatre through the previous three years; the search to regain a 'base audience' over the last year or two; the building up of an even more recent (successful) relationship with the Oxford Stage Company, and only *then* having the conviction to perform Trevor Griffiths' controversial play.

It is clear that many audiences, of different ages and genders, do find theatre more special as an event than television or film. It is also clear that, given the right local circumstances, many of them *enjoy* being confronted, made to feel uncomfortable about basic values, and experience 'a shift ... in one's attitudes, beliefs, feelings or prejudices'. Equally, these feelings of disturbance and change can adhere to both younger and older audiences.

With the passing of Griffiths' preferred 'broad church' of mass television, and the greater difficulty he has found getting access to television anyway, the focus for 'strategic penetration' may have shifted to the relationship of audiences with particular local theatres trying plays that are 'different to the trend' in very precise market conditions. In this sense, *Comedians*' postmodern critic in the Exeter audience may have been wrong. The fact that Trevor Griffiths himself has constructed the theatrical event of *Comedians* in terms of *specific live audiences and locations* encouraged not only a new audience methodology, as post-modern researchers examine local 'tales from the field' (Tulloch forthcoming), but also his emphasis on a live audience in the play's construction succeeded in generating widespread reflexivity and changing subjectivities in much of that local audience.

So we'll sing for tomorrow
If singing's no crime
And what's lacking we'll borrow
From the slow jig of time. (*March Time*, 1986)

There's times that Trevor Griffiths 'sings for tomorrow' without ever being heard, because his commissioned television and film writing has not been produced. In an interview in September 2003, I asked Griffiths about TV writing which he particularly regretted not going to air. 'The first one that didn't get made was the Tom Mann project, 1972/73, BBC. There is no play about Tom Mann ... The great transport strike of 1911 has still not really been written about.' Griffiths believes that his commissioned work about Mann, *Such Impossibilities*, wasn't made because ideologically 'it upset the apple cart of a series called *The Edwardians*'.

After *Such Impossibilities* there was nothing Griffiths wrote that wasn't produced for well over a decade.

Then rather a lot – the next major piece [that wasn't made] was one I wrote in the mid-80s called March Time, which was my first attempt to step outside the abiding, established structures of television film and television drama, and work from a very small power base ... run by a guy that had been working in trade union educational films for a decade up in the North-East. He had been having talks with independent drama producers at Channel 4 ... I spent a year writing a TV film that I thought, and still think, was important. (Griffiths, personal interview 2003)

Griffiths then spent two years trying to get Channel 4 to consider *March Time*, and failed. Also not produced at this time was a film Griffiths was working on for Warner Brothers called *Acts of Love*, about the secret workings of the African National Congress in South Africa.

This ... marked the beginning of the great reaction which made it difficult for people like me to get work done. It took Thatcher and her crowd and

Reagan and his crowd quite a while to get started with their kulturkampf, but eventually they caught up with a lot of people. The first to go were the touring theatre alternative groupings ... And then they started turning on television which was much harder to get at because of its through-put, and because of how it was owned and controlled. But they got there in the end.

Although *Acts of Love* and a long-term film project on Tom Paine have never been made, the remaining TV scripts that Griffiths wrote after *March Time*, a television version of *The Party, Hope in the Year Two* and *Food for Ravens* all got produced. Still, Griffiths says, there was intense political pressure 'in the ruling elite of the BBC' against his most recent television play, *Food for Ravens*, which New Labour supporters saw as profoundly critical.

> There were two things that emerged for me from Food for Ravens. One was a sense of wonder about what one can still do in the television drama medium ... and a great deal of pride in what was actually achieved in 17 and a half days of shooting. I found it such an uplifting experience to write and direct that piece. It is tragic then, that out of this feeling should come a sense close to certainty that ... I would never get the opportunity to do what I wanted to do in television again ... and that if I was to continue writing, it would probably have to be in the theatre ... [There are] strange little parts of British theatre which still prove a kind of hide-out from the people who would like to see your work only discussed historically, i.e. they don't want to see you do new work.

Griffiths had discussions with Granada in the late 1990s about writing a television version of *Doctor Zhivago* (originally developed with Trevor Nunn) which never got further. Later, without informing him, ITV went ahead with a musical version of *Zhivago*. Griffiths now says the fact that they didn't even acknowledge his idea made him aware that his TV writing days were probably at an end.

Whether Trevor Griffiths has finally been unplugged from television writing we shall see. What remains interesting, even with written works that did not go to air, was his development of changing forms for television – as between, for example, the politically optimistic, interventionist years for the Left of the early 1970s and the reaction of the Thatcher years. Griffiths still holds by the importance for their period of both *Such Impossibilities* and *March Time*, but these were very different forms of political work.

> March Time ... is a more important work than even I can imagine in terms of my own development in writing. I hadn't written a play up to 1985 that had quite such a striking device. It anticipates by a decade Hope in the Year Two and Food for Ravens in terms of the relationship of different

temporalities inside a text. It's quite interesting how ideas and devices can surface in one's work, are unused because the piece is not aired, seem to go back under, and then come back in a different form.

In contrast, reading the published script of *Such Impossibilities* today, one is aware both of the greater linearity of the narrative and the triumphalist, almost macho characterisation of Tom Mann, as Griffiths looked to enlarge 'our "usable past" and connect it with a lived present and to celebrate a victory' (1988, 181). 'Unity of action' is both the theme and the dominating temporality of this play. Tom Mann drives through it with a single-minded linearity of purpose hard to find elsewhere in Griffiths' work. Mann, as written, faces off the male militarism of the ruling-class as openly as he does the male machismo of the working-class militant Milligan. But the ruling-class is more devious. At the end of *Such Impossibilities*, Tom Mann, on his way to extend the struggle in Paris, is arrested on an Incitement to Mutiny charge for publishing an article encouraging young soldiers not to fight against their worker-comrades. He is given nine months in gaol.

His wife Ellen – 'late forties, small, grey, tired, dowsed ... hesitant, tiredly in control, but a little bewildered' – comes to see him in prison. She tells him, 'Why you do what you do, it's beyond me' (1988, 231). He draws her to him and tells her that while the state funeral of the Duke of Wellington forty years earlier attracted 120,000 people, today the funeral for a general labourer killed by police in Hyde Park was estimated at 150,000. She cries on his shoulder, experiencing and envisioning the loss of the personal in Mann's singular march of history towards insurrection. He responds to her tears, and the play ends with:

> Mann: 'Hey hey hey hey hey. You can't be crying. I'll not have you crying. The working-class don't cry, lass. We've nothing to cry for. We're winning.'
> (He kisses her on the forehead very gently. Pull out. Mann and Ellen stand there. He stands and watches her go. Roll: 'Actions that aim only at securing peace between employers and men are not only of no value in the fight for freedom, but are actually a serious hindrance and a menace to the interests of the workers. Political and industrial action direct must at all times be inspired by revolutionary principles. That is, the aim must ever be to change from capitalism to socialism as speedily as possible. Anything less than this means continued domination by the capitalist class.') (Tom Mann 1856–1941.)

In their book on Trevor Griffiths, Poole and Wyver discuss *Such Impossibilities* in the chapter on '*Occupations* and other dramas of revolution', and likewise Itzin describes this period of Griffiths' work as that of 'a revolutionary Marxist who believed that through various means of organisation, it would be possible to create an insurrectionary moment and then to exploit it for revolutionary purposes' (1980, 171). Ted Braun, otherwise an admirer of Griffiths' work, says of *Such Impossibilities*, 'there are no more than fleeting intimations of Tom Mann the *private* individual (as in the final scene with his wife, Ellen) and none of the contradictions found in *Occupations* and all the later works' (1988, 3). Mann is (nearly) all hard man, forged in the historical need to fight and defeat other hard men in exploring – and *calling* – that insurrectionary time; and even those moments in the play where tenderness begins to blossom, it is either in the male leader/novitiate relationship between Mann and the teenage steward, Groark, or else it is, as Braun suggests, an intimation of a relationship never developed, for example between Mann and the union stenographer Martha Clark (who herself is treated patriarchally by Mann, in sending her to buy sandwiches while he physically sorts out his male rival, Mulligan).

Between *Such Impossibilities* and *March Time* Griffiths had a decade of produced work to populate his 'long road' in representing gender and class. But the difference between the two plays is also a matter of formal and historical context. In this chapter, I want to examine these changes intertextually. I am comparing here two of Griffiths' plays written in some sense of continuity, in that they both relate to miners' strikes that were current at the time of writing, and each looked back to earlier victories and defeats for industrial militancy. Moreover, both plays – *Such Impossibilities* (1972) and *March Time* (1986) – were written for television and never produced. These plays, then, 'sing for tomorrow', but they 'borrow from the slow jig of time' in very different formal ways.

March Time

Trevor Griffiths wrote *March Time* in 1986, not long after the crushing of the coal miners' militancy against the Thatcher government in 1984/5. But *March Time* represents the 1984/5 militancy as part of a miners' march – a 'slow jig of time' – between the defeat for the working class in the General Strike of 1926 and the years after Thatcher's own defeat.

Whereas *Such Impossibilities* ends with a scene of hurt and misunderstanding between Tom and his wife Ellen after he has been sentenced to gaol, *March Time begins* with this kind of personal interaction, a scene set in court between the lead character, Jack Dunn and his wife, Mary. Like Mann, Dunn is completely unrepentant in his revolutionary aspirations as he faces up to the judge. And like Ellen, Mary faces bleakly an unending personal future of separation and loneliness.

Dunn: 'My lord, I will not waste your time with pleas of mitigation ... The so-called fellow-workers I am supposed to have assaulted were no such thing but the worthless gobs of vomit we call scabs, fished from the cesspits of the world by hard-hearted coal barons to steal our jobs and break our spirit ... And the so-called police officers I'm supposed to have obstructed were no such things, but agents of the owning class carrying out the work of their masters ...'

Close shot Dunn, the prisoner, 44, dark, contained scanning them from the dock ... Lands finally on a black-haired woman, late 30s, her arm around her son's shoulder, her gaze back at him hard and unyielding.

Dunn: 'As to contrition, my lord, I will not feign what I do not feel. For if a freeborn Englishman, in lawful union with his peers, may not defend his work and community without incurring the wrath of the courts, then this is indeed a sorry land, and I and many like me will not rest until these things are changed. We are already too many for your prisons, each day we grow in numbers and resolve. And we will make this our century, building peace and fairness where now there is only strife and greed. And there will be better days ...'

The gallery erupts with feeling. The judge gavels and flutes for silence. Dunn looks across at the woman, who shakes her head tautly in the gloom, buries her face in her hands. (1986, 1–2)

As this extract indicates, *March Time* begins no less hard-edged and masculinist in its interactions between workers, police and judges than *Such Impossibilities*. The play continues with Mary's voice-over, reading her farewell letter to Dunn. 'I suppose I know now you'll not change, not you, but I'm still young enough to start over, and that's what I'll do' (1986, 2). Not only Mary, but other women 'start over' too, so that the play does not follow the linear chronology to the final scene of an unrepentant Mann and his 'tired, dowsed' Ellen of *Such Impossibilities*. 'Starting over' is managed through the temporal innovations of *March Time* so that the class *energy* of men and women grows together, equal and unchanged.

In a series of phases, they travel from 1927 up to the War, come out of the War unchanged. The point about it is ... that they stay the same age, while everything else about them makes them seem as if they have lived the full amount of the life of a person marching for a job in 1949 and not 1929. So their clothing is different, their hair designs are different, their speech forms are some little way changed. They march in 1949/50 around a National Health hospital in Manchester. They walk past a pithead that has been invested in the National Coal Board. When one of them gets sick they get free medicine which they didn't have earlier ... These are the same people at the same age 20 years later, then 30 years later, then 40 years later. (Griffiths, personal interview 2003)

Early in the piece, Griffiths presents two different measures of time. The first is the long history and conjoint future of struggle which explicitly or implicitly marks all his works. The second is the local, sustained linearity of the workers' march to a mass demonstration in London. At first, this seems like the single temporality of *Such Impossibilities*. As Jack Dunn, recently released from prison for his 1926 militancy, prepares to lead a few Easley miners to join the miners' march to London, the union secretary speaks to the villagers.

All right, we lost the great battle of '26, some say betrayed by our leaders. But the war goes on. Their weapons now are unemployment, more hunger and starvation, more retrenchment of the services that make life possible for working men and women, more cuts in benefit and poor relief ... They're out to break us once and for all, return us to the base and spiritless servitude from which we've hauled ourselves over the long years ... Well, we're sending a message down to those people...Jack Dunn and the lads'll carry it, as will thousands upon thousands of others from all over this land. (VOICE LIFTING IN PASSION) We will not be broken. We will fight to the death for what we know to be ours; the right to work; and the right to the fruits of our labour. (CHEERS, APPLAUSE). Go well, bonnie lads. And godspeed. (1986, 5–6)

Here, in Griffiths' long history, the words are addressed as much to the defeated miners of 1984/5 as to those of 1926, and visually this march will be accompanied by 'ACTUALITY FILM. Slowed bleached sequence of hunger marchers from 20s and 30s: banners, programmes, thin faces, resolute eyes' (1986, 11), as well as by images of insurrections over several centuries, from the Levellers to the 1984 miners. Jack, his unruly friend Gypsy Armstrong, the older Percy Mann who is sick from coal dust in the lungs (with his own long history of struggle since 1872/3 when 'the owners'd sacked a whole shift for refusin' to work') and the tough, angry Scotsman Will Daly set out in Gypsy's cart drawn by an old, near-blind pit pony, Billy.

But then Griffiths introduces a third temporality – 'our time' embedded in 'their time' – which is signalled, as the long march is held up by a woman. They meet early on the road Ellen Pearson, joining the march in place of her miner husband who, crushed by unemployment, has recently drowned himself. This 'young woman, 25 maybe, slim, fair, a pack at her feet, dressed to walk, steps out from the side of the road to meet them' (1986, 8). She stands in the road before them as foursquare in her opposition to Jack as the honest and equally young Milligan of *Such Impossibilities* was to Tom Mann. But the resolution is quite different, not buried instantly in violent men's action but worked through growing and changing intimacies of comradeship. Ellen shrugs off the men's attempt to help her lift her pack, and will, unlike Martha in *Such Impossibilities*, certainly not be reduced to buying the sand-wiches while the men get on with the politics. Will Daly tells Ellen that marching is men's work, and Jack Dunn says 'it isn't a country ramble we're engaged [in]'. She responds with her own long history.

> If I can't keep up, sack me. But don't tell me this is men's work. Men've said it all my life and look where it's got us. My dad lived it ... and died of dust before he reached fifty. I'm not going to apologise for being a woman. Women are workers too, part of the class, part of the suffering, part of the struggle ... You're right, I don't have to do this. I choose to. (PAUSE) And it's not grief makes me. It's anger. (SHE STEPS BACK SUDDENLY, TO GIVE THEM THE ROAD). All right. The highways are free. I'll follow behind ...

Unlike the women of *Such Impossibilities* – and more like the politi-cally articulate and organised women of the 1984/5 British miners' strike – Ellen will stand at the centre of this play, defining its main actions, exploring its intimate relationships, and consistently *there* (as most of the men, including her lover Phelan, drift in and out of the central linear action of marching to London). Dunn agrees she go with them, and soon they find that the roads are not free for any of them. Police harass them along the way. In a south Durham town, the police and magis-trate have locked up a party of Scottish miners whom they were to join on the march to London. A wall of policemen block their way at the Westgate, and the magistrate is called to inspect them under the 'Public Order Act of 1926 as amended'. When he sees they are so few (and that there is a woman among them) he lets them pass, but the Scottish comrades remain behind bars. They are joined in the town by a young Irish newspaperman and Oxford student, Michael Phelan who becomes Ellen's lover (she is pregnant with her former husband Frank's child). Like Dunn, he has a socialist dream of going to Russia. But Phelan is also in mysterious contact with 'hard men' and unnamed authorities who have a hold on him through his imprisoned father in Ulster. He leaves a loving letter for Ellen and vanishes. 'I leave the march to make amends. When ... if ... I can feel decent again, call myself a comrade again, earn your respect again, I'll come and find you. Till then, go well, go forward. A wee song for you ... ' And he pens the words about singing for tomorrow with 'the slow jig of time'.

Dunn has earlier altered their route because of informers (one of them probably Phelan himself) alerting police to intercept them. They pass encamped soldiers and surrealistically imaged, empty armoured vehicles on the road. Dunn re-routes to Lancashire, where his son and wife Mary are now living with her militant union father. Griffiths has Dunn's journal voice speak of the march beginning to waste their energies: 'Percy's chest and feet, Will's persistent ill-humour, Ellen's grieving silences and a Spring as fickle and full of false promises as a British Labour Party in office.'

Griffiths' words thus articulate his third chronology of time in *March Time*, as 'Dunn's journal voice launches a montage sequence, sometimes mute, iconised, sometimes voiced, of their progress west and south into Lancashire. Versions of *Pit lie idle-o*, coming and going, bind the sequence of scenes and images. As previously, two time-codes are in play: theirs (about a fortnight); ours (around four years)' (1986, 22).

This third chronology – a continuous *popular-artistic play* between 'our time' and 'their time' – is enriched by an energising tapestry of songs and poems. *Pit lie idle-o* is one of the many songs out of the 'slow jig of time' – the pit band playing *The Internationale* near the beginning, the George Formby songs at the Manchester Miners' Hall, Gypsy's freedom song on the way, 'Now a hewer's no brains, As all wise people know. But a hewer can dream, From the dark down below'. Other songs from the 'jig of time' are stronger still – the freedom poetry and prose of Shelley, of Piers Plowman, of William Morris (which Ellen reads to the children of some cowherds who have mended their cart and fed them on the road to Manchester).

And now the streets seem gay, and the high stars glittering bright;
And for me I sing amongst them, for my heart is full and light.
I see the deeds to be done and the day to come on the earth,
And riches vanished away and sorrow turned to mirth;
I see the city squalor and the country stupor gone.
And we are part of it all – we twain no longer alone
In the days to come of the pleasure, in the days that are of the fight –
I was born once long ago; I am born again tonight. (1984, 32)

In this other temporality of songs, poetry and a woman's political-aesthetic history, many of Griffiths' most potent forms and themes work together, complexly yet with great simplicity and clarity: the different historical 'jigs of time'; the 'world historical' choices (here, between the 'global' need, voiced by Will of going to the Spanish Civil War and Dunn's insistence on the 'local' need of completing the miners' march to London); the private but also political decisions to be made – again and again – between the insurrectionary-hard, 'prison-cropped, eyes fierce' Dunn at the beginning and the man-of endurance, sensitised by his time on the road with Ellen, who is offered a Labour Party constituency seat near the end; the changing relationship between working-class men and women.

'Songs and Poems in the Slow Jig of Time'

The miners' march is an historical re-making as well as a contemporary strategy. The moment before we find Ellen retching in a stream in early pregnancy, Griffiths' instructions give us a 1932 Ministry of Health Report on the High Mortality Rate associated with pregnancy, and enjoining 'sound nutrition in a pregnant woman'. Ellen has been denied sound nutrition, both on the march and earlier as an unemployed teacher and unemployed miner's wife. Similarly denied is the sick and delirious Percy Mann, who as a march leader in the Winter of 1922 had allowed two older miners to come with them – and to die in the cold – because 'they'd earned the right to choose'. He himself now pleads with Dunn to choose not to be left behind. When denied doctors' help in Manchester, they are forced to take him to the Meanwood Workhouse and Hospital for the Poor, where the Master ignores him till Jack and Gypsy make a stand. But later, they have marched this other Mann though time to post-Second World War England, into the new dawn of a National Coal Board and welfare state, where they deliver him to a 'late '40's NHS hospital' – a future victory that Tom Mann worked for but never saw.

The march has thus far achieved its vision of 'sound nutrition' for pregnant women and a dignified treatment for the sick, poor and ageing working class. So, as well as the familiar temporalities of Griffiths' earlier work, linking between insurrectionary moments (often lost) past and present, there is in *March Time* this other chronology, where, as though in time travel, the marchers appear in a moment of victory partially gained – the establishment of the post-World War II welfare state. But it is time-travel as mediated by the experiential life-presence of Ellen, which is important because even within the continuing narrative of the play, this moment of victory will be lost again (we next see Coronation mania, with Dunn and Ellen marginalised from the nationalistic festivities), just as it had been in 1926 before the play started, and again in 1984/5 when the play was written. Near the end, Ellen shows her schoolteacher mother her sketch of her one-armed miner husband, asleep in his chair soon before he died (she has drawn the different, individualised workers during the march – especially the naked Phelan), announcing her thoughts of going to London to paint.

> Lily ... Everything's so ... strange just now...In movement. Beyond theory, somehow. (LONG PAUSE). Frank's death released so many things in me ... These last months have been ... bad, you called them ... no ... extraordinary. Transforming. Frightening ... Everything's important suddenly, every part of my life challenged, every part of my self reclaimable, reworkable. (PAUSES, SORTING IT OUT) This ... action, this march

... defines me anew, every mile we cover ... Gives me comrades ... Takes me to the edge of something ... a new politics, a new practice, a new ... person ... (SHE FINDS THE DRAWING OF PHELAN, LOOKS AT IT. HE STANDS ARMS FOLDED, UNAFRAID IN HIS NAKEDNESS, SMILING AT HER). I have no plans Lily. After [the march reaches] London ... perhaps I'll go back to school and learn how to paint. I might do that ... (1986, 86–7).

Those songs and poems in 'the slow jig of time' – 'Beyond theory' but not *instead* of theory – are Trevor Griffiths' own commitment. They are what he has always done, as history unfolds, is lost, and becomes 'reclaimable, reworkable'. But *March Time* is more reflexive than *Such Impossibilities*. Ellen in *March Time* is not only a much more developed woman than the Ellen of *Such Impossibilities*, Tom Mann's wife. She is also an artist 'beyond theory'. It is that potentiality of the artist to make and remake time, place and character – as in her representation of Phelan as both traitor to his comrades and as uncompromised, naïve, naked, working-class male, with his visions of Russia and his love of this woman – that Griffiths' wager, as an artist representing, but also re-making history resides.

World historical moments

At the beginning of *March Time* we see Dunn's angry response to his trial for assaulting scabs in 1926, followed, under the caption, 'March, 1927', by Griffiths' directions.

Fade up still image of long empty stretch of country lane in long shot ... After some moments a figure crests a rise in the far distance, headed for camera, a rolled kit-bag on his shoulder. Brings up sounds of a six-piece pit band tuning up and begin Titles. The advancing figure, still distant, holds the road alone for some while, then others appear, by twos and threes, optically inserted till the lane's dense with marching figures. Titles end as the crowded way gradually thins back to the solitary marcher, now almost at lane's end: It's Dunn, head prison-cropped, eyes fierce. The pit band slides gently into The Internationale, the shot pans the man into the approach to the village of Easley, where band and comrades are out in strength to greet his return. (1984, 2)

This is one version of 'march time', the optically inserted density of marching figures representing at least three historical moments: first, the many, many workers that Dunn and his few comrades will represent on the march to London at this crucial time of defeat and renewal in Britain; second, the history and future of other massive demonstrations against unemployment and class exploitation, such as at the time of the play's writing; third, as the 'crowded way gradually thins' of marchers, the *potentiality* of different 'world historical' temporalities and choices to be made at any one moment. 'March time' is about all these comrades, all these times, and – like *Such Impossibilities* – it is about leadership, honed here into the fine detail of the everyday minutiae of marching: the decision whether to let Ellen join, the debate whether to leave the sick Percy Mann to continue with them and maybe die; the naked swimming (as in *Hope in the Year Two*) as they refresh themselves along the way. But it is also about global/local choices in the working-class struggle, as in Dunn's decision when he meets the Manchester Miners' executive to continue the march. Even though Will Daly leaves to fight for the Republicans' cause in Spain, Dunn tells them,

> For myself, I'll go on with the march, as I hope many more will ... I agree the struggle's international ... But there's two fronts to the war. And abandoning the home front for all-out struggle abroad carries risks none of you seems to be interested in facing ... Beyond Spain, comrades, in five years or ten, money's going to need another war, possibly against Russia itself ... Imagine what the British working class're gonna make o' that, if we relinquish the field now to the leadership of the turncoat Labour Party and the collaborationist TUC. (1986, 39)

Near the end, when he has led his diminishing group of marchers – with him and Ellen in a new intimacy as comrades – into the post-war world of Labour Government and beyond that to the years of Thatcher, there are leadership decisions still to be made. He is offered membership of that 'turncoat' Labour Party in the place of Arthur Pointer. As the area secretary, NUM, Peter Tams tells Dunn, 'a certain feeling's grown up that maybe replacing damp union-fodder that Arthur – and scores like him, union-sponsored – have become with people who'll do the job that's needed wouldn't be all that bad an idea...Parliamentary cretinism's an endemic contagion that strikes down all, but the best (PAUSE) I'm prepared to stake you have immunity ...' (1986, 81).

And so Dunn and Ellen march on, comrade-idealism necessarily at its strongest, into the years of the Tories, where Griffiths' MAN says,

> The fight for peace was surrendered to the Tories. Macmillan was able to pose as the champion of the Summit and of understanding with the Soviet Union. Labour did not reply by exposing Tory policy on West German rearmament, NATO, the Cold War, the arms race and the insane policy of using the H-bomb first. On all these issues the Labour leaders declared their agreement with the Tories. Labour's policy boiled down to the claim that they would run capitalism better than the capitalists. It is not surprising that many electors should draw the conclusion that

in that case the job could well be left to the party of the capitalists – the Tories ... (1986, 102)

These are the bridge days between Aneurin Bevan's mountains march of the new welfare state in *Food for Ravens* and the post '60s radicalism of *Bill Brand*. The MAN's words are also the bridge between *Such Impossibilities* and *March Time*. Unlike Lukacs, Griffiths does not find his world historical moments simply in the great collisions of meta-orders, though these are certainly there. He locates them also in the *daily* moments (which Lukacs would look for only in the novel) – like Gypsy missing the beginning of the march to meet them on the bridge outside town with his 'ancient, peeling cart', his home-made bridle and harness and his blind, white 'comrade' pit pony, and his later love-making with a barmaid in Manchester in the cart, Billy still attached. This cart itself – and the endurance, energy, fun and sexuality in and around it – becomes a 'people's art', a continuing theme of the play – as also in Ellen's Clarice Cliff wedding-present tea mug, her sketches of each of the working men on the march, Gypsy's 'Hewer's Dream' songs, Phelan's harmonica, Ellen and Dunn swapping Shelley lines, and Ellen's reading of William Morris poems to the cowmen's children, to which Phelan, visibly moved, responds gently with the words, 'March time'. What Ellen says of her mug applies to all these everyday 'art' histories that keep the march comradely, sensuous – and alive 'There's nothing I own more beautiful ... People's art. It's everywhere. And it's invisible'.

Trevor Griffiths' women

As we saw in Chapter 3, the British media has by and large missed in Griffiths' work what was actually most central, his reflection on his own 'repressive tolerance' and suppressed emotion as a male member of a class where, traditionally, there had been 'no caresses or fondlings. Being a boy or a man meant remaining impassive, suppressing all emotion in the face, the hands, the set of the body' (*Times Educational Supplement*, June 25, 1976). This is the sense we have of the working-class, male leader Tom Mann at the end of *Such Impossibilities*. And just as in the case of Griffiths' own chemical process worker father who died (with few words to his son) of lung cancer at 54, so too the retired pitman Percy Mann may die without complaint at the end of *March Time*. But there is a difference now. Percy Mann (unlike the apparently dominantly healthy Tom Mann) also *lives* his sickness with erotic and liberated dreams.

The strength and belief in older men's choices to die without words on the march was also behind Percy Mann's (and the other men's) difficulty in admitting Ellen to the march in the first place. And the same 'historical explanation for every limitation in that man' (Griffiths TES, 1976) relates to Dunn's refusal of contrition in his opening 'worthless gobs of vomit we call scabs' speech to the judge at his trial in 1926, while his wife stands in court, gazing 'back at him hard and unyielding'. When Dunn sees Mary again, in Manchester, the scene reveals something new, some of the comradely tenderness of former partners that Griffiths showed between Dritterman, his former wife and sleeping son in his screenplay for *Fatherland* (Tulloch 1990, 107). Mary loves him still. Dunn says he dreams of going to Russia, and she implicitly asks for words of love from him in responding with her joking 'Happen I've done you a good turn then (HE SAYS NOTHING). Are you serious ...?' Then this hard, silent working-class man's words and emotions do spill out.

> (SUDDEN)... What do you want me to say, love? Ah'm broken? Ah miss ye? Ah canna live wi'out ye? Ah hate ye fer leavin me high an' dry? Ah canna say those things, they're not true, ah'm in one piece, ah can live wi'out ye, ye've allus 'ad the right to build a life wi'out me, an' the boy's yours more than 'e's mine, you've allus put more into 'im.' (1986, 43)

But, quite unlike Ellen's passive 'Crying at his shoulder' at the end of *Such Impossibilities* and Tom Mann's class-conscious rationality in response, here Mary 'watches the quiet pain work its slow way around his frame' as he then says '(LOW) Ah *do* miss ye, However ah've ... neglected things, you're a special person ... in my life love. Losin' it's hard'. They talk about Ellen who Dunn says is 'provin' a good comrade (A SMALL SMILE). Maybe that's the future, eh?' They spend the night together, he sees his boy in the morning, and Mary says 'Don't change, will you. I wouldn't want you ... any other way.' A 'slow smile, ironic and admiring, grows between them'. Both are stronger, more affective, and more reflexive at their parting. Dunn leaves his son a copy of Thomas More's *Utopia*, and marches on, committing to his journal, 'Two hundred years ago there was next to nothing. Two hundred years from now there'll be nothing again. Meanwhile, we live our lives'. Living our lives means more than the commitment to insurrectionary class struggle dominating the ending of *Such Impossibilities*. It means also Dunn emotionally sharing the past (with Mary), and finding new intimacies and strengthening comradeship in the present (with Ellen). Those relationships – of different personal intimacies and different historical moments of militant struggle – construct the very different temporalities of *March Time* and *Such Impossibilities*.

Living also means caring for the dying – Gypsy leaves the march to stay with Mann in hospital. But at the end Mann is still living, 'not ready for the knacker's yard just yet', fighting on, leaving the hospital, and this time Gypsy reappears in a pantechnicon which debouches his emblematic pony and cart. Dunn, Gypsy and Ellen walk on together, all those working-class words said and lived. In Oxford they are told by a Welsh miner that Phelan is suspected of having led the Scottish miners into the police ambush in Durham. Ellen traces Phelan to his college, confronts him in his room, and he reveals his betrayal of the Scottish marchers under Special Branch pressure on his 'sick old Republican' father, 'fitted up with a robbery charge they freely acknowledged they knew he couldn't have done'. Ellen softens, invites him back to the march, even while Gypsy and Dunn, waiting for her elsewhere in Oxford, read lessons from Engels and Germaine Greer on the gender politics of domesticity. The two men continue without Ellen on the march, Dunn confiding to his journal, 'Will Daly, Percy Mann, the Irishman, casualties of the road. And now the lass ... Pray God the rest have fared better or we'll prove the sorriest huddle ever seen on Parliament Hill.'

But once again Ellen appears in their road, 'bag on shoulder, blocking their way'. She invites Phelan down from some trees beside the road, he acknowledges the Durham betrayal, and Gypsy 'smacks him to the ground with a single blow'. But here the man-on-man violence is surrounded by a more complex politics than Tom Mann's action against Milligan in *Such Impossibilities*. This time the woman, Ellen, is there for the action, and is central to Dunn's decision to accept Phelan back. She influences him both by her words ('You're *pathetic*, all of you ... All right, he betrayed us, he betrayed his people, but the lesson's been learnt, damn you, and he's *here*, asking, asking...he doesn't need your anger, he needs your intelligence and your understanding') and by her refusal to blackmail the men – she will go on to London with the men, she tells Dunn, even if they don't accept Phelan. They all go on together, their tiny, renewed solidarity all the more important in the immediate context Griffiths provides of Special Branch personnel surveying the scene from a furniture van through binoculars. 'OK, looks as if they're on the move again...Irishman too, well, well, well ... Little bastard thinks 'e's given us the slip, little bastard does ...'

Endings

They walk, dragging their cart – very Brechtian – up Parliament Hill
at night, and all the torches are burning, and there are thousands and
thousands and thousands of marchers encamped on the way, and they're
walking through them. And they start with Lollards in the fourteenth
and fifteenth centuries, and then we come to the fifteenth century and
the Levelllers and the Diggers, and then we're in the eighteenth century
with the Luddites. (Griffiths, personal interview August 2003)

The march has expanded its numbers in time and through time on
its way from Oxford to London, as each historical moment of industrial militancy – including the 1972 miners' strike which inspired *Such
Impossibilities*, and the 1984/5 strike which inspired *March Time* – and
each betrayal is marked by moments of sound and vision: the 'hard'
sounds of the strikers of '72' and '74'; the softer, emotional visuals of
('Dunn, Armstrong, Phelan, Ellen, Albert and the Durham contingent
sit[ting] in silence amid beer and sandwiches to watch the miners' 1985
return to work on the bar-slung colour TV. Ellen weeps quietly. Gyp
watches, numb. Dunn glances at two maps spread ... on the table ...
Dunn's hands remove the road map of central London, reveal a second
map ... London-Nicaragua has been thickly recoloured in black biro').
Above all, the continuity of political betrayal is signified repetitively by
the alienating devices of a succession of furniture vans (each containing
Special Branch agents) 'writing' the periods marched through with
'Heath & Co., Light Removals', 'Wilson & Callaghan Ltd., "We move
People"', 'Thatcher & Co., Demolitions'.

At the very end of Griffiths' first version of *March Time*, as the
marchers queue on Parliament Hill at tables for accreditation (in a
scene that replicates much more positively the opening scene of sailors
signing-on in *Such Impossibilities*), Dunn meets Will Daly again. It is
Daly, not the shipping owners' aggressive doctor of *Such Impossibilities*,
who now sits behind the table, processing the workers. Daly is back, not
from the 1930s Spain he left for earlier, but from 1980s Nicaragua, and
Dunn watches his maimed comrade swing away on crutches to meet
with other marchers. New era historical dreams (of Nicaragua) replace
old dreams (of Stalin's Russia) within the characters' re-energised life-
spans (and we are reminded that Dunn, too, had his map of Nicaragua
over that of London). The play ends, as Griffiths' *Fatherland* did, with
thousands of lights in the dark, in a determined optimism of the will
that faces the continuing history of leadership betrayal, and of police/
military surveillance and oppression. '*EXT. NIGHT. The din from the
hill, voices in their hundreds pulsing down the long grass slope, grows on their
approach. Fires flick and leap, lamps swing in the night.*'

It is this mix of each new era's utopian thinking (Griffiths' parting gift to his audiences – like Dunn's gift to his son of More's *Utopia*), of personal/local/global narratives, of mixed temporalities and of Brechtian devices that ends *March Time*. Although formally *Such Imposibilities* and *March Time* are very different plays, they also carry, in addition to their common industrial militancy subject matter, a strong continuity. In *Such Impossibilities*, Tom Mann reads Thomas Carlyle:

> There is not a horse in England willing and able to work but has due food and lodgings ... And you say it is impossible. Brothers, I answer, if for you it be impossible, what is to become of you? It is impossible for us to believe it is impossible. The human brain, looking at those sleek English horses, refuses to believe in such impossibilities for Englishmen. (1988, 200)

The words refer us forward intertextually to the scene in the stables between Sir Frederick and the hop-pickers in Griffiths' *Country*; but also to Dunn's words to Ellen's mother in *March Time*. 'Lenin said ... Think the impossible. Demand the impossible. Be a realist' (1986, 94). It is that undiminished critical realism which underpins Griffiths' utopianism, and his 'Slow Jig of Time' between *Such Impossibilities* and *March Time*.

March Time then and now

Trevor Griffiths began writing *March Time* in 1985, and presented it to Channel 4 in late 1986/early 1987. 'It was turned down comprehensively' (Griffiths, 2003) and languished on his shelf. In 1994 Stuart McKinnon, director and producer of Trade Films, who had been dealing with *March Time*, approached Griffiths again because a former Channel 4 producer who had shown interest in the piece now had a key job at the BBC, and was interested. Griffiths' recent success with *Hope in the Year Two* on the BBC may have cued this interest.

> I was pretty reluctant to get started back into March Time because it seemed to me to belong to the wrong period ... The idea of finishing it 7 or 8 years later for a new dispensation in a new era politically and culturally was going to be quite difficult .... It was when I came to look at how it might be finished given the additional eight years of lived political history for me to absorb into the lives of these people on the march that I began to see ways in which the idea could be taken forward, and that became draft 2. (Griffiths, personal interview October 2003)

Griffiths made virtually no changes in the first 80 pages.

The real changes occur towards the end of the piece when they are ... on the outskirts of London. They encounter a great deal more surveillance, which is taken from the first draft, but amplified. And then run into this a major explosion in the city street, which at the superficial level takes in IRA bombings which were a feature of the 70s and 80s in mainland Britain, but which also lead inexorably to the secret state and all the resources at its disposal, which are easily and often deployed against people on a long march for social justice. And what I came up with was a rather dystopian dream for seven pages or so – a sort of dream space into which they are blown, which seems like a hospital but becomes a site of subtle but increasingly ugly interrogation by officers of the state, the people who have had them under surveillance since they set off in 1927. (Griffiths, October 2003)

These pages are among the most sombre, frightening and powerful that Griffiths has ever written. It begins with the appearance of one of *March Time*'s alienating pantechnicons. Gypsy leads Billy to it, thinking it is the horse box taking the old pit pony to his green-fields retirement.

The truck explodes. Smoke, flame, glass, screams, sirens, silence, moans, calls. Slow hovering track of the pavement, bodies, glass, the randomly scattered contents of store windows loom ghost-like from the thick hang of smoke. Through it all, the Tory Conference standing ovation [for Thatcher] continues. Sirens, closing. The shot reaches Dunn, crumpled, lifeless, bloodied. Holds. His eyes open suddenly, see nothing, close. Bleed in local radio beeps and news headlines. Terror bomb in High Street, two dead, twenty injured, inner-city riots, third day, unemployment, 2.5 million, thousands join the March for Jobs ...

The harshest parts of this new text are not the explosion itself (which may well be by the 'secret state' itself), but the frightening medical institution where the survivors find themselves interrogated ruthlessly and cruelly, watched via monitors by the same agents who have watched them all along. Ellen is casually and cruelly told of the death of Phelan (who had shielded her from the blast with his body) by a 'sympathetic' fellow female patient, who is trying to get personal details from her ('if you've anybody needs calling, just jot down the number'). Ellen loses the baby, nearly dies, and is hauled out by the silent watchers. But Dunn, canny, sees the camera.

Whitecoat: 'Yes, yes, you've located the camera, a man of your experience, you're bound to have an edge ...(Removes white coat) Believe it or not, it's for your own protection, ensures we don't overstep the mark of our zeal to put the bloody murderers away for the rest of their miserable lives ...'

Dunn: 'We? ...'

Whitecoat: 'We're the state, Mr Dunn. Or is it comrade? We defend the realm. Against scum like yourself. Shall we get on? (He flicks the statement across the desk). There's nothing we can't back up with hard evidence, Dunn, you were there at the lorry with your co-conspirators... Armstrong, the women Pearson and our friend Phelan, all right? Just sign at the bottom and we can wrap the thing up. Friend Phelan's dead, by the way, so if you want to lay most of it on him that's fine by us, but we need your signature, OK?' (Hands him the pen). 'Shall we?'

Dunn takes the paper and signs.

Whitecoat: 'I think you're going to have to sign your own name, sunshine, we've got Mickey Mouse inside already.'

Dunn: 'Sorry. Best I can do.'

Whitecoat: 'We'll see. Maybe it's escaped your notice in your hectic dash to change the world friend, but we're running the show now, not scum-bags like you and your murderous mates ... Think it over.'

In a garden outside, Gypsy is being equally cruelly interrogated. 'Do you remember the pony ... What did you call him, Billy was it? ... Blown to buggery anyway. He'll be Whiskas by now.' Gypsy resists, apparently impassive.

Whitecoat: 'There's twenty years of subversion in the dossier, strikes, marches, demonstrations, sit-ins, so-called Anti-Nazi League, peace demos, anti-poll tax shenanigans, it's all there friend, we've logged your every fart and belch for years, so make no mistake, we'll wear you down, whether you sign or not...You hearing me?'

Armstrong: 'S'funny, I thought this were a hospital.'

Whitecoat: 'S'a private clinic.'

Armstrong: 'Private clinic. What can I say. I've lost me memory. I don't know nothing ... What is this place?'

Whitecoat: (A smile) 'This? This is England.'

They are released, again from a large van, into 'the rot and rubbish of a post-eighties British city'. The radio announces the second ballot for the Tory leadership (after Thatcher) and a new pit closure programme.

In part the toughness of this is in the writing, with the laconic cruelty of the whitecoats' sense of natural control. In part, it is the loss by the narrative of its 'good' hospital dreams, seen earlier in the optimism of the National Health Service late-1940s. In part, it is the dystopic concentration of a secret state which in effect is more complete but still *continuous* with the start of the march in 1927. In part, it is the ruthless destruction of the growing unity of the marchers. In part, as always with Griffiths, it is in the screen directions in his head as he writes, and now as he re-writes his never-to-be screened text. 'It's in this dream that their unity of relationship and purpose gets destroyed or very seriously damaged. Phelan is lost ... Dunn is injured. Ellen loses her child. Billy is lost to the march. And there's a sense of the overall mode of the peace having been violated.'

Griffiths noted in interview in late 2003, that 'when I look at this now it's as long since I wrote draft 2 as it was between writing the first draft and the second. And I can see that there's a kind of unprepared-ness [in the ending]. On the other hand, I think [the redraft] contains the germ of something quite ... extraordinary' (October 2003). By the time of that interview, Griffiths had had the experience of directing *Food for Ravens*.

> Even with the writing that's there in March Time, it's possible to see and feel a way of directing it which I think is instinctive within the lines and words – which is to do with this notion of a dream of whiteness, the white-coatedness of things ... That it would be slowed down. The sound would be odd, refracted, difficult. There would be bleached qualities in the imaging that would make it dystopic and clinical – everything pared down to brutal essentials. And that muffled, awful thing would gradu-ally give way – give back to – the reality of the march again, this time in the late 80s and early 90s, in other words in a new temporality beyond that recent historical moment. And then you could have the ambient sounds bleeding back. I guess what I'm saying is that this is work in progress. And that the tragic thing...is that it's work in progress that nobody's funding.

Griffiths' writing, whether in 1985, 1994 or 2003 is always histori-cally immediate and intertextual, and the secret state theme had been strongly present working through his texts: his film with Ken Loach, *Fatherland*, his play, *Thatcher's Children*, and his never produced film for Warner Brothers, *Acts of Love* 'about ... the work of some underground ANC people in Johannesburg – based on a true story and very much about the secret state and oppositions to it, including explosions and bombings' (October 2003). But the secret state was also in *The Last Place on Earth* – a series 'which was very much in my mind when I started writing *March Time* .... It represented that part of the secret state which operates ... full-frontal, and we call it 'the Establishment'. So it's the head of the Royal Geographical Society, several key judges and generals, and the important wife who meet without minutes – rather like prime-ministerial meetings today– and they chisel away at an edited version of Scott's texts that will keep the squeamish on board and will not interfere with the good taste of the nation' (personal interview, October 2003).

Looking back from 2003, Griffiths re-recognised what had become submerged for him, that there is a critical link between Scott's journal voice in *The Last Place on Earth* and Dunn's journal voice in *March Time*. Both these journals speak directly about the harshness of the 'march'. But in *March Time* 'I was trying to *reclaim* working-class history for working-class leaders, for people who lived it as they led it. ..In that earlier period of history, the journal was the tool of the officer class [like Scott]... And yet we know that the working class kept diaries, but we never see it in literature. Here was a way that you could inset that reality into a narrative' (Griffiths, October 2003). It is this set of conjoint narratives – journal, poetry, songs and crafts – which is the reflexive, creative relationship Griffiths has with this history, as writer.

However, in the inserted 'secret state' pages of the second draft, all of these voices are stopped. There is no poetry. The marchers are separated from each other. Virtually the only thing they can do is resist their interrogators and say nothing. Dunn signs his name 'Mickey Mouse', which is saying nothing. There then comes a writing problem for Griffiths, of how to lift the finale to the same level of strength as that 'bleached' dystopia.

> Clearly not enough time was spent on exploring and taking into account what an explosive, detonative event I'd created in those new pages ... When the Parliament Hill sequence came on top of the original earlier sequences in draft 1, it was a climax. You were going uphill, you were seeing the very, very strange dreamlike world of six centuries of march and struggle and contestation and class definition. But when you come out of the 80's that I've written in the second draft, you need some writing and directing to negotiate between that bleached, sepulchered, dystopic dream and this other dream ... with the Lollards, and the Levellers, and the framebreakers, and on each side in the darkness of night the fires, the red faces, the camaraderie, discourse and intensity and context ... Somehow you've got to make that dream bounce against the horror of the previous passage. As it is written they are too baldly set against each other ... Something's got to happen between the one and the other that negotiates.

In draft 1 Will Daly is in the finale, and his transformation from 1930s Spain to 1980s Nicaragua works in continuity with the changing chronologies and temporalities of the entire text. But that is lost in the later version because Daly is missing, Nicaragua is not there, and Griffiths instead invents two kinds of solidarities: a) the 'good Lefties' from the earlier text – Mary, their son, her radical father, Left Labour workers, the cowmen; b) the history of the Levellers etc. But there is no new movement of temporalities to contrast with the melodramatic bleaching of the new 'explosive' text. Overall, *March Time*'s form is picaresque, until it is suddenly wrenched into the dystopic dream of draft 2, after which the finale seems 'out of form'. Griffiths now argues that in draft one Will Daly's return in '87 is 'within the temporalities of the movements of these people and of the writing. He went to Spain in '38 and he came back from Nicaragua in '86/87. All of that makes sense because Nicaragua was a recent thing then.' But by the time of the 1994 redraft 'Nicaragua is already remote ... In draft 2, it would probably have worked to bring Daly back earlier, even before the explosion'. The disjuncture between the two dreams (one dystopic, the other utopic) that ends draft 2 lies in the 'oversight in writing' of failing to carry Will Daly's 'story through the piece, because that has been the conceit of the play, going out and then coming back. Old Percy for example, in the '30s in Lancashire not being able to get a hospital, but in the 1940s finding the National Health hospital .... That's the convention, that's how things work in this piece, and Daly is lost to that.' The *energy* of the play has been in that mix of temporalities. 'That's the haste of picking up eight years later and driving it hard hoping to get a production out of it...There's almost a tacit acknowledgment that the *means* of the united struggle have been destroyed, that's what the 80s sequence means ... And worse, it ends going back to Jack in the past, like a history loop.' (personal interview, October 2003).

For Griffiths, 'as draft 2 stands it is Orwellian ... Do I think that the forces of what I call progress are losing the battle, here and now, in this bleak moment? My answer has to be no. But I think over the twenty years it has been a very close run thing, and it will remain so, probably for another hundred years.' The difficult thing, Griffiths argues, 'if you want to be true to what you understand as well as true to what you hope for', is ending a play 'as if time has stopped, and of course it hasn't. Tom Mann, in *Such Impossibilities*, is very interesting here. Given that I'm dealing with one of the very few strikes that were major, seminal, determinate strikes that reshaped the next twenty or thirty years, given that I'm dealing with one of the very few that actually achieved what it set out to do, even that is not a euphoric play ... It's 1972 when there are days of hope but there are also days of despair' (October 2003). For Griffiths, *March Time* 'is one of the most powerful pieces I've written. It's also one of the most difficult plays to find a resolution for, which is one of the reasons it was left unfinished.'

Still, dystopia and utopia have always been Griffiths' two material worlds – witness Cosgrove's criticism of the utopian ending of *Oi for England* (Chapter 1). And Trevor Griffiths has already written the space of Will Daly's next return. 'Trevor Griffiths, Palestine, Summer 1995'.

Trevor Griffiths' television productions

Adam Smith – (two series, 11 episodes written by Trevor Griffiths under the pseudonym Ben Rae), with Tom Conti, Brigit Forsyth, Andrew Keir – Granada, 1972/73.

The Silver Mask – (in the series *Between the Wars*), with Joyce Redman, Joan Peart, Anthony Roye, Zoe Wanamaker; dir. Alastair Reid – London Weekend, June 15, 1973.

All Good Men – with Jack Shepherd, Bill Fraser, Ronald Pickup, Frances de la Tour; dir. Michael Lindsay Hogg – BBC1 *Play for Today*, January 31, 1974.

Absolute Beginners – (in the series *Fall of Eagles*), with Patrick Stewart, Lynn Farleigh, Mary Wimbush, Michael Kitchen and Bruce Purchase; dir. Stuart Burge, BBC1, April 19, 1974.

Occupations – with Jack Shepherd, Donald Pleasance, Natasha Parry, Georgina Hale and Nigel Hawthorne; dir. Michael Lindsay Hogg – Granada TV, September 1, 1974.

Through the Night – with Jack Shepherd, and Alison Steadman; dir. Michael Lindsay Hogg, – BBC1 *Play for Today*, December 2, 1975.

Bill Brand – (11–part series), with Jack Shepherd, Arthur Lowe, Cheri Lunghi, Alan Badel, Lynn Farleigh, Allan Surtees; dir. Michael Lindsay Hogg, Roland Joffe, Stuart Burge – Thames TV, June 7 –August 16, 1976.

Comedians – with Jonathan Pryce, Bill Fraser, Ralph Nossek; dir. Richard Eyre, BBC1 *Play for Today*, October 25, 1979.

Sons and Lovers – (7–part adaptation of D.H. Lawrence's novel) with Tom Bell, Eileen Atkins, Jack Shepherd, Geoffrey Burridge, Karl Johnson, Leonie Mellinger, Lynn Dearth; dir. Stuart Burge, BBC2, January 14– February 25, 1981.

The Cherry Orchard – with Judi Dench, Bill Paterson, Timothy Spall, Paul Curran, Harriet Walter, Frederick Treves, Anna Massey, Anton Lesser, David Rintoul, Wensley Pithey, Suzanne Burden, Frances Low; dir. Richard Eyre, BBC1 *Play for Today*, October 13, 1981.

Country – with James Fox, Wendy Hiller, Leo McKern, Joan Greenwood, Penelope Wilton, Frederick Treves, Jill Bennett; dir. Richard Eyre, BBC1 *Play for Today*, October 20, 1981.

Oi for England – with Neil Pearson, Gavin Richards, Adam Kotz, Lisa Lewis; dir. Tony Smith, Central TV, April 17, 1982.

The Last Place on Earth – (7–part series) with Martin Shaw, Max von Sydow, Sverre Anker Ousdal, Susan Wooldridge; dir. Ferdinand Fairfax, Central TV, Central TV, February 18– March 27, 1985.

The Party – with Kenneth Cranham, Jack Shepherd, Andrew Keir; dir. Sebastian Graham Jones, BBC1 Scotland, March 9, 1988.

Hope in the Year Two – with Jack Shepherd; dir. Elijah Moshinsky, BBC2, May 11, 1994.

Food for Ravens – with Brian Cox, Sinead Cusack; dir. Trevor Griffiths, BBC Wales, November 18, 1997. Winner of Royal Television Society and Welsh BAFTA awards.

Trevor Griffiths won the BAFTA Writer's Award in 1982 for his television work.

References

Alvarado, M. and Buscombe, J. (1978) *Hazell: The making of a TV series* (London, British Film Institute).

Auslander, P. (1999) *Liveness: Performance in a mediatized culture* (London, Routledge).

Bennett, S. (1997) *Theatre Audiences: A theory of production and reception* (London, Routledge).

Bennett, T. and Woollacott, J. (1987) *Bond and Beyond* (Basingstoke, Macmillan).

Bignell, J. (1994) 'Trevor Griffiths's Political Theatre: From *Oi for England* to *The Gulf between Us*', *New Theatre Quarterly*, 10(37): 49–56.

Braun, E. (1988) 'Introduction' to T. Griffiths, *Collected Plays for Television: All Good men, Absolute Beginners, Through the Night, Such Impossibilities, Country: 'A Tory Story', Oi for England* (London, Faber and Faber), 1–31.

Brunsdon, C. (1981) '*Crossroads* – Notes on soap opera', *Screen*, 22(4), 32–7.

Bull, J. (1984) 'Trevor Griffiths: Strategic Dialectics', in *New British Political Dramatists: Howard Brenton, David Hare, Trevor Griffiths and David Edgar* (Basingstoke, Macmillan), 118–50.

Carlson, M. (1990) 'Theatre Audiences and the Reading of Performance', *Theatre Semiotics* (Indiana), 10–25.

Clark, R. (1999) 'From Text to Performance; Interpretation or Traduction? Trevor Griffiths' *Fatherland*, as directed by Ken Loach', *Language and Literature*, 8(2): 99–123.

Cosgrove, S. (1983) 'Refusing Consent: The *Oi for England* Project', *Screen*, 24(1): 92–6.

Creeber, G. (2001) 'The Single Play', in G. Creeber (ed.) *The Television Genre Book* (London, BFI Publishing), 9–13.

Creeber, G. (2001) 'The Mini-Series', G. Creeber (ed.) *The Television Genre Book* (London, BFI Publishing), 35–8.

Cremona, V.A., Eversmann, P., van Maanen, H., Sauter, W. and Tulloch, J. (2004) *Theatrical Events: Borders, dynamics, frames* (Amsterdam, FIRT/ Rodopi B.V.).

Free, W.J. (1994) 'Class Values and Theatrical Space in Trevor Griffiths' in

K.V. Hartigan (ed.) *Sam, Sam, Within the Dramatic Spectrum*, Lanham, University of Florida, 45–53.

Garner Jr., S.B. (1995) 'History in the Year Two: Trevor Griffiths's Danton', *New Theatre Quarterly*, 11(44): 333–41.

Garner Jr., S.B. (1996) 'Politics over the Gulf': Trevor Griffiths in the Nineties', *Modern Drama*, 39: 381–91.

Garner Jr., S.B. (1999) *Trevor Griffiths: Politics, drama, history* (Ann Arbor, University of Michigan Press).

Gilbert, W. Stephen (1976) 'Brand X', *City Limits*, June 4–10, 7.

Gillespie, M. (1993) 'The Mahabharata. From Sanskrit to sacred soap: a case study of the reception of two contemporary televisual versions', in D. Buckingham (ed.) *Reading Audiences: Young people and the media* (Manchester, Manchester University Press), 48–73.

Griffin-Beale, C. (1981) 'Can film techniques invade the electronic factory', *Broadcast*, November 2: 24–5.

Griffiths, T. (1977) 'Author's Preface' to *Through the Night* and *Such Impossibilities: Two Plays for Television by Trevor Griffiths* (London, Faber), 7–12.

Griffiths, T. (1980) 'Trevor Griffiths: Politics and populist culture', interviewed by A. Summers, *Canadian Theatre Review* (summer): 25.

Griffiths, T. (1982) 'Introduction', in *Sons and Lovers* (Nottingham, Russell Press), 7–12.

Griffiths, T. (1982) *Sons and Lovers. Trevor Griffiths' screenplay of the novel by D.H. Lawrence* (London, Spokesman).

Griffiths, T. (1982) 'Countering Consent: An interview with John Wyver', in F. Pike (ed.) *Ah! Mischief: The writer and television* (London, Faber), 38.

Griffiths, T. (1986), *Judgement over the Dead:* Screenplay for *The Last Place on Earth* (London, Verso).

Griffiths, T. (1986) interviewed by N. Boireau, *Coup de Theatre* (May) 1985.

Griffiths, T. (1986/1994) *March Time: An original screenplay* (Boston Spa).

Griffiths, T. (1988) *Collected Plays for Television: All Good Men, Absolute Beginners, Through the Night, Such Impossibilities, Country: 'A Tory Story', Oi for England* (London, Faber and Faber).

Griffiths, T. (1990) 'Author's Preface', *Piano* (London, Faber and Faber).

Griffiths, T. (1994) *Hope in the Year Two* and *Thatcher's Children* (London, Faber and Faber).

Griffiths, T. (1995) 'Introduction', in *Occupations*, in *Plays One: Occupations, The Party, Comedians, Real Dreams* (London, Faber and Faber).

Griffiths, T. (1996) cited in 'Spinning Yarns, Trevor Griffiths talks to David Jays about his stage work', *Plays International*, 11(6): 11.

Hall, S. (1976) 'A Critical Survey of the Theoretical and Practical Achievements of the Last Ten Years', in F. Barker, J. Coombes, P. Hulme, D. Musselwhite and R. Osborne (eds) *Literature, Society and the Sociology of Literature*: Proceedings of the conference held at the University of Essex, July 1976, 2–7.

Hobson, D. (1982) *Crossroads: The drama of a soap opera* ((London, Methuen).

Inverso, M. (1993) '*Der Straf-block*: Performance and Execution in Barnes, Griffiths, and Wertenbaker', *Modern Drama*, 36: 420–30.

Itzin, C. (1973) 'Trevor Griffiths', in *Stages in the Revolution: Political theatre in Britain since 1968* (London, Eyre Methuen), 165–75.

Jackson, B. and Marsden, D. (1966) *Education and the Working Class* (Harmondsworth, Pelican).

Jacobs, J. (2001) 'Hospital Drama', in G. Creeber (ed.) *The Television Genre Book* (London, BFI Publishing), 23–26.

Jenkins, H. (1992) *Textual Poachers: Television fans and participatory culture* (New York, Routledge).

Johnstone, R. (1985) 'Television Drama and the People's War: David Hare's *Licking Hitler*, Ian McEwan's *The Imitation Game*, and Trevor Griffiths's *Country*', *Modern Drama*, 28: 189–97.

Lewis, J. (1991) *The Ideological Octopus: An exploration of television and its audiences* (New York, Routledge).

Lukacs, G. (1964) *Studies in European Realism* (New York, Grosset & Dunlap).

Millington, B. and Nelson, R. (1986) *Boys from the Blackstuff: The making of a TV drama* (London, Comedia).

Morley, D. (1981) *The 'Nationwide' Audience* (London, British Film Institute).

Nelson, R. (2001) 'Costume Drama', in G. Creeber (ed.) *The Television Genre Book* (London, BFI Publishing), 38–40.

Poole, M. and Wyver, J. (1984) *Powerplays: Trevor Griffiths in television* (London, British Film Institute).

Reinelt, J. (1994) 'Trevor Griffiths: Counterpoint to a Brechtian Aesthetic', *After Brecht: British Epic Theatre* (Ann Arbor, University of Michigan Press), 143–75.

Tulloch, J. (1980) *Chekhov: A structuralist study.* (London and Basingstoke, Macmillan).

Personal interview with J. Tulloch (1982) by T. Griffiths.

Tulloch, J. and Alvarado, M. (1983) *Doctor Who: The unfolding text* (Basingstoke, Macmillan).

Tulloch, J. (1985) 'Chekhov Abroad: Western Criticism', in T.W. Clyman (ed.) *A Chekhov Companion* (Westport, Greenwood), 185–206.

Tulloch, J. and Moran, A. (1986) *A Country Practice: 'Quality Soap'* (Sydney, Currency Press).

Tulloch, J. (1990) *Television Drama: agency, audience and myth* (London, Routledge).

Tulloch, J. and Jenkins, H. (1995) *Science Fiction Audiences: Watching Doctor Who and Star Trek* (London, Routledge).

Tulloch, J., Burvill, T. and Hood, A. (1999) 'Rediscovering or Reinhabiting *The Cherry Orchard*: Class and history in performing Chekhov', *New Theatre Quarterly*, 53 (February), 318–28.

Tulloch, J. (1999) *Performing Culture: Stories of expertise and the everyday* (London, Routledge).

Tulloch, J. (2000) 'Multiple Authorship in TV Drama: Trevor Griffiths' version of *The Cherry Orchard*', J. Bignell, S. Lacey and M. Macmurraugh-Kavanagh (eds) *British Television Drama: Past, present and future* (Houndmills, Palgrave).

Tulloch, J. (2000) *Watching Television Audiences: Cultural theories and methods* (London, Arnold).

Tulloch, J. (2005) *Shakespeare and Chekhov in Production and Reception: Theatrical Events and their Audiences* (Ohio, University of Ohio Press).

Wandor, M. (1993) *Drama Today: A critical guide to British drama 1970–1990* (London, Longman in association with the British Council), 10–11.

Wheeler, W.J. and Griffiths, T.R. (1992) 'Staging "The Other Scene": A psychoanalytic approach to contemporary British political drama', in A. Page (ed.), *The Death of the Playwright? Modern British drama and literary theory* (Basingstoke, Macmillan), 186–207.

Wertheim, A. (1981) 'Trevor Griffiths: Playwriting and politics', in H. Bock and A. Wertheim, *Essays in Contemporary British Drama* (Munich, Huber), 267–81.

Williams, R. (1968) *Drama from Ibsen to Elliot* (London, Peregrine)

Williams, R. (1977) *Marxism and Literature* (Oxford, Oxford University Press).

Wolff, J. '*Bill Brand*, 'Trevor Griffiths, and the Debate about Political Theatre', *Red Dwarf*, 56–61.

Wolff, J., Ryan, S., McGuigan, J. and McKiernan, D. (1976) 'Problems of Radical Drama: The plays and productions of Trevor Griffiths', in F. Barker, J. Coombes, P. Hulme, D. Musselwhite and R. Osborne (eds), *Literature, Society and the Sociology of Literature*: Proceedings of the conference held at the University of Essex, July 1976, 133–53.

Wyver, J. (1981) 'How "the best play of the twentieth century" Took to the Air', *City Limits*, October 9–15, 50–4.

Index